Mary's Message
of Divine Love

THE GOLDEN WORD OF MARY SERIES

Mary's Message for a New Day

Mary's Message of Divine Love

Mary's Message of Divine Love

Mark L. Prophet
Elizabeth Clare Prophet

SUMMIT UNIVERSITY PRESS®

To all devotees
of the Blessed Mother
and of her Son
Jesus Christ

MARY'S MESSAGE OF DIVINE LOVE
by Mark L. Prophet and Elizabeth Clare Prophet
Copyright © 2004 by Summit University Press
All rights reserved

Design and layout: Brad Davis

Library of Congress Control Number: 2004108211
ISBN: 0-922729-89-1

SUMMIT UNIVERSITY 🌙 PRESS®

Contents

PART TWO
The Love Aspect of the Holy Spirit
Five Mysteries of the Rosary by the
  Mother for Her Children

MARY'S SCRIPTURAL ROSARY
FOR THE NEW AGE

The Inspiration Mysteries
Monday Evening – The First Secret Ray

The Action Mysteries
Tuesday Evening – The Second Secret Ray

PART THREE
The Power Aspect of the Holy Spirit
Fourteen Messages of the Word of Life
   to the Children of the Mother

Illustrations

Note: Eight rosaries—one for each morning of the week and Sunday evening—are published in *Mary's Message for a New Day*, the first volume of The Golden Word of Mary series.

A Word from the Author

As I was brought up Protestant, I did not have an appreciation of Mother Mary, although my natural inclination was to enter all the Catholic churches and to engage in prayer there. However, I had no instruction concerning this and I was rather indoctrinated in a prejudice against the person of Mother Mary for what seemed the idolatry of Catholics deifying her, having statues to her, having medals to her.

Without even realizing it, I had developed that same antipathy toward the Blessed Mother. It was a great lesson to me because I saw that it is so easy from one's upbringing to have prejudice against those things one does not understand, to merely accept what one hears and think it's one's own thought.

I can remember, when I was a student at Boston University, seeing a painting of Mother Mary in the public subway with stars around her head. And it said that this is Mary, the Mother of Jesus, the Queen of Heaven. To me the terminology was so strange, and I thought, "How can she allow herself, if she is the being she is, to be the object of all of this idolatry?" Every time I took the subway, I would see this image and I would experience the same disturbance in my being.

Well, I had a very wondrous experience one day. It was a personal conversion. I was just walking down the street and I looked up and before me I saw Mother Mary. I saw her in all the beauty and sweetness and presence and love of the being we know her to be. I was so moved and so touched by her reality, instead of the unreality that I had been programmed to feel, that I literally ran to the nearest Catholic church. I knelt before her statue—which is something unusual for a Protestant, as you know—and I asked for forgiveness for these thoughts and feelings I had held. I also gave to her my life and asked her to use me as an instrument of her mothering of all people.

The joy that I've had ever since then of having Mother Mary as a constant companion and adviser in my life is simply boundless. And I am so grateful that Mother Mary was concerned enough about one person to actually show me her presence and her reality, which instantaneously dissolved all of a lifetime's worth of indoctrination. I realized that had she not done this, I would not have had that conversion of the Holy Spirit that she conveyed and I would have been left in ignorance. I would have been left in a state of making that karma of actually disputing the office and presence and person of this one who serves as the Blessed Mother.

In knowing Mary as she really is, I have come to see her as a relentless and constant force, challenging the oppression of her children everywhere, in every faith, in every religion. She is a World Mother, and I have seen this in her tremendous mastery of life. Her knowledge of administration and organization, as she has conveyed it to me, has given me the real teaching of how to administer this organization and with a very capable staff bring it to this level of complexity of service that we are all enjoying.

I want to give acknowledgment to Mother Mary as the great teacher of this order and organization, because some do not realize that that quality of administration is a quality of the Mother flame. When we want to master the details of life in any field, we realize that it is the Mother aspect of God that actually corresponds to Matter or the Matter universe, as *mater* is the Latin for Mother. And so, here on earth, if we are going to accomplish anything, we must invoke the Mother flame. We must understand the Hindu conception of the Mother aspect of God as the Shakti, the active principle, the force that brings into manifestation the Father's will.

As a number of theologians have said, when it comes to the soul, we are all feminine beings. In that polarity of being feminine, we identify God as Father, which is as it should be. But we understand that Father also contains the feminine principle, as in the allegory of Adam and Eve. Eve comes forth out of Adam, symbolizing the breaking apart of the T'ai Chi of Alpha and Omega.

And so, we see that the universal presence of the Mother is actually the reason for the manifestation of our physical bodies. Our spirits are very masculine, or yang, and our spirits are intended to carry the force and the power of the Holy Ghost. But the details of life, our daily jobs, what we accomplish in a twenty-four-hour period—all of this has to do with that mastery of the Mother flame, which is the white light in the base-of-the-spine chakra. The Hindus call it the Kundalini fire. It is the ascension flame. It is the power of locomotion, of movement in this octave.

So if you want to know how to get things done and how to get them done because your aim is helping people and glorifying God—which is our only reason for being—then ask Mother Mary. And you will find that she is truly a master and not an ignorant peasant woman who happened to be called to give birth to beloved Jesus, as some would have us believe.

We know Mother Mary as an angel. We understand in God's divine plan that over a million years and more, many angels of heaven have taken embodiment on earth out of a concern for God's children, to minister to them. And thus you find upon earth people of a very devotional nature who love to serve, who are in many fields—doctors, nurses, waitresses, hairdressers, even secretaries, people who are performing a service to others. There are all kinds of occupations that these angels take up, but their love is to help others realize their goal. And so you find them among the support system to the executives and the driving people who get things done, and they enjoy that role.

Angels historically have taken embodiment to become ministers to life. They are characterized as people with great feeling and an abundance of love. They may not always be the most brilliant because they have not necessarily worked in fields of the development of the mind. Rather they have developed the feelings, because angels as orders of heavenly beings actually exist to impart to the sons and daughters of God faith, hope, constancy, compassion and love—these very necessary feelings that we must have in order to get along with each other and to help each other.

Without those uplifting feelings we could become very dreary and cynical and hopeless. We might not get through the crisis of death or the various calamities that come upon us. And so, in those moments of great need we sometimes feel an overwhelming presence of love and support, and it is God extending his care to us through the invisible angels. And sometimes he does this through angels in embodiment.

Mother Mary is of the hierarchy and evolution of angels. These hierarchies also serve on the seven rays of the Godhead that emerge through the prism of the Christ consciousness. Mother Mary's ray is the fifth ray, the ray of emerald green, the ray of healing. It is the ray of science, of medicine, of supply and abundance. The economy also comes under the fifth ray. Those who serve on it and master that ray also become masters of precipitation, which means bringing down the energy of God into practical application in form.

Mother Mary, then, has great talents in many areas. I don't think there is a field of human endeavor where she does not have the expertise and understanding to teach others how to realize and implement the highest and best goals. Mother Mary's mind is vast, vast beyond comprehension.

In Catholic pictures that retain somewhat of a traditional image of the Mother, we see perhaps the Mother of Sorrows or the heart pierced or the sense of the immaculate virgin. But as we see

Mother Mary in the present day, we move to the understanding of a woman in our midst—a Mother Mary who is as modern, as liberated, as tough, as determined as many of the finest women you might meet on earth who are fighting for various causes.

We need to see her as friend, as companion, as sister, although she may rightfully be called "goddess" because of the tremendous God consciousness she has. We must not place her on the pedestal that forces us to become idolaters of her image. But we should revere her in the sense that she has great attainment and great standing in heaven and was chosen to be the mother of Christ because she had the ability to hold the light and the balance for his entire mission.

So we have to realize the meaning of reverence and respect as opposed to worship or that sense of ourselves as the abject sinner and herself as the unreachable Virgin. We have to understand that God has not created the gap between ourselves and the hosts of heaven. This has come through mass guilt imposed upon the race by self-condemnation, by a tremendous emphasis upon sin and guilt rather than upon the joy of forgiveness, repentance, reunion with God and absolute freedom from our past.

When God forgives, he forgives permanently. But upon this planetary home, people do not readily forget one's past, one's mistakes, even though one may have gone miles and miles from that point and sincerely regret the error. So when we know we have received God's forgiveness, we must leave the dregs of an existence of guilt and condemnation, thinking we can never rise again.

I read a story recently of a very devout young woman, Catholic, serving in her church with great joy. And all of a sudden this girl mysteriously died—or was killed or even perhaps committed suicide. From the moment I heard her name and saw this article in the paper in Los Angeles, my heart was gripped with a sense that here was a soul who met a crisis she could not face.

Something happened to her. Perhaps she made a mistake. Perhaps she did something that in her eyes was not equal to the life of devotion she had begun. But I wept over her death, and I felt such a great loss of this beautiful soul of light.

One evening before I went to bed, I went outside to meditate and be at peace for a while. I called to Mother Mary for the assistance to her soul, and Mother Mary showed me this particular one. She was being borne by Mother Mary's angels, and she was wrapped in a swaddling garment of light. The soul of this young woman appeared as it would appear in its native innocence, almost in the childhood or baby state, and yet it had the full presence as she was when she passed from the screen of life.

I saw how she was being borne to other realms and truly cared for. And yet I had the sense that if I had been near that young woman in the hour of her crisis, if I could have held her hand and prayed with her, that that death would have not come to pass.

It burdened my heart because I see so many times the emphasis upon sin and all the accusations that people face—whether from their communities or through the press or the media—condemnation heaped upon condemnation. Many people are not able to bear the censure and the scorn of public opinion that decides, according to its moral codes or whatever, that this is the unforgivable sin. And under the weight of public opinion, people take their lives or they quit their helping people. They resign from their jobs; they resign from public life. They are not able to face even the truth of saying to the world or to those who are their friends, "Yes, I have made a mistake; I have made an error. Forgive me, and let me continue to serve."

I think that this is prevalent all over the world. I think there is a tremendous sense of guilt if people are not living up to certain codes of behavior. And as I have been in the heart of Mother Mary since last evening I feel these are the things that are on her heart.

And were she to ask us a favor in this hour, it would be to pray for the alleviation of that burden of suffering of people who suffer under this censure of others.

And so, the Mother comes to heal us all of our sense of sin regarding ourselves or other people. She comes to liberate us, especially in the Christian world, of the enormous division that renders Christianity ineffective. And, of course, she comes carrying the sorrow of the people of every single nation on the planet and the determination to help them as we give the prayers and the calls.

One of the greatest teachers I have known in the past twenty-five years is Mother Mary. From her heart come two great teachings. Mother Mary has taught us the cosmic clock, charting the cycles of our returning karma and our initiations. Those teachings are a wonder to behold, and you can find them in numerous books and tapes which we have available.[1]

The second teaching is the rosary, the walking of the fourteen stations of the cross, understanding the cross as the symbol of world karma and individual karma. The cross that Jesus bore on those fourteen stations on the way to Calvary was the cross of the weight of world karma, bearing the sins of mankind, sin and karma being synonymous terms.

Walking the fourteen stations with Jesus and the Mother has been an exercise in the transmutation of world karma, coming to understand what it means to bear our brother's burden, to bear one another's burden, which is the admonishment of Christ.

What is your burden? Your burden is always your karma. Even the heaviness of the gravitation of the earth is actually an effect of planetary karma. The full weight of all transgressions upon the law of God of all humanity of all centuries remains until transmuted, until consumed by the sacred fire in answer to our call. This is why it is so difficult to resolve planetary problems, why people never stop their disputes in the Middle East, for example.

They cannot get over their arguments because they are based on an ancient karma. They have to give up the desire to conquer the other one, to get even for that past sin. When will they ever cease getting even for something that happened a half a century and more ago? One has to forgive in order to be free of one's past karma. One has to say, "We will not go on killing to get even for what happened a century ago or ten thousand years ago." Unless you do this, you will never be free from karma. So, you see, forgiveness and freedom can only come when there is a change of heart, a change of spirit and soul.

It takes a lot to say, "I am no longer going to hold this thing against you. You burned my house down. You caused the death of my mother. You did all these things to me." You can either let go of it and put it into the flame, or you can carry it with you for ten lifetimes. You may not remember why you hate this person, but when you meet him you hate him on sight because in your soul you have never forgiven, you've never resolved the hatred, you've never put it into the flame. You are bound by that hatred, and you are binding the other person or a whole nation. If the Jews, for example, never forgive the German people for what the Nazis have done, they will remain bound. It's as simple as that.

At some point you have to say, "Christ is greater than all these things," and realize that being wronged is really a test to see if you can contain the quality of mercy, if you can be Christlike. Or are you a follower of him in lip service only? If you can't forgive, don't call yourself a follower of Christ.

Now the rosary is given to us in bearing world and personal karma on those fourteen stations of the cross.[2] El Morya came to me in June of 1972 as I was meditating in a Catholic church in Hawaii and he said, "You will begin walking these stations on June 27, 1972." And so, certain events came to pass where it was very clear that I was walking these stations and that I should exercise the Science of the Spoken Word in giving the Our Father, the

Hail Mary, the invocations to Archangel Michael to transmute the effects of the burden and weight of those stations—the weight of the condemnation of Christ, world condemnation, the weight of world karma.

Mother Mary says that when we say, "Hail, Mary," we are not giving in an idolatrous way our worship to a figure, a person; but we are saluting the Mother ray, the Ma-ray, which is what the name Mary means. We are giving devotion to the principle of God that is Mother. This is universal in all cultures and religions, even in primitive cultures. The acknowledgment of the Mother principle, whether as a goddess of fertility or in many other guises, is fundamental to life, to birth, to crops, and so forth.

So we salute the Mother ray in God, in the universe, in Mother Mary. Truly we give adoration to the light in each of the saints— to the one light that is God—rather than to the personality. Worship one God, then, adore the light, and realize the light is also in yourselves.

Elizabeth Clare Prophet

The Flame of Freedom Speaks conference
July 3, 1984

Foreword

This work is a tribute to the World Mother and to Mary, who, as the Mother of Jesus, was her foremost representative in the Piscean age. It is a trilogy of wisdom, love and power that flows from the heart of the Mother to her children. It contains not only the worded revelations of Mary through our messengership, but also the light emanations of her Presence made manifest to us. Thus we would bear witness to her immortal soul that does continually magnify the LORD.

The three parts of each of the three books of the Golden Word of Mary series fulfill the words of Jesus "The kingdom of heaven is like unto leaven which a woman took and hid in three measures of meal, till the whole was leavened."[1] The leaven is the Christ consciousness, the woman is the Divine Mother, and the three measures of meal are the three aspects of God made manifest in man as the Holy Trinity.

We have endeavored to make a measure of the Trinity understandable in each book. Book One shows forth the glorious wisdom of the Son, Book Two reflects the comforting love of the Holy Spirit, and Book Three defines the perfection of the Father's goodwill.*

The whole of humanity's consciousness will ultimately be leavened by the wisdom of the Mother as she raises her children to the true awareness of Father, Son and Holy Spirit. The Mother teaches the law of the great Three-in-One through the understanding she imparts of the Holy of holies and the Christ flame that burns upon the altar of the heart. This threefold flame is the spark of his Spirit, the flame of his flame, that is God's gift of life

---

* Book One is *Mary's Message for a New Day*. Book Two is *Mary's Message of Divine Love*. Book Three is forthcoming.

to every one of his sons and daughters.

Part One of this book is composed of "Fourteen Letters from a Mother to Her Children" and is intended to anchor the wisdom aspect of the Holy Spirit within the self-awareness of the disciple. These letters were dictated by Mother Mary to us as messengers for the heavenly hierarchy in the hope that her children might "stay with the dream of God, shut out the clamoring wakefulness of the outer mind, and never lose touch with the components of Reality in all parts of life."[2]

The instruction in these fourteen letters also introduces the devotee of Mary to an illumined awareness of the fourteen stations of the cross, whose challenge each soul destined for the immortal reunion with the Spirit of God must one day meet.

These letters, originally distributed as *Pearls of Wisdom* to disciples of Mary's son throughout the world, are the gift of the Cosmic Mother for the tutoring of the heart in her wisdom and in the immaculate concept she holds for all of her children. Entrusted to her by the Father, this image pure and undefiled of the perfection of each one, immaculately held in heart and mind, is the hope, the faith, the charity of the Godhead toward an evolving humanity.

Part Two of this book includes "Five Mysteries of the Rosary by the Mother for Her Children"; it shows forth the love aspect of the Holy Spirit. These mysteries were dictated by Mother Mary to me as the Mother of the Flame.

They continue the rosaries included in Book One in this series, which has the seven rosaries for the seven mornings of the week (corresponding to the seven rays of the Christic light that emerge from the Holy Spirit) and the eighth mystery, given Sunday evening (which focuses the power of the eighth ray).

By daily giving the rosary in this format, devotees of the Mother anchor the love of Mother Mary within their heart's chalice, thereby consecrating their life's energies to the expansion of the Mother's light throughout the planetary body.

When Mother Mary came to me and told me of her desire to have devotees throughout the world give a Scriptural Rosary for the New Age, she first announced the seven mysteries for the seven rays, together with the prayer format that was to be used.

These mysteries are: The First Ray: The Joyful Mysteries, which amplify the will of God; The Second Ray: The Teaching Mysteries, which extol the wisdom of God; The Third Ray: The Love Mysteries, which magnetize the love of God; The Fourth Ray: The Glorious Mysteries, which show forth the purity of God; The Fifth Ray: The Healing Mysteries, which demonstrate the truth and the science of God; The Sixth Ray: The Initiatic Mysteries, which exemplify the ministration and service of God; and The Seventh Ray: The Miracle Mysteries, which bear witness to the transmutation, the freedom and the forgiveness of God.

When these rosaries were completed under her direction, the Blessed Mother released The Masterful Mysteries for the eighth ray, which focalize the majesty and the mastery of God. In her third appearance, the Holy Virgin presented the mysteries and the prayer format for the five secret rays, which she said were to be given at eventide Monday through Friday.

These secret-ray rosaries, which are released in this volume, are: The First Secret Ray: The Inspiration Mysteries; The Second Secret Ray: The Action Mysteries; The Third Secret Ray: The Revelation Mysteries; The Fourth Secret Ray: The Declaration Mysteries; and The Fifth Secret Ray: The Exhortation Mysteries. Mother Mary said that when a sufficient number of people would have established their daily ritual of reciting these rosaries she would dictate the fourteenth rosary, which is to be released in Book Three.

Mary's Scriptural Rosary for the New Age teaches the disciple the devotional aspect of the love of Mother and Son—their love for him and his love for them—while reinforcing the pattern of the life and works of Mary and Jesus as they set forth for all the highest and best example of the Christian way of life and laid the foundation for the Christian dispensation.

The giving of this rosary, formulated by our spiritual Mother to meet the needs of the hour, affords a universally Christic experience calculated by heaven to awaken the soul to the realities of the Divine Woman and the Manchild. For it is their light that goes forth from each one who elects to be a part of the rosary of life that garlands the earth. This living rosary is composed of every son and daughter of the flame who daily consecrates his energies both in heaven and on earth in the ongoing service of Jesus and Mary.

The rosary of souls is an endless chain of floral offerings to the Mother, which she receives, blesses and returns to her children to make them one—heart, soul and mind—as the great body of Christ[3] on earth, the living Church Universal and Triumphant. These prayers are the true and lasting praise of the saints who shall overcome the accuser of our brethren by the blood (the essence of the sacred fire) of the Lamb (of the Christ). This is the word (the spoken Word) of their testimony—of them that loved not their lives unto the death.[4]

And when the oneness of the children of the light is made manifest in the flow of their communion with the Father and the Mother—affirming "I and my Father are One/I and my Mother are One"—then shall they be found with one accord in one place.[5] And they shall hear "a great voice out of heaven saying, Behold, the tabernacle of God is with men, and he will dwell with them, and they shall be his people, and God himself shall be with them and be their God."[6]

Christians have prayed to God through Jesus and Mary from the founding of the early church to the present. Thus it will be seen that the giving of the rosary is the exaltation of the Motherhood of God and of the divine Sonship that can never be confined to one church or one dogma. Just as the theme of the Son of God conceived of the Cosmic Virgin is heard over and again in many of the world's religions, so all mankind will one day revere the Mother as the source of life and the Son of God as the Saviour of the Christic light within all.

The "Adorations of the Rosary," which precede the mysteries in Part Two, consist of the prayers outlined by Mother Mary for the five secret rays. And in "Mary's Ritual of the Rosary," the giving of the rosary is explained in fourteen steps so that all who read and feel the love of the Mother may return that love by immediately offering these meditations, salutations and affirmations even while they recall the sacred events in the life of our Lord, whose grace is sufficient for us and whose hope is our eternal salvation.

Part Three of this book is a collection of "Fourteen Messages of the Word of Life" dictated by Mother Mary to us as we have journeyed throughout the world preaching the gospel of the kingdom.[7] As a part of the mission of the heavenly hierarchy to the age, the spoken Word of God has been delivered through our twin flames from the body of saints whom we know as ascended masters. In this giving of the testimony of the sacred fire and of the Law of the Logos, hierarchy has proclaimed that the work of the two witnesses[8] has been accomplished.

The Word of Mary set forth in these fourteen messages also prepares the individual consciousness for the initiatic experiences of Jesus' last days on earth. As the disciple assimilates Mother Mary's own awareness of the perfect will of God for every son and daughter, he is blessed by Jesus' momentum of overcoming at each of the fourteen stations (initiations) on the *via dolorosa*.

To know Mary the Mother we must become aware of the appearance of the individualization of her God flame during the centuries of her service to the Father, to the Son and to the Holy Spirit. Therefore in our Introduction, "The Soul of Mary in Heaven," we have desired to acquaint the children of the Mother—

those who have known and acknowledged her flame and those who have not—with new insight and a better understanding of the functions of this ascended lady master. For as the patroness of the youth of the world, she holds a key position in the hierarchy of ascended masters who have set forth the scriptures for the golden age in the teachings and publications of The Summit Lighthouse.

Mother Mary has bequeathed to humanity the archetype of the New Age woman. By her example and constancy, she calls forth the Divine Woman in us all. She not only shows us *how* the feminine principle can be redeemed, but *why* it must be redeemed in order that the Divine Manchild as the unfolding Christed man and Christed woman might appear within every son and daughter beloved of God.

This is the Divine Manchild who must go forth to rule all nations—every aspect of the human consciousness—with the rod of iron.[9] The meaning of *rod* is "radiance of divinity." The meaning of *iron* is "I," or the I AM, "rule over nature." And nature includes the four planes of God's consciousness designated as fire, air, water and earth, which correspond to the four lower bodies of man and of the planet.

The ruling of the nations with the rod of iron is the "radiance of divinity in the I AM rule over nations." The establishment of this rule is the goal of the incarnation of the feminine ray in this and every age. The culmination of the mission of the divine Feminine, the energy spiral of Omega in both man and woman, is the realization of the Christ consciousness.

Until the feminine principle of the Godhead is ennobled in each man and each woman, the Christ cannot be born. And until Christ is born in the individual, the evolving identity of man and woman cannot experience the new birth. Thus the rebirth of the Christ in man and woman, often referred to as the Second Coming, is necessary for the salvation of the soul; indeed the individual Christ Self is the Saviour of the world of the individual.

When the Christ is born in the heart of man and woman, his consciousness dethrones the Antichrist, whom Paul referred to as the carnal mind that is enmity against God.[10] For the Son of God comes forth to slay the dragon of the lower self—the human ego—which must be put down that the Divine Ego may appear.

Without the Mother there can be no Son. Therefore this trilogy is dedicated to all devotees of the Blessed Mother and of her Son, Jesus Christ, who personified the glory of the only begotten Son of God that we might behold his light—"the true light which lighteth every man that cometh into the world"[11]—thus be molded in his image.

It is the fond hope of the Mother and her fervent faith that her children, following the precepts of the Father, shall succeed beyond their farthest dreams. Thus she beckons with a poem and a smile:

> The house of divine Sonship
> Holds open still the door.
> The darkness of the mortal mind
> Cannot, shall not, be anymore.
>
> For just beyond the mortal sunset
> Lies the light's immortal dawn,
> Trembling on the face of morning,
> Shining promise from now on.
>
> Day of life's immortal gladness
> Echoes from the dim-lit past,
> Shimmering freshness of the Daystar,
> Crystal diamonds in the grass.
>
> Like a dewdrop ever fairer
> You reveal the bright new day;
> In the fervor ever nearer
> Christ's own face is seen today.

Like a gossamer veil atremble
With the thunder of the sun,
Beauteous doorway of forever
Swings wide open for each one!

In Her service I remain

Elizabeth Clare Prophet

Introduction
The Soul of Mary in Heaven

Mother Mary is of the angelic kingdom, chosen by Alpha and Omega, Father-Mother God, to incarnate in the planes of Matter to give birth to the Christ, the Word incarnate. In holding the immaculate concept for the incarnation of the Word in Jesus Christ, she set the archetypal pattern of the Christ for the sixth root race.[1] Realizing in her soul the fullness of the Presence of God as Mother, through her "magnifying" of the Lord or "law" of being, she set the example for the culmination of true womanhood and the rise of the feminine principle in the Piscean age.

Mary serves on the fifth ray of truth, concentration, constancy, science, healing and precipitation. She says, "Because the flame of the fifth ray relates to precipitation in Mater* and because the feminine aspect of the flame is directly involved in the spirals of God-realization descending from the formless into form, I was chosen by Alpha and Omega to incarnate in this system of worlds, to set forth in time and space the example of the Divine Woman reaching full self-realization in and as the Divine Mother [of the Christ consciousness incarnate]."[2]

While her twin flame, Archangel Raphael, remained in the planes of Spirit, Mary took incarnation in the planes of Matter to manifest the balance of the flow of truth "as Above, so below," to be on earth as in heaven the ensoulment of the Mother ray. She is one among the archeiai[†] who has experienced directly the veil of human tears, one who—like the avatars, Buddhas and Christed ones of every age—has volunteered to work through the form of

---

* *Mater*, Latin for "mother," used interchangeably with *Matter*.
† *archeiai* (plural): the feminine complements or twin flames of the archangels (singular, *archeia*).

flesh and blood to save the lost sheep of the house of Israel. As she has said: "Take comfort, O my children! There is not a place on earth where you can be that I also have not been."[3]

To know Mary the Mother we must become aware of the appearance of the individualization of her God flame during the centuries of her service to the Father, to the Son and to the Holy Spirit. The soul of Mary merited and received the training of the priests of the sacred fire in the science of the Great Law. Both in former embodiments of consecration to the flame and between incarnations while she served in the retreats of the Great White Brotherhood,[4] through diligence and a right heart, Mary was able to transfer her momentums of mastery gained in the angelic kingdom to avenues of service in the world of evolving humanity.

Through obedience and unselfish love, the divine complement of Archangel Raphael earned a position in hierarchy to which many aspire but few attain. To this one who offered her life as an open door for heaven's love to be consummated on earth, heaven opened its doors. Mary frequented the temples of the archangels and was welcomed by the hierarchs of the retreats of the Brotherhood, who received her in the role of disciple as well as master.

The solicitation of God's messengers, of seraphim and cherubim both before and after her soul's descent into the form provided by Anna and Joachim was a tangible manifestation of the grace of God that assisted her in keeping the delicate instrument of her consciousness tuned to the celestial truths of inner spheres, which she had known and mastered long ago. These angelic beings also assisted her in the focusing of the consciousness of listening grace.

Mary dwelt on Venus prior to taking embodiment on earth, to which planet she was assigned by the Lords of Karma[5] to show forth the raising of the feminine ray subsequent to the fall of Eve. There she served among the evolutions whose energies focalize on the etheric plane and who for thousands of years have sustained, through the laws of harmony and love, the culture of the Divine Mother.

The souls evolving under Sanat Kumara and the seven holy Kumaras and Lady Master Venus are those who have applied themselves to the laws of nonattachment—humility, chastity and obedience, selflessness, harmlessness and desirelessness—and are thereby wholly free to be agents for the flow of the creative energies of the Central Sun.*

Mary, then, through a long period of sojourn on Hesper (Venus), was prepared to come to earth and to challenge mankind's perversion of the cosmic honor flame—of the fiery crystal spirals of obedience to God's laws that sustain the very movements of the atoms and the rhythm of heavenly bodies. She came bearing a generous portion of the fires of Lady Venus, charged with her love, and carrying the responsibility to redeem the feminine nature in all mankind. Through her own momentum of grace, combined with that of Raphael, Mary pursued her calling—"operation regeneration"—in the constancy of the emerald ray, the fifth ray. To assist her in the operation, the LORD assigned the full complement of angels and hierarchies serving under Archangel Raphael to etch upon the consciousness—the body, the soul and the mind—of earth's evolutions the laws of truth, the transforming power of truth and the science of truth.

Holding the balance of Alpha and Omega in the center of the spherical mandala of this order of angelic hosts, Raphael and Mary offered themselves to the God and Goddess Meru.⁶ Before the great altar of the feminine ray in their etheric retreat, the Temple of Illumination, at Lake Titicaca, they came—-archangel and archeia—to pronounce their vows to bring truth to the entire evolution of souls who were to embody under the sixth dispensation sponsored by Lord and Lady Meru. For through these magnificent

---

*the point of origin of all physical-spiritual creation.

twin flames representing Helios and Vesta—Father-Mother Center
of our solar system—the lifewave, or soul group, known as the
sixth root race would receive the impetus of the spirals of Alpha
and Omega.

Embodiment on Earth

Under the tutelage of the hierarchs of the sixth dispensation,
Jesus incarnated to set forth in body, mind and soul the archetypal
pattern of the Son of God, the Christ, while Mary came forth to
typify the incarnation of the feminine ray as it relates to Father, to
Son and to Holy Spirit. She appears as the Mother of God incarnate, the favorite daughter of the Most High, a sister of the sacred
fire, of kings and priests unto God,[7] of the spirits of nature and of
all walking the homeward path. She leads us to the ultimate goal
of the divine Feminine, to the culminating matrix of divine womanhood in all its glory—to be the bride of the Holy Spirit.[8]

After serving a novitiate in the retreat of Lord and Lady Meru,
during which time she also journeyed with Raphael and the
angelic hosts to apply herself to the disciplines of several of the
retreats of the Brotherhood, the time came for her to embody in
Nazareth to initiate the spirals of the Piscean age and the victory
over death through the mastery of the fires of the divine Feminine.
The record shows that through her application to the Mother ray,
the spirals of white fire infolding and enfolding within her heart
comprised a cosmos in itself. And thus the regenerative stream of
God's mind concentrated and consecrated there was to provide
the energy and the way for millions of evolutions to come to the
reality of their own God-potential through the sacred heart of
Mary. So pure is the stream of fire kept within the heart of Mary
by her devotion that it is as a reservoir of light to all peoples and
all nations. The light of her heart is a veritable sun in itself, a
source of succor to all who call upon God in her name.

When devotees of the Mother pray for the consecration of

loved ones—of those who are passing from this plane to the next or of nations and peoples in need—to the Immaculate Heart of Mary, the response is immediate. Streams of light pouring forth from her heart supply the pure energies needed to carry a planet and its people through their darkest hours. The fires of the heart of Mary are golden-pink liquid light that infuse souls and bodies and minds with healing, with inspiration, with guidance and an ever-present help.

Although many glorious beings are arrayed among the hosts of heaven to serve humanity's needs, there is no one who can replace the image of Mary within the heart of one who has beheld her glory. She comes at any hour of the day or night to enfold in her arms of love and her mantle of protection all who call to God and seek the comfort of the Cosmic Mother. As Saint Bernard said, no one who has ever fled to her protection or asked her intercession was left unaided. Her golden, flowing hair, her deep blue-green eyes, her perfect features glowing in an oval face, her form delicate but strong, her stature graceful, imposing but not too tall, she comes draped in the robes of a heavenly goddess and reveals to us the light of her heart as sparkling diamonds so brilliant that we can scarcely look upon them, so dazzling is this focus of the Central Sun. Those who have been privileged to observe this aspect of her cosmic consciousness often speak of Mary's diamond heart, offering praise to the light of God's holy will that is concentrated there for the nourishment of earth's evolutions.

In the Temple of Illumination, the Lord and Lady Meru anchored within the mental and etheric bodies of Mary those precepts that she imparted to Jesus when he was a child. These etheric-mental patterns also provided the matrices through which the energy spirals flowed while Mary carried Jesus in her womb. Thus the full momentum of the feminine ray from high in the Andes was made tangible in the body of Jesus through the soul of Mary. The anchoring of the masculine ray from the retreat of Lord

Himalaya in the Himalayan mountains was accomplished in his early years when Jesus himself journeyed to the East between the ages of twelve and thirty[9] and frequented many of the retreats of the Brotherhood.

Just as Mary had been prepared for thousands of years for the role she was to play in the great drama of the Piscean age whereby the Lord would make himself known to his people as the flame of God-mastery, so Joseph was also prepared to focus the flame of the Father and to provide the protection required for the threefold flame as the basis for the divine family and for the entire Christian dispensation.

Today Joseph is known as the Master of Freedom, Saint Germain. As Mary is called the Mother of God, so he has earned the right to be called the God of Freedom to the earth and the Master of the Aquarian Age. The return to the unity of the family, wherein each member thereof holds sacred his office and his position in the trinity, is the beginning of the return of civilization to the golden-age standard.

In Joseph the father, in Jesus the son, in Mary the mother who is wed to the Holy Spirit, we see the foundation for the golden city of the sun, the City Foursquare, to become the kingdom of God in manifestation upon earth. Joseph heard the warning of the angel to depart into Egypt after the birth of Jesus, because Herod sought to kill the one who had been prophesied to be king of the Jews, the one who would hold the key to the incarnation of God among the Israelites.[10] Thus, while the innocents were being slaughtered,[11] Mary and Joseph fled to Egypt and took Jesus to the Ascension Temple at Luxor, where in early childhood he studied the disciplines of the Law and the alchemical principles which he was to publicly demonstrate during the final three years of his mission.

The writings of the early church fathers record many instances of the infancy of Jesus that have not been included in the four

Gospels. Jesus returned to Jerusalem after the death of Herod "that it might be fulfilled which was spoken of the Lord by the prophet, saying, Out of Egypt have I called my son."[12]

At the age of twelve, Jesus was found conversing in the temple and confounding the doctors.[13] At an early age he was baptized of the Holy Spirit; and during the years that followed, he studied in the retreats of the Brotherhood in the Far East, in the Retreat of the Blue Lotus under Lord Himalaya, and under his guru, Lord Maitreya, and other ascended and unascended masters. Here he learned the mastery of the four planes of Spirit and Mater through the mantras and meditations and the transfiguring affirmations, which he taught to his disciples. One of the most important of these was "I AM the resurrection and the life."[14]

Although there was anchored within the soul of Jesus all that was required for him to fulfill his mission, the preparation for the final three years of the public demonstration of the Law was given to him that he might anchor in his four lower bodies the sacred symbols and hieroglyphs, the matrices of perfection. All of this was in preparation for the ultimate victory, the public demonstration of life over death and the raising of the physical body by the power of the resurrection flame. When Jesus was prepared to enter public life, having humbled himself before members of the hierarchy who would rather have chosen to be his students than his guru, he revealed step by step the thirty-three tests that must come to everyone who desires to reunite with the God flame.

The early and later years of Jesus and his teachings on the initiatic path will be the subject of another volume.[15] In this introduction to the soul of Mary we are attempting to show her relationship to Jesus. With all her strength and light and devotion, the final three years of Jesus' mission was a period of great testing and trial for the Mother. Nevertheless, it was her concentrated momentum on the fifth ray that enabled her to sustain the matrix of the triumph of truth through the miraculous life of Jesus unto the hour of his crucifixion, his resurrection and his victory in the light.

Jesus' parting words to his mother before his death on the cross were, referring to the beloved disciple John, "Woman, behold thy son!" and to the disciple, "Behold thy mother!" Thus the mantle of the son—the Son of God—was passed in that moment to the foremost disciple of Jesus, and it is written that from that hour the disciple took her unto his own home. [16]

Later Years

After the forty-day period during which Jesus appeared to the apostles and the holy women in the upper room, Mary gathered together the inner circle of devotees who had made themselves ready to partake of the initiatic mysteries, gathering often to receive instruction, to receive the sacred Word of Jesus Christ. By the descent of the Holy Spirit on the day of Pentecost these were made the body of God upon earth whose souls by their consecration formed the foundation of the Christian Church.

Mary the Mother was the acknowledged head of that community of lightbearers—the center of the circle of apostles, disciples and holy women. She was the veritable fountainhead of Christic energies that flowed throughout the Holy Land, the Mediterranean and Asia Minor, wherever the good news of Christ the light of the world was spread abroad. From Mary's heart concentric rings of fire—the fire of the Holy Ghost—moved outward as the ever-widening embrace of the Father-Mother that holds all of humanity in the geometry of love.

After a time, according to the instruction given by Jesus and the Archangel Raphael, Mary, with the help of John the Beloved and Joseph of Arimathea, organized a journey through Egypt, across the Mediterranean and to the British Isles to anchor the Christic light for the Piscean dispensation.

They traveled to the retreat of the Brotherhood at Luxor, Egypt, to the Temple of Truth on the island of Crete, across the

Mediterranean Sea, stopping in southern Italy, southern France and Portugal, and then on through the Strait of Gibraltar to Glastonbury in the British Isles and to Ireland.

In all these places, seven devotees drew forth the seven rays of the Holy Spirit that would enable those following the light of the Christic path to outpicture the seven aspects of the Christ consciousness[17] over the next two thousand years. Mary herself drew down the focus of the fifth ray from the retreat of Archangel Raphael that is located over Fátima, Portugal, where she later, from the ascended state, would appear to the holy children and perform miracles before the multitudes. In each of these places the flame of truth to which her heart had been dedicated so long was anchored. The healing focus at Lourdes, in southern France, is the divine manifestation of Mary's services both in earth and in heaven.

According to legend, the Holy Grail, the cup used by Jesus at the Last Supper, was buried in a well in Glastonbury. Here Jesus appeared and planted the flame of the Christ, which later inspired El Morya, embodied as King Arthur, to form the Knights of the Round Table and to enfire them in the quest for the Holy Grail. The focus of the threefold flame placed in Ireland was later drawn upon by Saint Patrick, who taught the mystery of the Trinity through the shamrock, illustrating therewith the individed oneness of Father, Son and Holy Spirit. He also invoked the sword of truth to rebuke the plague of serpents that threatened the land of Eire.

The emerald-green healing flame remains to this day the symbol of Ireland and a remembrance of a journey long ago traveled by those seven representatives of light whose devotion to the seven rays enabled them to succeed in paving the way for the expansion of Christianity throughout Europe and ultimately the entire Western Hemisphere.

It is believed that Mary spent the last years of her life in Jerusalem and made her transition from the Holy City about the year 48. According to local tradition, John took Mary to Ephesus for a time to escape persecution in Jerusalem. Examining the various traditions surrounding the passing of Mary, we find that evidence takes us back to the Cenacle, the upper room in which the Last Supper was held and in which the apostles met after Jesus' departure from their midst. In the Acts of the Apostles we read that the apostles "all continued with one accord in prayer and supplication with the women and Mary the mother of Jesus and with his brethren."[18]

It is said that the Mother of the early Church kept the flame of the Mother on behalf of earth's evolutions on Mount Zion in a house overlooking the city and the temple, the Cedron Valley, and the Mount of Olives. There in the upper chamber that became the gathering place of the disciples and where the first Christian church was established, Mary served the Logos during her final years of glory. It is in this place that Christians guard the memory of the dormition, or "falling asleep," of the Blessed Mother.

Saint John of Damascus, an eighth-century Greek Father of the Church, describes the passing of Mary with the apostles at her bedside. He tells how they were moved by divine grace to sing hymns of farewell, how angelic choirs sang to the Divine Mother, and how they carried her bier on their shoulders through the streets of the Holy City followed by the entire Christian congregation while angels accompanied the procession, praising God and covering the coffin with their wings as pinions of protection.[19]

It is said that Mary was laid to rest in a sepulchre near the Grotto of Gethsemane. On the third day Thomas, who had been absent, came to the tomb and the disciples opened it for him that he might both see and believe. It is recounted that the tomb was empty save for beautiful roses and white lilies. God had received her unto himself through the ritual of the ascension, known as the Assumption of the Blessed Virgin.

From these writings of the early Christians we glimpse the

glory of the beautiful soul pattern of a daughter of the Most High chosen to magnify the LORD from the hour of her immaculate conception in the heart of the Father-Mother God. In her final incarnation, Mary held from infancy the focus both for the Mother flame and for the Word that was to be made flesh and dwell among us.[20] This holding of the immaculate concept in mind and heart as the image most holy proved to be her great genius in every life she lived for truth.

In this perfect realization of the divine Feminine, Mary countermanded the fall of Eve, even as Jesus had reversed the spiral of the sin of Adam. By their proving of the Law in the masculine and feminine cycles of the Godhead, they charted the course whereby every man and woman who applied himself could master the energies of the Piscean age and return to the Eden of God's oneness. Through the Sacred Heart of Jesus and the Immaculate Heart of Mary, man and woman can call forth the power, the wisdom and the love of the Woman and the Manchild to resurrect all of the energies of life that have ever flowed through their being and to restore the mind (Father) and heart (Mother) of self to the divine wholeness.

The coronation of Mary referred to in the Catholic Church is the crowning of the Blessed Mother with the twelve stars of glory, signifying her mastery of the twelve initiatic mysteries through the mastery of the energies of the twelve solar hierarchies.[21] Her position as Queen of Angels and Queen of All Saints is understood in the light of the fact that in each dispensation, in each two-thousand-year cycle, a masculine and a feminine member of the heavenly hierarchy holds the office of the Christ and of the Divine Mother. Hence during the Piscean age Jesus and Mary have held this position in hierarchy. Their triumph over the last enemy is the open door for sons and daughters of God to walk through and inherit immortal life. "I AM the open door which no man can shut!"[22]

Mary's Appearances Since Her Ascension

Although all ascended lady masters keep the flame for the World Mother, Christians revere Mary as the Mother of Mothers, the archetype of motherhood. Since her ascension, Mary has made several famous appearances and continues today to respond immediately to the call of any and all of her children on earth.

Guadalupe

Her appearance in sixteenth-century Mexico had a profound effect on the spread of Christianity in the New World. In what is now Guadalupe, Mexico, Mary appeared to Juan Diego, a fifty-seven-year-old Aztec Indian born of the servant class. He and his uncle Juan Bernardino, had been among the first Indians converted to Christianity.

On December 9, 1531, Juan Diego was on his way to honor Mary at Saturday morning Mass when a sudden and unexpected symphony of birds' song brought him to a halt. As he stopped to listen, the singing abruptly stopped. Through the silence a sweet voice beckoned him by name.

Juan Diego climbed the frozen hill that hid from him the source of that sweet voice and there atop the hill beheld a Mexican maiden of radiant beauty. She appeared to be about fourteen years old. Golden beams of light streamed from her in every direction. All that touched her radiant beauty was bathed in an ethereal magnificence. Rocks and trees and cacti sparkled like jewels and gold. Raised up by the glory he witnessed, Juan Diego calmly regarded the maiden as she said to him, "I am the ever-virgin Mary, Mother of the true God." Mary explained that she wanted a church built on the hill from where "I will show my compassion to your people and to all people who sincerely ask my help in their work and in their sorrow."[23]

Conveying the Blessed Virgin's request, Juan Diego twice visited the Lord Bishop in Mexico City, who requested of him an authenticating sign. Mary promised to give Juan the sign on Monday, the following morning. Juan missed his appointment with Mary while caring for Juan Bernardino, who had fallen ill with a deadly fever. Juan Diego passed the holy hill on Tuesday morning while on his way to find a priest who would administer the Last Rites to his uncle. Mother Mary descended the hill and met him on the road. She told him that Juan Bernardino was healed and that as she had effectively attended to his errand, he could now freely attend to hers.

Mary instructed Juan Diego to climb the frozen hill and gather the flowers he would find growing there. And there amid the frost-capped grass and frozen rocks, Juan found growing magnificent Castilian roses, fragrant and fresh with dew. Juan filled his *tilma*, or cape, with the wonderful roses and returned to the Virgin, who carefully arranged the roses in his tilma, tied the bottom of the garment around his neck, and sent him to the bishop.

With the bishop were several of his staff. Juan Diego faithfully told the bishop everything that the Blessed Virgin had wanted him to tell and then reaching up, loosed from around his neck the tilma that held the requested sign. The roses fell in a heap to the floor. The bishop was suddenly up out of his chair and kneeling before Juan Diego. Everyone else in the room soon joined the bishop and appeared to be praying to Juan.

This confused him until he looked down at his tilma and saw what the bishop and his staff saw. The Blessed Virgin had indeed given them a sign, for there emblazoned on his tilma was the image of the Virgin as he had first seen her three days earlier, wonderfully radiant and beautiful. The bishop finally rose and removed the imaged tilma to be enshrined first in his chapel, then in the first little church built on the holy hill.

Several of the bishop's advisers traveled with Juan Diego to see his uncle. When they arrived at Juan Bernardino's dwelling, they found him relaxing in the sun. He told them how he had been on the edge of death when the darkness that had been engulfing him was dispersed by the light of a young lady who suddenly stood beside him radiating peace and love. She informed him that he would be well, that she had intercepted Juan Diego and that she had sent him to the bishop with a picture of herself that would be enshrined on the rocky hill. "Call me and call my image," she told him, "Santa Maria de Guadalupe."[24]

Today, more than four hundred years later, the perfectly preserved image of Our Lady of Guadalupe remains displayed and venerated in the new basilica, completed in 1976. Through the intercession of beloved Mother Mary, and galvanized by this miraculous sign, millions of Aztecs swiftly embraced Christianity. Blessing the New World with her appearance and intercession, Mary plainly demonstrated the universal love of the Divine Mother for her children.

Lourdes

Mary's appearances at Lourdes are among her most famous, and led to the establishment of a pilgrimage center that has drawn millions from all over the world. Bernadette Soubirous was the eldest child of a poor milling family from the village of Lourdes, in southwest France at the foot of the Pyrenees. On February 11, 1858, Bernadette was gathering firewood near a rocky grotto. Alerted by a noise like a storm, she turned towards the grotto. There in one of the openings of the rock she saw a lone rosebush that waved as if blown by a secret wind. A golden cloud formed there and soon after a lady of magnificent beauty appeared above the rosebush.

She looked to be sixteen or seventeen years old and was dressed in a long white robe that was tied at the waist with a flowing blue ribbon. A long white veil almost covered her hair and fell down at the back to below her waist. Her feet were bare but for the last folds of her robe and the gleaming yellow rose that graced each foot. On her right arm was a rosary of white beads and a gold chain that, like the roses on her feet, shone as though made of the sun.

Bernadette took her rosary in hand and knelt on the ground. The Lady led the rosary in silence but prayed aloud with Bernadette each "Glory be to the Father." Bernadette did not yet know with whom she prayed. When the rosary was completed, the Lady returned to the golden-clouded hollow of the rock and disappeared.

Mary visited the child eighteen times at the grotto. Bernadette was told to bring a lighted candle on her visits and to pray for sinners. At the eighth visit, Mary exhorted her with the statement, "Penitence! Penitence! Penitence!" On the ninth visit, Mary told Bernadette to "drink from the fountain and bathe in it."[25] Bernadette was puzzled, since there was no source of water in the grotto. She began to dig at the ground with her fingers. In moments a bubbling pool was formed from which Bernadette drank and washed her face.

Large crowds accompanied Bernadette on her visits to the grotto. Clerical and secular investigations and harassments had been initiated. Bernadette stood for her Lady before all and courageously continued to visit the grotto. In the thirteenth visit, Mary asked Bernadette to have the clergy build a chapel at the grotto and have the people go there in procession.

At their sixteenth visit, Mary revealed her identity by declaring, "I am the Immaculate Conception."[26] Bernadette did not know what "Immaculate Conception" meant, but it became a phrase that sealed in hearts and minds the world around the beauty, validity and God-magnificence of that radiant Lady who blessed Bernadette and the entire world with her presence.

The pool that flowed to the hand of Bernadette at the command of beloved Mother Mary is charged with miraculous healing properties. Today its flowing waters minister to the mental, emotional, spiritual and physical needs of those who come in faith to bathe in its waters.

Some time after the pool appeared, a crippled man left his crutches propped against the grotto rock as a sign of his miraculous healing. Today thousands of crutches and candles blaze a message of gratitude for the merciful bounty of the Mother of God. An international board of medical examiners verifies the stream of legitimate healings that yet flows from the shrine of Our Lady of the Immaculate Conception. Verified against the highest standards of professional inquiry, the healings at Mary's fountain of living water continue to bear witness on earth of the eternal wisdom of our Father-Mother God in heaven.

Fátima

In 1917, the Blessed Mother appeared to three shepherd children near Fátima, Portugal. At that time, World War I was raging across Europe and the Bolsheviks were plotting their revolution in Russia.

Holy Amethyst, divine consort of Archangel Zadkiel, spoke to us of Mary's visitation in the rocky meadows of Portugal:

"One of the tremendous appearances that Mary made in your own time was the appearance at Fátima, when the great miracle was performed before the eyes of the three holy children selected by karmic law and recompense to receive a manifestation of this Blessed Mother.

"I call to your attention that those three holy children that received that vision were also in the Essene community and knew her in her state of imperfection, and they were chief among the critics of her at that time. It came to pass, then, that it was given to their eyes to see her in her glory in performance and fulfillment of the great truth of God, which he has spoken, saying, 'And I will bring thine enemies to thy feet that they may know how much I have loved thee.'"[27]

Prior to Mother Mary's visitations, the Angel of Peace appeared three times to the children—Lucia dos Santos, age nine, and to Jacinta and Francisco Marto, her cousins, age six and eight respectively. It was the summer of 1916.

In his first appearance, the children saw a great dazzling light that moved over the valley from east to west. As the light drew near the cave where they were playing, they saw the form of a young man of about fourteen or fifteen years of age, "transparent as crystal when the sun shines through it, and of great beauty."[28]

As they beheld his countenance filled with glory, he spoke: "I am the Angel of Peace. Pray with me." He then knelt, touching his forehead to the ground, and prayed: "O my God, I believe, I adore, I hope and I love thee. I ask pardon for those who do not believe, do not adore, do not hope and do not love thee." The angel gave this prayer three times, the children repeating it after him. Then rising to his feet, he told the children to pray in this manner, for "the hearts of Jesus and Mary are attentive to the voice of your supplications."[29]

On his second visitation to the three children, whose hearts the hierarchy employed to focus a threefold action of the flame of peace, the angel identified himself as the Guardian Angel of Portugal. He adjured them to "Pray, pray a great deal! The hearts of Jesus and of Mary have merciful designs for you. Offer prayers and sacrifices constantly to the Most High." Lucia, focusing the love of the Holy Spirit, asked how they were to sacrifice, and the angel replied: "With all your power offer a sacrifice as an act of reparation for the sinners by whom He is offended, and of supplication for the conversion of sinners. Thus draw peace upon your country. I am its Guardian Angel, the Angel of Portugal. Above all accept and endure with submission the suffering which the Lord will send you."[30]

In his third and last appearance, in September or October of 1916, the angel descended in the crystalline light, holding a chalice with the Lord's host suspended above it. These remained in the air as he knelt down and addressed the Deity:

"Most Holy Trinity—Father, Son, and Holy Spirit—I adore thee profoundly. I offer thee the most precious Body, Blood, Soul and Divinity of Jesus Christ, present in all the tabernacles of the world, in reparation for the outrages, sacrileges and indifferences whereby he is offended. And through the infinite merits of his most Sacred Heart and the Immaculate Heart of Mary, I beg of thee the conversion of poor sinners."[31]

He then administered the Sacred Eucharist to the children, saying: "Take and drink the Body and the Blood of Jesus Christ, horribly insulted by ungrateful men. Make reparation for their crimes and console your God."[32] They saw drops of blood falling from the host into the cup. The angel placed the host on the tongue of Lucia, and to Jacinta and Francisco he gave the chalice (for they had not received their first Communion) and they partook of it. Once again the angel prostrated himself and pronounced the prayer three times, the children saying it with him.

As we shall see, this bright angel came as a messenger of the Divine Mother to prepare the children's consciousness for her visitation and to test them to see if they were ready to be obedient to her representative and to pray as he had instructed them to do. Should they pass this initiation in hierarchy, then they would become worthy to receive the Blessed Virgin herself.

This Angel of Peace has revealed himself to us as the head of a band of angels known as the Legion of Peace. And from the Keeper of the Scrolls we learn that he assisted Jesus in amplifying the flame of peace during his Galilean ministry. He was also one of the ministering angels who, together with Holy Amethyst, kept the vigil with Jesus in the Garden of Gethsemane. He was one of the heavenly hosts sent by God to sustain Jesus after he had prayed, "Father, if thou be willing, remove this cup from me: nevertheless not my will, but thine, be done."[33]

Although the Father, acting in conformity to his own Law, did not "remove this cup," he did send his archangels and archeiai and, among others, this Angel of Peace to strengthen Jesus in his resolve to do the will of God. The fiery presence of these angels served as electrodes to magnetize the flames of peace and power, healing and truth, faith and hope and reality from Jesus' own causal body, thereby aiding Jesus in bringing the full momentum of his own light to bear upon the betrayal, the trial and the crucifixion that lay before him.

The three appearances of the Angel of Peace served to establish in heart and mind, in body and soul of the three children the aspects of the holy Trinity. In the first instance the angel gives the command to "pray with me." He is testing their obedience, their faith and their love of the will of God. He teaches them how to invoke the law of forgiveness on behalf of those whose sin stands between them and their God.

All manifestations of sin, which represents the individual's abrogation of the sacred covenants of the law, focus a weight of density, or a karmic weight, within the aura or forcefield of the individual. When the faithful call upon the flame and the law of forgiveness on behalf of those whose sin so easily besets them,[34] the LORD God of hosts responds with the action of mercy. He sets aside a portion of this weight that mankind, being set apart for a time from the human will, might know the freedom of striving to overcome in the joy of God's will.

Promising them the solicitation of Jesus and Mary, assuring them that out of their heart's light their calls would be answered, he departed from them that their faith and their obedience to his communication might be tested.

In this account of the intercession of the angelic hosts we have on divine authority the teaching of the LORD on several aspects of prayer: (1) that prayer is a necessary form of communication between man and God; (2) that the godly are called upon to pray for the ungodly, the righteous for the unrighteous; (3) that it is within the right of all who adore, hope and love the LORD to beg the pardon of those who do not, that the act of calling for forgiveness not only for oneself but for others is thus within the province of God's children; (4) that prayer is more effective when it is repeated—specifically, when it is repeated three times—and that the repetition of prayer when performed in faith and hope and charity does not constitute vain repetition; (5) that man may pray to God and receive assistance from the hearts of heavenly beings such as Jesus and Mary.

Here, then, is proof of a heavenly order, or hierarchy of beings, serving under God on behalf of evolving humanity, and that the hearts of these beings, kindled with love, respond with light to the voice of the supplicant. This shows us that it is necessary to pray aloud. According to the Teachings of the Ascended Masters,[35] we know that it is the power of the spoken Word that makes prayer effective.

In his second visitation, the Angel of Peace sheds illumination upon his commands; and as a reward for their obedience, he explains another aspect of the law of prayer. He commanded them to "pray a great deal," showing again the necessity for constancy and repetition in prayer to build a momentum of mercy and forgiveness on behalf of mankind. He told them that Jesus and Mary had merciful designs for them, implying that these could not be accorded to them without their constant supplication. And then he told them also to sacrifice.

To sacrifice is to surrender something that is precious to the self, and the ultimate sacrifice is the total surrender of the self. Each time a child of God offers something of himself unto the Deity, the Deity can return that gift a thousandfold to the supplicant and through him to all mankind.

When a portion of the human race act singularly or concertedly or jointly in defiance of the Law, they accumulate offenses or a karmic weight that can only be balanced by the sacrifice of the saints. Thus the Angel of Peace appealed to the children to sacrifice, that peace might come upon their land. This is the law of the atonement whereby the light of the Christ in every heart is amplified to hold the balance for mankind's karma. He urged them to submit to the will of God, to accept and endure any suffering that would be sent by the LORD, not only to test and strengthen them but also as a counterbalance to the weight of injustices incurred in World War I.

In his third appearance, the Angel of Peace displays the epitome of the love of the Holy Spirit through the ritual of Holy Communion. With fervent adoration the angel offers unto the Most High God the Three-in-One, the Body, Blood, Soul and Divinity of Jesus Christ, which he pronounces is present in all the tabernacles of the world.

The reference to the tabernacles of the earth is most interesting. What are these tabernacles? Jesus said, "Destroy this temple, and in three days I will raise it up."[36] Clearly he was referring to the body temple. Paul said, "What? know ye not that your body is the temple of the Holy Ghost which is in you, which ye have of God, and ye are not your own?" And again he says, "For we know that if our earthly house of this tabernacle were dissolved, we have a building of God, an house not made with hands, eternal in the heavens."[37]

Preaching to the men of Athens, Paul affirmed that "God that made the world and all things therein, seeing that he is Lord of heaven and earth, dwelleth not in temples made with hands."[38] Our meditation upon this unique expression of the angel can only lead us to conclude in the light of scripture, as well as in the light of the ascended masters' teachings, that the precious body, blood, soul and divinity of Jesus Christ is present in the tabernacle, or dwelling place, of the souls of every man, woman and child evolving upon earth.

Why, then, is it necessary for the angel to offer these four aspects of the Christ consciousness to the most holy Trinity? It is necessary because the evolutions of earth have not yet consecrated the divinity of the Christ that God has placed within them. Thus the angel speaks on their behalf, hoping to attain the reparation for the "outrages, sacrileges and indifferences" with which the Christ in every man has been offended.

The angel pleads before the throne of the Almighty in the presence of the three holy children for the conversion of "poor sinners"—those who have not recognized the inherent life of God nor perceived that in him they "live and move and have their being."[39] The angel pleads his case before the Almighty according to the law of the sacred covenant whereby through the attainment won by sacrifice, the infinite merit of the most Sacred Heart of Jesus and the Immaculate Heart of Mary, souls desiring to be free may pass through the open door of the consciousness of Jesus and Mary and find therein forgiveness of sin, atonement through Holy Communion, and an opportunity to be found in the image of the Christ and in the image of the Divine Mother.

Having thus spoken three times, having pleaded his case before the courts of heaven on behalf of sinful humanity according to the law of the cycle of the three, the angel, in the role of priest of the Order of Melchizedek,[40] administers Communion, offering the Body, or Matter principle, and Blood, or Spirit principle, of Jesus Christ to those whom the LORD found worthy to receive it in his name.

Again he pleads, this time for the children to make reparation for the crimes of mankind and to console their God. This they will henceforth do in the power of the Holy Ghost, which it was his office to bestow upon them. And thus before taking leave of them, he prostrates himself once again and affirms the prayer three times with the children repeating it after him. How great are the lessons of God's angelic messengers.

Almost a year after the angel's appearances, on May 13, 1917, the children halted before a small evergreen tree. A lady "all of white, more brilliant than the sun"[41] stood atop the tree in a sphere of blazing light. The gold-edged veil and gown that hung to her feet were, like the rosary she held in her fingers, made of the same brilliant light. Her hands were held as in prayer before her heart.

Mary asked the children to come to the tree at the same time on the thirteenth day of each of the next five months. In October she would tell them who she was and what she wanted. She asked if they wanted to offer themselves to God, to pray for the conversion of sinners, and to help atone for the sins of the world by accepting whatever suffering God would send them. The children immediately agreed. "Then you will have much to suffer," she told them. "But the grace of God will be your comfort."[42] She asked them to say the rosary every day to obtain peace for the world and the end of the war. Our Lady then arose, until like a star she disappeared in the vastness of the East.

In June and July, the Lady told the children to pray the rosary every day in honor of Our Lady of the Rosary, who would be able to bring the world peace. She promised to perform a miracle in October so that everyone will see and believe. She gave the children two visions. The first vision was of the Immaculate Heart of Mary pierced by a crown of thorns that was formed by the sins of man.

The second vision, given in July, was of a sea of fire filled with demons and tortured souls. "You have seen hell [the astral plane]," she told them, "where the souls of poor sinners go. To save them God wishes to establish in the world the devotion to my Immaculate Heart."[43]

She warned that a greater war and much suffering would be meted out to mankind if they did not stop offending God. She asked for the Communion of Reparation on the first Saturdays and that Russia be consecrated to her Immaculate Heart. If her requests were granted, she said, Russia would be converted and there would be peace. If not, Russia "will spread her errors throughout the entire world, provoking wars and persecution of the Church. The good will suffer martyrdom. The Holy Father will suffer much. Different nations will be annihilated. But in the end my Immaculate Heart will triumph."[44] Mary then entrusted the children with a secret that they were not to reveal.

By this time the children had become the objects of much criticism and curiosity. Thousands of people joined them on their monthly pilgrimage. Their families were divided against them. They were being questioned by the local clergy, and the government administrator for Fátima was determined to stop the affair. He kidnapped the children on the morning of August thirteenth and caused them to miss their appointed meeting with the Lady. Though thrown in jail and threatened with torturous death, the children did not reveal the Lady's secret. They were released on the third day.

On August nineteenth and September thirteenth, Mary asked the children to continue their prayers, rosaries and sacrifices. "Many souls go to hell," she explained, "because they have no one to sacrifice and pray for them."[45]

On October thirteenth, the day of the promised miracle, it was cloud-covered and rainy. Seventy thousand people had gathered to witness the miracle. Mary spoke: "I am the Lady of the Rosary. Let them continue to say the Rosary every day. The war is going to end, and the soldiers will soon return to their homes." She said people must amend their lives and ask pardon for their sins. "Let them offend our Lord no more, for he is already much offended."[46]

The Lady of the Rosary then opened her hands and beamed a ray of light into the sky. The clouds rolled back and the sun shone brilliantly upon the crowd. Mary merged into the light from her hand and appeared high in the atmosphere with Saint Joseph, who held the infant Jesus in his arms. Jesus and Joseph blessed the world three times with the sign of the cross.

Then in the second vision, given only to Lucy, Mary appeared as she did on the way to Calvary and Jesus was by her side. Jesus looked compassionately upon the crowd and blessed them with the sign of the cross. In the last vision, Mary, with her infant son upon her knee, reigned as queen of heaven and earth. The Holy Queen then worked her miracle.

The blazing sun grew pale and began to whirl and dance and change colors in the sky. It rotated madly on its axis and spewed out gigantic flames that blazed and reflected their colors on the face of the people and the earth. Three times it danced the dizzying dance. It then toppled and plunged zig-zagging toward the earth. It seemed the end of the world. People fell to their knees and cried and prayed. The heat increased and increased until the sun halted suddenly in its earthbound course and returned to the place of its natural order. The all-surpassing power of Almighty God blazed upon the hearts and minds and world of the seventy thousand pilgrims who witnessed Mary's miracle of the sun.

"When I appeared at Fátima," Mother Mary tells us, "and the flow of my love poured out to stir a nation and a world, to sound a warning to mankind, it was to convey the same universal tide of love and light that flowed forth and ushered into the world the first Christmas: Peace on earth, good will toward men. Where is it now? Where but in the hearts of those who respond to it."[47]

Zeitoun

For three years, from April 1968 to early 1971, thousands gathered nightly outside the Coptic church in Zeitoun, a suburb of Cairo, Egypt, to witness the appearances of the Blessed Mother. Unlike Mary's other apparitions, everyone in the crowds, of any race and religion and belief, was able to see her. The apparitions were photographed by hundreds of professional photographers and were even broadcast by Egyptian TV.

Eyewitnesses said Mary's appearances over the church, which lasted anywhere from a few minutes to several hours, were heralded by flashing lights and the coming of large dovelike birds. On occasion, Jesus and Joseph accompanied the Blessed Mother. Published photographs taken during the apparitions show the figure of the Mother of Christ next to the dome of the church with a luminous bird hovering over her head. During the Zeitoun apparitions, hundreds said they were spontaneously healed, and reports of cures and miracles continued even after the apparitions had ceased.[48]

Medjugorje

Mother Mary has also desired to bring her sons and daughters closer to her heart through her appearances to six youths in the small village of Medjugorje. She began appearing to them on June 24, 1981, and has continued her appearances on a daily basis to the present day. Medjugorje is in what was then Yugoslavia but is now Bosnia-Herzegovina.

These appearances have also been met with skepticism and persecution. The seers were aged ten to sixteen when the apparitions began. They were interrogated by authorities of the Communist government and the Catholic Church. At one point, the local police detained the youths, told them to recant and threatened to have them committed to a mental asylum.

The parish pastor and other priests at first doubted the authenticity of the apparitions. This caused one of the seers, Ivanka, to remark, "The only ones who do not believe us are the priests and the police!"[49]

The youths were subjected to medical, psychological and psychiatric examinations to determine if their behavior was being caused by drugs, hypnosis or other factors. And they were also closely examined while in the state of ecstasy during the Blessed Mother's visitations.

As the throngs of believers continued to increase, the Communist government became alarmed at the religious revival taking place. Huge crowds of people would gather on a hillside overlooking Medjugorje to witness the apparitions. The authorities took repressive measures and several priests and nuns were arrested. For almost two years the police forbade anyone to visit the place of the apparitions.

For about six months during this time, the appearances took place at various other sites—such as fields, woods and the homes of the youths and many others in the village. Beginning in January 1982, the Blessed Mother appeared in the rectory, the sacristy and the choir loft of the parish church.

The children said that during her Medjugorje visitations the Blessed Mother gave them messages stressing peace, conversion, prayer, fasting, penance and a sacramental life. Mirjana, one of the seers, said, "Our Lady continues to invite us to prayer and fasting, saying: 'You have forgotten that with prayer and fasting you can ward off wars, suspend natural laws.'"[50]

The messages from the Blessed Mother are still being given to the visionaries. And in addition to these messages, Mother Mary has said that she will give to each of them a total of ten "secrets"— prophecies of events that will occur on earth in the near future.

Although the Catholic Church has declined to confirm that the visitations are authentic, Mother Mary said to us in a 1987 dictation that she was indeed appearing to the youths. More than twenty million people have made a pilgrimage to Medjugorje and many report having been spiritually strengthened and even transformed by their experiences there.

Mary's Ongoing Service

Until 1954, Jesus together with Mary held the focus of the masculine and feminine rays for the sixth, or Christian dispensation.

At that time, their responsibilities as directors for the coming age were assumed by Saint Germain and Portia, representatives of the seventh ray—the ray of freedom, transmutation, alchemy, mercy and justice—for the seventh, or Aquarian, dispensation. Mary today works with the ascended master El Morya and the Darjeeling Council in their service to the will of God on behalf of all mankind.

When called upon, Mary will place her blue cape around all who are in need of the protection of a mother's love. Her cape focuses the will of God and its intense protection for the Christ consciousness emerging within every soul. With Archangel Raphael, Mother Mary renders assistance teaching parents their responsibilities, preparing the way for incoming children and guiding the precious body elementals in the forming of physical bodies.

Her focus of the immaculate heart in the Resurrection Temple over the Holy Land is the focus of the threefold flame commemorating the mission of the Christ, of the Holy Trinity, and of her service with Saint Germain and Jesus that laid the foundation for two thousand years of Christian worship and service. Mother Mary's blue, which we associate with her love, is almost an aqua, a blue tinged with the healing radiation of her devotion to all who call for her assistance. Her flame flower and fragrance is the lily of the valley.

PART ONE

The Wisdom Aspect of the Holy Spirit
Fourteen Letters from a Mother to Her Children

New Alignments of Receptivity

Children! Children! Children!

Dipped in the life-essence of God,
The souls of men take on new luster.
The radiance of immortality
Shineth unto the present hour
In men and women of good will.

I know the human types,
The hard and the soft—
Those who shelve the feeling of love
In pursuit of an ideal
And are consistently driving forward
And those who are moved by every appeal,
Almost to a weeping of heart.
Both in the name of God
Mingle with those of the middle way;
They may appear to be divided in method,
But their purpose is one.

I plead for Christ-orientation
Which receives holy truth and rejects error,
Seeing no man's person
But only the gift of love
He brings to the altar
As his dedication to Reality.

Every earthly tie must one day be severed;
Even memory needs to die to pain.
Only then can God muster from the dust
The living souls who, in the patterns of the present,
Shall see the reality of paradise.

The whole world crumbles,
Yet, unafraid, the lamentation of Christ
Gathers the many devotees
Into new alignments of receptivity.

Forgiveness is so carelessly uttered
When memory is retained
And every recurrent activation of episode
Intensifies the hurt.
Forgive and release
Those who ignorantly harm you,
For these know not what they do.
One day a clearer morn shall dawn for all.
But for those who can hear, I plead:
Live in Christ charity,
Forgive one another continually,
And move on to world and personal perfection!

The day is far spent.
Stand!

Your Mother,
Mary

1

The Reality of Heaven
Is All around You

To Those Who Rejoice to Fulfill His Holy Will:

As the dancing light in the eyes of a child speaks of realms other than those of this earth, so do highlights often glimmer in the young men and women of the world when in unspoiled freshness of heart and mind they unfold the joyous expectancy of hope for life at hand. In the quietness of a garden, in the contemplation of nature bursting into bud do the strands of hope eternally renewed come into manifestation year after year.

As a mother watches her young child expand his tiny limbs until together with mind and consciousness they aspire afar, so does the flame of God posited within the soul gaze upon each child as Father-Mother Spirit Most Holy, hoping against hope that that one (returned to embodiment in the world of form to renew old associations, right old wrongs and win new victories) will be successful in the carrying-out of the divine aims implanted within.

That the beautiful aims and lovely ideas of God and his holy angels seem too faint to be sensed by the aspiring consciousness may seem a pity to many. However, let this feeling of sadness concerning the still small voice of God be not held. Let it not rule in your heart. For as we gaze upon the records of the lives of mankind individually and compare the world situation to that which it was in centuries past, we are aware that regardless of appearances, there are more souls today who can clearly discern the voice of God than there were in the olden days.

Men and women who have perpetrated crimes against

individuals, society and even against the Deity—those who in so doing have desecrated their own souls—are the many whose shortened life spans are the result of their dissipations of God's holy energy, which practice has produced for them scarcely any of the fruits of happiness; whereas the men and women of vision who have served their fellowman, their community and their God to the best of their ability (although they may have realized only in increments the hand of opportunity extended as the promise of immortal life) have derived therefrom incomprehensible happiness. The momentum of their happiness in fulfilling his will, and of their victory in so doing, floods the world today and occupies a stratum within the atmosphere that can be contacted by the heart and consciousness of mankind.

As a bird in flight hovers near the earth, near a friendly tree or a verdant terrain, so those who are able to go apart in consciousness and quietly commune with God can live in the wonders of his Being and Presence right while the most sordid conditions exist all around them. I do not mean to imply that it is not advantageous to seek refuge away from the multitudes where the templed atmosphere enables one to draw closer to heaven and God. But I wish to convey that no circumstance in the world of form is permanent; therefore, it cannot forever delay the perfect manifestation of the divine plan within you.

In days gone by, it was my joy to contemplate the mastery of my Son Jesus. Today, I regard all of the children of the world as my own. And when one of them reaches up heart, head or hand in divine seeking or out of a longing to serve the cause of the kingdom, I cannot fail to respond if and when I am called upon.

But for those who have reservations about my office in hierarchy and my mission to the world, those who have accepted the restrictions of the Reformation (which have prevented millions from prayerfully seeking my intercession and that of the saints and ascended beings), for those who still consider statues created in my honor, which focus the flame of my Presence, to be objects of idolatry, I withdraw in gentle love into the folds of heaven's grace and from afar pray for that soul. But to those who wish to draw nigh unto God by embracing the compassion of my heart, which belongs so completely unto him, I will impart the comfort of my love and the powerful momentum of grace that God has given to me.

So it is with all those who have gone on before, those who have attained and in bliss eternal do enjoy the felicity of heaven. They, too, are willing to respond to the devotees who elect to call upon them. This is never a question of idolatry or a tearing away of the heart from God. It is simply the soul's assimilation of the light and friendship of brothers and sisters in higher octaves. For those who yet require communion with the personal aspect of God's consciousness, it is a means of establishing personal ties with those who have ascended into the Presence of God. Being wholly perfect, these beings are incapable of contaminating souls who seek their aid with anything that is less than divine.

There is never any desecration of the Holy Trinity or any other aspect of God's Spirit when man communes in prayer with the Christ Self of any member of the Lord's body if the motive be pure and dedication to the Eternal Father be the goal of the soul. Did not our Lord say, "Love one another"?[1] How can true love desecrate the object of its affection?

Purity and right motive are the determinant factors in the blending of the aspirations of the soul with God-realization. Beauty and strength go hand in hand, and the sense of beauty is decisive in developing both beauty and strength.

In order to ready oneself for a Gethsemane, for a Golgotha, for a resurrection or for the final victory and triumph of the ascension, one must realize that the requirements are high. Unyielding faith is a prerequisite to the completion of the task. To sense that you are not alone, bereft of either friends or companions along the way, is helpful. But to know that the spiritual forerunners of past ages are watching your progress still and are not so far removed from you in time or space or by the cynical concepts of contemporary man is a great blessing to those who can accept it.

We are your contemporaries, more so than many of those ephemeral ones who walk beside you in the marketplace. They often seek their own gains or to tear from you some beautiful softness of soul which they themselves cannot accept and would but desecrate in order to feel a moment of mortal triumph. By contrast, we would restore to you the great communion of hearts that makes one wide world and one beautiful cosmos.

The kingdom of God is within you; that is to say, the key is there. You must place it in the golden door, as did my Son Jesus, and accept the reality of heaven that is all around you.

The emptiness of atheism and the travesty of agnosticism are symbols of the incomplete. Men and women who have mastered languages, the arts and sciences and other finite possibilities of worldly learning are often lacking in their understanding of cosmic adventure. They live but a moment upon the wind and then they are scattered to a new seed time. But the LORD abideth forever.

Those who love the great magnetism of his heart of love will tremble in joy and anticipation to fulfill his holy will. As did my Son and your beloved Saint Germain, they will seek freedom's star, both near and far. They will triumph, and they will win.

I love you always,

Mother Mary

March 20, 1966

2

Give Yourself Wholeheartedly to the Path of Christ

Blessed Children of My Heart,

Children of the white-fire light which descends as a mighty flame from the heart of creation, know ye not that the Father who gavest thee life and being and allness hath established thy purpose from everlasting unto everlasting?

O sacred fire, descend now, I pray, this day upon all those who read these words, that they may know that the Motherhood of God is vested within me, that they may know the Fatherhood of God as it was manifested by my Son, the Christ—the holy one who has become one with the Father and serves upon the cosmic ray of infinite Christhood on behalf of all mankind evolving upon this orb of freedom's destiny.

Beloved ones, it is time to think upon immortal destiny and the origin of that destiny. Can you not realize that because you have come forth from the great source of all life, your destiny is preempted and preordained by the very nature of that origin? Life is not hopeless. Life is not without direction, without cause or purpose or being or salvation. The very one who gave you breath has also framed and fashioned the worlds. And he has created an ultimate goal for each and every Manchild who is in the process of becoming one with the Father.

During this holy season, which commemorates those days when the beloved Jesus walked once again among his disciples in his refined body of light, preparatory to his ascension, I would remind you of the great understanding of the Christian mysteries which can be gleaned from the Christ each year during the period when mankind celebrate his victory over death and the cross. Life in all of its immaculate stillness breathed forth into that blessed one the fullness of heaven while he yet walked among mankind. And Jesus did appear in the closed room and did teach not only the disciples who had followed him but also the holy women who had assisted him throughout his ministry.

The teachings of the risen Christ are transcendent indeed and far more advanced than those recorded in the scripture which he gave in parable to the multitudes. Today the Great White Brotherhood would impart to mankind the fullness of those teachings. And we stand at the portal of humanity ready to impart the knowledge which he gained after that final triumph, when the world could no longer touch him. He remained a part of the world and yet he had overcome the world even before his Passion. As he said, "Be of good cheer; I have overcome the world."[1] Not even the force of gravity could hold his body earthbound. But by conscious will, he remained to give his final service to the evolutions of earth.

Beloved ones, do you know the great sacrifice that it was for him to remain with the disciples after his resurrection and also to descend into the astral planes, the level which mankind call hell, or hades, where those souls slept who had not been reborn since the Atlantean days due to their extreme infringements of the Great Law? Do you know what it meant for the Christ to remain to teach, to give the very ultimate of his being before his ascension and then, having said all, having given all, to walk up Bethany's hill to stand in the place marked by the sacred fire? Do you know what it meant for him to stand in the center of the blazing white-fire cross and to feel the mighty ascension currents pulsating, pulsating, pulsating, until they took complete control within his lower bodies and raised him into the final glory of reunion with the Holy One, the mighty I AM Presence of all life?[2]

Those final hours of deliverance to the captives are recorded in akasha, and the teachings are there for all who can approach the spirit of the resurrection flame, for all who can become one with the mission of Christhood, which is the joy and privilege of every man, woman and child who has gone forth from the heart of the Father. Blessed ones, I am calling today for a conscious reunion with the spirit of Christhood, that you might enter into the Holy of Holies—to that place where the fullness of the divine teachings may flow from your own Christ Presence into the very cells of your brains to awaken you to the knowledge of life without end, life without beginning.

I come to you this day to inspire you to search the meaning of all things that pertain to the manifestation of your own Christ-identity with its transcendent possibilities. Realize that the Father who gave you life and birth could not have done so without imparting unto you the seed containing all that which you shall ultimately become as you discover your Divine Selfhood, which was created and is sustained in his image and likeness. The fullness of your divine potential is already a part of your true being. You have but to claim it, to commune with it, to adore it, and to be one with the Presence of the Lord of hosts.

Strive daily, then, to be children of the one God, followers of the high calling,³ as Christs, as sons and daughters of the Most High. Little by little, like sand falling in the hourglass, the knowledge of divine union will descend into your lower self and enable you to have the reunion which you desire with the great wisdom of your Higher Mind. Nothing is impossible to him who believes in the promise and the fulfillment of the Christ for every man.

Most assuredly, Jesus gave himself for the sins of mankind—not that mankind throughout all ages should be exonerated for wrongdoing because he died, but because he lived they, too, might find the glory of the resurrection and know the fullness of their own Christ Self. Jesus did not place himself upon the cross to atone for your sins, precious ones; only you can do that. But the Christ, through him, offered himself as a balance of light's power, wisdom and love against the total weight of world darkness, that you in your time might also overcome. Jesus set the example for the age that you might realize that you too can be an overcomer of all things through the light momentum of his glorious overcoming.

The footsteps of the cross are not sorrowful ones, precious children. They are the footsteps of the overcomer; they are the steps of initiation which each one must pass. But because my Son manifested them for you, the pathway is made easier for your lifestream. The Christ would not deprive any one of God's children of the great joys upon the path of overcoming. God would not confine salvation to one son when all must find the fullness of his Presence here on earth in order to rise into the heavenly bliss which comes from fulfillment and from self-mastery.

Beloved ones, the path of the Christ is not one to be shunned; it is one to be embraced. Give yourself wholeheartedly to the pursuit of this high calling, for no greater joy exists. You think that in the pleasures of the world there is happiness, that in the indulgences of the senses you will find oneness. How false are mankind's conceptions of bliss, for joy is found only in the presence of the Joyous One. Absence from the Lord is not life; on the contrary, it is nonexistence. It is separation, incompleteness, a cutting off from the Divine Source, which can only result in unhappiness, fruitlessness and death.

I AM the resurrection and the life![4] So simple is this statement of the Christ, yet it reveals the fullness of the Law. But how men do wander in search of the answer which lies before them and to which all nature attests. O mankind, reverse the flow, reestablish the patterns of divine unity, and you will find the joy of the Lord in his Presence.

I, Mother Mary, wish to reaffirm to you this day our solemn union with all those upon earth who are struggling to see—with those who walk in darkness and yearn to see the great light. I declare to you this day that we who have gone on before you are never absent from you in your hours of trial when the advocates of sin would tempt you with all manner of folly and deceit. And when you vanquish the invisible forces which oppose the Christ, we are there to applaud your victory, to give you our hand and to say, "Come up higher! Well done! Thou hast been faithful over a few things. Continue in the fight and you will win the full crown to become ruler over many."[5]

The joy of that crown—the joy of victory, the joy of freedom in the heart of God—is worth all giving and all giving up of the earth. Beloved ones, you can enjoy the beauties of this world, which are the beauties of God, without being overcome by the world. We are not here to advocate extreme austerity and a bed of nails as the key to salvation. Nay, we are here to tell you that the embracing of life and of love in all creation is reunion with the Father. To praise God in all men is to know the true I AM.[6] For he is in you all, and all men are fashioned of his supreme essence and light.

All else is naught. Shun it, then. Divest yourselves of that which would impede the flow of light within you and create burdens too dense to be taken to the summit height.

> O starry night,
> Flood forth the light!
> Let mankind know that high
> Within those infinite orbs
> The might and right
> And light of infinite hands
> Have sparked in the manifestation, man,
> So much light
> So much fire of his heart
> That the entire universe may behold
> The glory of those who have overcome.

Be ye therefore overcomers:
The Christ way is the only way
Follow his footsteps through the night
Learn the power when truth is right
Within your heart, ne'er to depart
Till all have come to know the way.

The day of reckoning is at hand;
Let every heart throughout the land
Be receptive to the Christ within,
Forever shun the bane of sin.

Mankind must rise this hour
Lest the victory be postponed to a latter day
For if ye do not seize this hour—
The mighty I AM, its strength, its power—
The cosmic cycle will have turned
And ye know not when opportunity shall return.

This is the cosmic hour
This is the appointed time
Now is come salvation, now is come the Lord.
Receive him—receive him now
To his light and love all bow.

For glory and honor and peace are his
No more shall mankind be deceived.
The time is here; the Christ doth appear
In the hearts of all who have the courage bold
To lift the banner, to have, to hold.

No man can take from another the flame of life.
It is in your hands—there is no strife
For God is nigh, and he has said,
"The light shall expand, the darkness has fled!
Go forth, ye sons! Go forth tonight!
Bear the power of victory's might

Conquer, then, in Christ's own name
Conquer, then, by Christ's own flame."

Do not fear to tread the Path
It has been paved for you to win at last:
You will win this very day
If you heed the call
From those who point the way,
For God on high is ever nigh
And will not let one go astray
If he will watch and wait and pray.

I AM the Cosmic Mother
I stand within God's flame
My hand is offered unto all
Who will look to me and make the call.
You are the children of my heart
I have given my all that you may start
Upon the homeward path of light
Where angels guard all through the night.

You are the chosen ones so blest
Stand steadfast, God will do the rest
Never let your faith be replaced
By clouds of darkness and disgrace
For none can challenge the light of Christ
None can disillusion the children of light
I AM here, I AM near
To guide and guard you all the way.

Lovingly in the name of the ascended Christ,

I AM your
Mother Mary

May 1, 1966

3

Accept Your Individual
Oneness with God

To Those Who Would Lift Up Their Hearts as a Chalice unto God:

There is a most intimate means of communication involving the heart behind the heart, the attunement of the inner flame with the flame of the Creator in the heart of the Central Sun. Upon establishing intimate personal contact with the God flame in the Sun, a pathway of light is woven down the corridors of the years and cycles, producing a unity of self and God. Then the star of the Christ, the inner radiance that exists both in the Macrocosm and the microcosm, is magnetized to the world of the disciple, producing Christ-awareness and the ever-new sense of him who has indeed received the white stone and the new name which no man knoweth, saving he who has received it.[1]

As the cycle of the year draws toward its rhythmic close and to the time of solstice, thoughts turn with increasing power and definition toward my Son and his mission. Although he was actually born in the spring of the year, long ago the decision was made to celebrate his birth in concordance with the time of the winter solstice, the annual darkening of humanity's consciousness being a most propitious time for the appearance of the brighter light.

Take heart, O men of earth, and understand that his mission of hope to the world, together with his teaching in all of its simplicity, demands that God be not denied as possible of attainment for every man. His mission was clearly defined as one in which the Son of man came not into the world to condemn the world, but that the world through him might be saved.[2] For did he not say, "I AM come that ye might have life and that more abundantly"?[3] These two tests—the elimination of condemnation as the chief deterrent to the flame of God-power and the amplification of the abundant life as the key to God-mastery—have not been passed by many precious souls who have come into embodiment seeking a salvation born out of the hope of a greater manifestation of their dawning God Selves.

Men have commanded the sun to stand still within the domain of the self in its finite capacity. They have longed to fulfill their purpose in life. But in so doing, they have followed the patterns and tangled skeins of mortal weaving. Pain and sorrow have been their lot, whereas glory and peace were the divine intent. Just as the many herald the mission of my Son, so there are those who say that he failed to persuade mankind to follow his example. I am certain that devotees of truth will quickly recognize that the failure was not in my Son nor in his mission. And yet, I bear no reverence for his sonship that I do not also, as a World Mother, transfer in hope to every son of God in whom the star of hope is appearing.

Historical modes can never successfully cry, "Halt!" to the Deity. In every past age, in the present hour, and in all time to come, there will always be room in the inn of my being for the latent son of God who seeks to develop the divine qualities of the eternal One within himself. This is why I suggest, in this hour of mortal trial, that men apply their thoughts diligently to the acceptance of their individual oneness with God. For this is a time when the earth herself is being sorely tried by her sins and inequities, when individuals are meeting personal Golgothas, crucifixions on the cross of mortal error, and in many cases suffering the pangs of death without acceptance of the hope of the Christ, which, although it floods the world, is not seen by the blind.

It is difficult for them to hold awareness of infinite purpose or to realize the God-concern which the eternal Father has for each son of his heart. A sense of separation has kept from mankind the glories of communion and its holy strands. The strident voices of the world seem to dull mankind's senses that would inwardly attune his being to the realm of the great imponderables of eternity.

Do men long to commune with God? God longs to commune with man. He who long ago promised Abraham, saying, "I will multiply thy seed as the stars of the heaven and as the sand of the seashore innumerable,"⁴ did create and send waves of his glory across the heavens, that no part of space should be bereft of the hallowed radiance that comes from the Central Sun.

Celestial choirs sing not alone upon the advent of the Christ or at the period of one planet's celebration of a winter solstice. For there is a universal harmony that pervades all, and the star of the Christ is the star of hope and of universality that shines twenty-four hours a day and forever. The crown for which each man longs—that the many seek to win, that the few find and that God would give to all—is first attained by the weaving of strands of holy personal communication between the individual and the Divine Presence.

> Do men fear?
> The All-Seeing Eye does behold all,
> And from that eye
> Naught can be concealed.
> Better that all should cast themselves
> Upon the lap of God
> As weary and tired children,
> That his hand, resting upon their brows,
> Should wipe away all tears from their eyes
> And point them to celestial skies
> Where dawns without fear

The light of God shining clear.
The balm of comfort
In each earthly mother's heart
In cosmic mothers does impart
A new birth, a new head start
For all who will revere it.

Precious ones, the advent of the Cosmic Mother is always made manifest simultaneously with the advent of the Cosmic Christ. And as Cosmic Man is born to fulfill the divine plan which is uniquely identifiable with each lifestream's release from the imprisoned splendor of God's heart, so does the hour dawn for each individual when he will willingly seek God without ceasing!

The finding of God
Is no erasing of opportunity,
But rather the opening of the Book of Life
Upon whose clean white pages
Will be recorded, then, no strife
But only the sacred tomes of the sages
Who throughout history have seen
The advent of the star of God
With brilliance all serene.
The quick and the dead ought both to arise
And see the glory from the skies,
Streaming 'round his tiny head,
A new world dawning just ahead.
Through cycle of the years
Appears—as fragments from afar
Beaming as his star—
Choiring might of angelic band.
God's peace I bring in my right hand
To take dominion o'er the world

As law of life to all unfurls
My banner, as the Lamb of God
To feed his sheep who neath the rod
Of holy law the Path do trod
To ever-new vistas, whose whitened way
Shineth hope for each new day.

I AM your Mother of eternal comfort,

Mary

December 4, 1966

4

Alone with God

Children of My Heart,

Far, far from the madding crowd, in divine quietude, man comes face to face with himself. And when this is accomplished, behold the man in whom dwells the spirit of truth.

In mortal togetherness there is a way that seemeth to be brotherhood. But if you will examine the fabric of history—especially the record pertaining to those sons of God who came down to perform a service to the Cosmic Mother on behalf of her errant children—you will see that each such blessed individual came apart from the multitude and did enter into the closet of his being to commune with the one God.[1]

Whereas there is much to be gained from fellowship with friends and from companionship along the way, and the gregarious nature of man is not without divine design, there is also a dominant theme active within the universal principle of life. That is the silent night of man's contemplation wherein he enters into the consoling vibratory action of the divine heart and returns to the world with the blessedness which only that heart can give.

From time to time it is well to communicate with one another, and surely it has been well said that men should not forget to communicate.[2] Be it so, I am concerned with the increasing tendency of individuals to seek without for that which is always within. There is not, nor can there be, a substitute for the doorway of self. And surely the clamor and clash of the world and the world mind are designed, methinks deliberately, to tear men from the subtle fineness of the voice of the soul.

As I come to you this week, then, joining El Morya at the portal of the year, it is to point out to all who would achieve their true celestial greatness, according to the divine design, that they must spend a certain amount of time alone with God. Oh, we do understand how mankind become caught up in a round of humanitarian activities. And then too, the craving of self-expression looms large on the horizon while the pull of family and friends is often strong. Yet we who are your spiritual family, and who know that your real strength to better serve all humanity comes from above, plead with you now to consider the necessity for balance in all that you do.

Just as it is not good for man to be alone, so it is not good for man never to be alone. For in the aloneness of self-communication, there are woven giant strands of cosmic light-substance which generate in the world of the seeker the tremendous God-impulse which can never be denied. The reality of this impulse to do and to further the Father's kingdom upon the planet is always achieved in the bright ray of holy communion between the beloved Son and the Father.

Does it seem strange to you that I who am your Cosmic Mother, that I who mingle my energies with the rays of Cosmic Motherhood should express concern for each lifestream upon the planetary body, that they forget not to communicate with God? I hope not. For in this specific appeal, there is the potential garnering of strength for all of the body of God upon earth, whose members can this very year produce those miracles of Christ-perfection for which they have long called.

We cannot afford to listen to the voices of world negation and the unfortunate myths with which the children of men surround us, and neither can you. To do so is an act of self-destruction. As Peter said long ago, "If the righteous scarcely be saved, where shall the ungodly and the sinner appear?"[3]

Applying these words to this concept, if the ascended masters

with their infinite power do not and cannot afford the indulgence
of negative contemplation, how can mankind—caught in the net
of mortal delusion, dwelling below the sun of the Presence yet
subject to receipt of its rays—deny the splendid shining of those
rays by clouds of mortal negation?

They ought not to, blessed ones—but, oh, they do! And it is
a lack of faith in the power of the Presence of God that has denied
so many individuals the required strength through past years
and cycles. Will you not, then, this very year, as we enter into a
greater impetus, renew your faith in the immortal doings of the
celestial mentors of light's momentum?

The LORD's hosts have drawn very nigh unto the earth, challenging by their very presence mankind's endless meanderings in
the old and tired stream of human history. The dullness of repetition and the cycles of perfidy are timeworn, and the souls of
men cry out for freedom from the nets of darkness they themselves have woven.

Let us resolve, then, that our joint faith, the faith of the children of God united with our own, shall mount up with wings as
eagles.[4] Let us resolve that no thing, place, person or condition
shall have the power to alter the strands of that mounting faith as
we carry the steadfast ones toward heaven in the victorious overcoming of the entire planetary body.

Oh, how many children call out to me daily and with what
tireless energies! It often seems to me that the combined currents
of their faith should be enough to provide the answer for the
whole world, so beautiful and bright are the energies of their
hearts' devotions as they rise to me. Yet the pitiful neglect on the
part of the multitudes to communicate with their God Presence,
the angelic hosts, the ascended masters, and with the momentum
of their holiness has rendered the earth spiritually impotent.

The power of our grace is being magnified hour by hour and
day by day. Won't you resolve to do that which can reestablish in

all whom you contact the vibration of hopeful renewal? Won't you rectify past errors, making the crooked paths straight and the rough places plain?[5] Won't you maintain hope in the appearance of my beloved son in all human affairs?

Mortal shadows have their long lines of despair, but the sunlight of divine truth that is everywhere needs an opening in thyself. I AM the door, the open door that no man can shut.[6] In the bond of world need, I remain your friend,

Mary

January 22, 1967

5

Shaping the Hard Wood

To Those Who Would Intercede for a Cessation of World Conflict:

I urge upon every praying mother, and upon every woman in whose heart there is a sustaining momentum of God's love, to intercede with me during the coming weeks for a cessation of world conflict.

Some do not know that born of the necessity of mankind's own karma, the hierarchy has been forced to withdraw from interference in some of the war-connected activities. This has resulted in a temporary worsening of conditions, calculated by heaven to dramatize for mankind—through their direct confrontation with the horrors of war—the necessity to produce its permanent end.

To wage peace rather than war is the requirement of the hour, and the prognosis of peace can only be assured when men are willing to give their all to its cause. This my Son sought to convey to those around him, and those who accepted his teaching received the divine approbation "Blessed are the peacemakers, for they shall be called the children of God."[1] Throughout all ages the saints have obeyed his commandment, which is based on karmic law, "Thou shalt love the Lord thy God with all thy heart,…and thy neighbor as thyself."[2]

It is an absence of love, then, first for oneself and then for one's fellowman, an absence of self-respect (which is reflected in an absence of respect for others), an absence of consideration between peoples and of faith in the Christ, who lives in all, and indeed a great lack of faith in oneself, in the Real Self, that permits the attitudes of war to enter the consciousness of mankind.

Saint Germain, your beloved friend of light, has said that

soldiers who are forced into battle—who are obliged to kill in the heat of battle and yet have no hatred in their hearts but do so out of a sense of duty to comrade and country—are partially exonerated of the karma of war. This knowledge should give some hope to those whose sons are forced into strange and uncompromising situations.

The world situation today is a breeding ground for violence. And it is to elucidate the law of cause and effect that we would point out to all that the effect of war cannot be mitigated in the realm of effects, but only in the realm of causes.

There are many agencies in the world as well as many individuals who are devoted to the cause of peace. These do not always understand that much of the preparation for launching warfare on a world scale is carried on every day as people continue to feed the stream of the mass consciousness with feelings of hatred (and even mild dislike), criticism and condemnation, ignorance and misunderstanding. The accumulation of the energies that are released in the clashes that ensue between individuals is causative in the outbreaks of violence that stir the planetary aura.

Now, the solution to all conflict, both inner and outer, personal and planetary, can be found in the magnification of the ancient desire of the soul to become a Son of God—a ray of the eternal Sun, a fragment of the coals of the altars of heaven, a manifestation of the law in mortal form, an indissoluble link with the eternal nature. In fact, the pursuit of the divine Sonship is the only means of establishing permanent ties between the domain of the world's consciousness and the domain of God's consciousness.

The tranquility of heaven is to be found in the peaceful coolness of the Garden of Eden—a place in consciousness where thought can stand still and see the salvation of God,[3] a place where thought can reproduce in the mind the creative energies that originally brought it forth. Thus, only out of the creative fires of perfect love, out of the peace that passeth all understanding can permanent changes be wrought within. This change can be as the changes that were wrought in the multitudes by my Son the Lord Christ Jesus.

Each and every person upon the planet who will daily make the effort to consciously attune with me can receive my ministration as a Cosmic Mother, my watchful care over their energies, which are indeed the energies of God, and my guidance on behalf of the Divine Manchild. For God longs to produce many sons and to bring them into captivity to his holy will.

"Blessed are the peacemakers, for they shall be called the children of God." Do you not see that peace must be forged by action? Peace is not a cessation of activity but rather a stepping up of the tempo of life's purposes within you and the demonstration of courage to honorably defend the right, and to do so with the grace and power of the Lord's Spirit.

It is never wise to attempt to stamp out violence with violence—as some say, to fight fire with fire. Instead, quench the hot coals of hotheadedness by pouring the refreshing water of life upon the seething emotional vortex of mankind's devious energies. For the creations of hatred always issue out of the void where there is no love or understanding.

I do not intend herein to examine the entire fabric of world ethic as it represents or misrepresents the divine ethic, especially in regard to the complexities of war. For certainly there are those who would agree with what I would say, and there are others who would disagree partially or even in toto.

Rather than explore the intricacies of the Law in this release, I say to all, this is an area in which you must find your own way. For if heaven sought to dominate your thoughts, you might very well rebel against this encroachment upon your free will, and understandably so. And if you rejected our concepts, you might also reject the healing ministrations of our angelic band and thus hinder the progress of the entire planet.

It is by the acceptance and magnification of love, by the acceptance and magnification of peace, and by the acceptance and magnification of every godly quality that individuals finally come to the place where they know that their treasure lies within their heart.[4] And it is in the heart of the consciousness of the Presence of God, in the heart of the recognition that life is one, and in the heart of the realization that the Christ is native to all people that your conceptions of life as God become fertile and abundant.

I recall one morning when beloved Jesus was yet a small lad that he came to me with a very hard piece of wood that he was trying to whittle. He desired that I should persuade Joseph to exchange it for a softer piece, one that would lend itself more easily to molding.

I sat him on my knee, and I proceeded to explain to him that there was an ingrained quality that of old had been placed within the tree, making one to possess a harder quality and another a softer quality. I told him that the soft wood would easily mar and that, were he to use it, the little image that he sought to whittle would not endure the knocks and tumbles that might later come to it, whereas a carving made of hard wood would endure more substantially. I also told him that the wood enjoyed being shapened by his hands and that the only difference between the soft and the hard wood would be that of a greater use of patience on his part.

He brushed back his hair, which had fallen across his eyes, and with great and quick gentleness planted a kiss upon both of my cheeks. I noticed a trace of a tear in one eye as he dashed away to continue his work of shaping the hard wood.

Thus, in your patience possess ye your souls.[5] For God works with people of diverse origins and perverse thoughts, seeking to restore all to their God-estate.

Lovingly in Christ's name, I remain

Your Mother of Light,

Mary

March 3, 1968

6

God Loves You

My Beloved Sons and Daughters,

So there are times when you do not feel like going on. The light seems far away, and you question your favor with heaven. The weight of returning misdeeds seems heavy on the scale of manifestation, and the comforting word far away. On top of it all, a spirit of fatigue adds to your outer distress and inner turmoil.

If, then, the words of the ascended ones seem to you to be as platitudes, as oft-repeated statements, believe it not. For God loves you, and his love is tender, sweet and understanding. Those who have erred much in the past, who come to him now with heavy burdens, he will not turn away. The children of the light, the elder brothers of the race, the ascended masters and the comforting angels are also real. They will not turn you away as long as you do not turn yourself away from the light, and herein lies the danger.

Man is made to feel by conspiratorial circumstances that all is lost, that he is cast out, that seedtime has come, summer and harvest, and that his fruitage is lacking. But the love of the Infinite, the eternal plan and the etchings of tests must be taken into account. For the soul must be given the opportunity to have her fullest test in the realm of experience.

We are not forbidden to reach out into the domain of men and to extend a more than ordinary passion toward embodied mankind. Have we not walked the *via dolorosa*? Have we not stood in the Presence of the living God? Have we not lingered in the valleys and watched from the snow-crowned summits as the sun went down, washing in splendid gold the land, the air and the sea?

O blessed ones, if only you would understand as you look at the lamps lit in the heavens that the fingers of God that placed them there, so far away from this terrestrial globe, are as near as the doorway of your hearts! If only you would understand that the fingers of God reach out to the meek and the lowly, to the poor and the tired, to the despairing and the joyous. For the fingers of God touch also the joyous lest they be lifted up to such a height that they could not bear a descending cycle.

The sound of far-off worlds is heard in the hearts of the lonely ones, and they are lonely no longer. The collapse of the universe into the microcosm of man is the surrender of the eternal One to the individual. The flame caresses the soul; and as God draws nigh within the flame, understanding is born and all of the pieces of the strange puzzle of life rise into place as a cosmic picture of celestial hope.

"I AM the way," he said.[1] My Son spake thus. And the Christ of every man, which spoke in him, speaks yet today. I too, in the name of the Spirit of the Resurrection, hold the immaculate concept for everyone who loves God. And how wondrous is the love of God! It is a mother's kiss planted on the forehead of a child. It is the tenderness of a father's watchful care as the fever breaks with the dawn and the heart is flooded with the promise and the hope of a new day: things will be better. The angels also whisper hope to the listening hearts of men. And midst turmoil and confusion, the artistry of God is seen afresh.

I cannot, in these dark hours of the nations, refrain from reaching out to touch individual man. While many are concerned with national crisis, with world-shaking events, to me, to a universal Mother, each child is important. And as a representative of the Divine Mother, I must express her love to each one.

To go and do likewise[2] is to place your hand in the hand of the trembling ones who grope in the dark. They have no one else to turn to among men but yourselves. In the days to come many will reach out into the dark to touch the hand of God, and they will find your own. The chain of the Spirit must not be broken. Whether from near or from far, wherever the cry rises up, the answer must come. Hope must be bestowed and tears wiped away. The blindness of despair must be shown to be a passing thing.

The universal plan lingers in the air, but it is also in the hearts of men. Little light rays from near and far are pulling together the scattered pieces of universality. God's will is being done even when men tremble and quaver and react as though the darkness in them were real—as though they must protect it from the covetous ones who would steal the shadowed misconceptions of their worlds because they, too, believe that they are real.

Nothing is real, blessed ones, but the light and the truth and the Spirit of God. His love transcends all things in life. The sting of death cannot stand before the face of God, for he is life. As the untoiling lilies[3] are arrayed in white, in fragrant garments, so will everyone be whose faith is deep enough to move the heart of God, to evoke a response from him.

He knoweth your needs before you ask. Yet they do not always seem to manifest. What is the reason, blessed ones?

There is no reason, for they do manifest. God responds at his level with the immediate answer to every need of men. But they must learn the art of finding it, of accepting it, of receiving in grace the divine yes or the divine no. And sometimes the no is greater than the yes, for God knoweth what is best for men. And if they wisely say, "Do unto me whatsoever is best—not my will, but thine be done,"[4] they may meet their Gethsemane, their Golgotha, their *via dolorosa*. But this will be followed by the resurrection, by the ascension and by unity with truth.

"Inasmuch as ye have done it unto one of the least of these my brethren, ye have done it unto me."[5] Let us remember his words always.

Lovingly, I remain your Mother,
Mary

September 29, 1968

7

Something Must Be Done

Friends of God's Heart,

Outcries from the inmost being of men rise to solicit our aid. We cannot fail to respond. Everywhere tumult causes the hearts of men to shudder. And in the face of nature's sun, where hope should radiate its burning message, the numbing chill of fear reveals the deepening dark in the world community.

While the seams have been torn again and again by human selfishness and inconsideration, we have again and again mended the rents. The yawning gap between ministering heavenly hands, such as I recently offered in Cairo, Egypt,[1] and the petty grievances that men amplify seems to be an almost uncrossable abyss. Yet men cry out, and we in our councils debate the answer.

Certainly something must be done. Things cannot continue as they are in the world order, else undesirable dissolution will occur and the forces of nature radically effect man's defection from universal purpose.

The magnanimity of one heart, such as that of my Son Jesus, can for two thousand years and longer sustain the heartbeat of a Christlike momentum on behalf of a planet. Countless sages have echoed and reechoed his message. They have seen how the clever machinations of Antichrist have sought on a world scale the destruction of the mainstream of God-identity in every man.

The cutting-off of belief in God in the schools and colleges of the earth by those who proclaim a militant atheism has torn from the minds of the young the one sublime hope that would have sustained them throughout life. Mothers all over the world vary in their understanding of their children. Some offer them a prayer, whereas others give them a cigarette. This gamut, from the sublime to the ridiculous, is only a sample of life as it is currently manifesting.

Beautiful hope, revealed in the magnificence and ruggedness of nature, speaks to man of the sculpturing of his identity according to the plan of the eternal Father. But first we must restore to the people of this age a correct understanding of the inner flames of their own real beings—the divine spark of life that is the gift of God to every man. This seemingly simple matter of recognizing the God who lives in every man must be included in the most complex patterns of civilized living. But because this truth is obvious, it is overlooked even by the devotee of years' standing.

Well might men say, "Open my eyes that I may see." For the breathing of this prayer, by reason of its humility, keeps the soul on guard against the choking weeds of delusion and all that would equate mankind with a world scheme in which, as instruments of the state, they lose their identity.

What is one of the major plots of the Antichrist in the world today? It is the downgrading of human life, the downgrading of man's opportunity, the downgrading of the soul. For if men can be made to feel that they are worthless creatures, they will not be overly concerned when they cast aside their lives and opportunities. Their pleasure madness is not so much a result of inordinate desires as it is the result of a failure to perceive a sense of mission for themselves.

I have recently sat at the Darjeeling Council table with my Son Jesus, Master El Morya, beloved Kuthumi and a host of others whose every concern is for the welfare of the children of this planet. The plots of the Antichrist and the disturbing conditions of the world were discussed, strange as it may seem to some among mankind who believe that heaven holds in hand a separate solution to every human problem. We realize full well that the solution was given in the Beginning. Our task is but to tutor

men and to develop in them that self-reliance which will enable
them to seize and reestablish dominion over their worlds according to that original and perfect solution which was affirmed of old
by the universal Christ.

Mindful, then, of the need for greater commitment on the
part of all who seek to serve the cause of guiding a distraught and
straying humanity, we urge every son of heaven to persevere continually in prayer and attunement with the higher octaves of life.
Just as no angel or deva in heaven is insignificant, so no soul upon
earth is bereft of meaning. All are loved. And in that love of God
for the lost and straying sheep,[2] there is hope also for those who
are closely following in the footsteps of the Good Shepherd.[3]

All should perceive their great need to maintain contact with
us in thought, in word and in deed. For in the reading and contemplation of our words, there is to be found the inspiration for
daily good deeds. Thus, through Christ-ordained activity, the
body of God upon earth is knit together into one salutary action
that produces the fruit of rightful strivings among men. For the
crown is ever raised above the cross, and achievement stems from
many small victories.

All these matters and many more were discussed at our recent
council meeting. For we who identify so much with the Word,
with the Logos, maintain a steadfast communication with one
another and with our blessed Divine Presence, the eternal Father.

Born from the council's recent sessions were many fervent
ideas for the illumination of mankind. Human ignorance, by reason of its contrast to divine truth, seems more virulent than ever.
For the intellect of man has become a two-edged sword to drive
him from the Eden that he seeks and the knowledge that heaven
would convey. The statement was made by one of the wisest of
the masters that man's ignorance of himself is greater than his
ignorance of the world around him. In this twentieth century, the
average person knows far more about nature and nature's

processes than he knows about his own psyche.

Therefore, the idea was born that some treatment of the subject of the consciousness and being of man should be given in the *Pearls of Wisdom* in a forthcoming series.[4] This would prove an invaluable aid to men of every race and creed, and it would provide insight so badly needed to people in all walks of life.

The valiant combination of the instruction of the World Teacher Kuthumi released from his beautiful temple in Kashmir, India, the meditations of beloved Lord Lanto given from the retreat in the Grand Teton, and commentaries on the age directed by the beloved God Meru from the Temple of Illumination in South America will, I am certain, bring forth a splendid series born out of the wisdom of God that is calculated to assist individual man in finding his place in the divine scheme. The series will also help him to understand the juxtaposition of forces that seek his doom and show him how he might better carry on a service to himself and to all life.

Living free from fear and in a constant state of listening grace, man is able to spread the message of the divine radiance far and wide. Hopefully and by the grace of God, he is able to penetrate the facade of this age, the strange front of mortal illusion. Then there will be revealed before his very eyes, in a new and vitalizing manner, the hand of the Eternal as he extends that hand through us all to redeem the world order and to call forth from among men the coming race.

Victoriously, for the freedom of every Manchild, I remain
Your Cosmic Mother,

Mary

June 15, 1969

8

The Self Is the Gateway to God

Cherished Children of My Heart,

We would ease tension and not create it. Yet we cannot fail to tell you that mankind's appalling waste of time in the pursuit of trivial affairs may one day be regretted. People say that they do not have time to pursue spiritual studies, prayerful intercession on behalf of those in need, meditation and the things of the Spirit. And many shun faith in spiritual endeavors until they themselves come to the place where they are sorely in need of assistance from on high.

Last week Lord Maitreya delved into one of the problems that is currently facing humanity on a world scale which engages their energies not in producing the miracle love of the kingdom of the Christ, but in spreading the blight of division and hatred across the face of the earth. At this time I would like to deal with certain problems that arise in the field of religion which are often most disturbing to the children of men.

Many of you will recall my Son's words to Peter: "Satan hath desired to have you, that he may sift you as wheat."[1] The phenomenon of sifting the spiritual man or woman as wheat has often been observed, even in your time. This sifting of men's devotions does hurt to the children of God who yearn to pledge their faith not only to him but also to embodied men and women who are about their Father's business.[2]

When those who are supposedly engaged in the business of serving the spiritual needs of man (whether in the East or in the West) do not uphold the principles of truth and honor, when they manifest a spirit of criticism toward individuals or segments of society, and their own lives afford meager example of Christly virtue, those who look to them to set the example for the age are often keenly disappointed.

Most spiritual seekers have at some time in their lives manifested great idealism. This idealism causes them to yearn to bring into their lives elements of spirituality that will draw them very near to God and to their fellowmen. When they see those who claim to espouse the divine cause, those who profess to be teachers of righteousness (ministers, priests, learned pundits or church officials) engaging in practices that are unkind, unholy, unethical or that compromise in any way the true teachings of the Christ, these idealists are sometimes driven, almost in a spirit of despair, to discontinue their own search for God or to reject the reality of God in themselves and in others.

The damage that is done by these would-be leaders, who go forth in my Son's name but carry not his Spirit, is incalculable. Yet I would speak to those who have suffered the pangs of disillusionment, and I would say to you, one and all: Remember, in order to have disillusionment, you must first have illusion. Look only to the real, which God has implanted in every man, and then you will not be disappointed in the unreal, which man himself has unwittingly created or accepted in his world.

Strange as it may seem, there are some individuals who have consciously sought to manifest evil. These dark spirits, pursuers of Luciferian tendencies, mistakenly think that the knowledge of the world is the brilliance of Reality which they seek. And they look upon the kingdom of God and his wisdom as though they were foolishness.

Observing the great caravan of lives returning to the heart of the Father, we are concerned* that the simple beauty of the pure in heart will one day be the goal of every man. If man looks for purity of heart in himself, he will also look for it in others. And

---

*concerned: i.e., interested in seeing.

if he does not find it, he will want to invoke it. Yet in this strange drama of living, to rise in an ever-ascending spiral of cosmic reality men must also understand the importance of true discrimination. My Son said, "By their fruits ye shall know them....Do men gather grapes of thorns or figs of thistles?"[3]

Whereas we have again and again stressed that men ought not to speak ill of one another or to gossip (pointing out the corrosive dangers involved in such activities, which border on condemnation and judgment), we have also said that spiritual people should realize the importance of learning to discern the difference between good and evil. How else shall the follower of the Christ understand the meaning of the words spoken by Paul to the Corinthians: "What fellowship hath righteousness with unrighteousness? And what communion hath light with darkness? And what concord hath Christ with Belial? Or what part hath he that believeth with an infidel?"[4]

Evil deeds are self-declaring, whether they are practiced by saint or sinner. And if the saint be truly all that the name implies and he commit one or more mistakes while his life is filled with good deeds, if he is a saint, if he is truly a child of God, he will be grateful to have pointed out to him the error of his ways. But if he stand behind the shield of personal egoism, defending himself as one who can do no wrong, he will not retain the purity of heart that will enable him to see clearly the path that lies ahead.

In this connection may I say to all, to those of learning and to those who are struggling to master their worlds, bear in mind that the love of God is tangible and real. You should strive continually to express it.

But you should also realize the difference between the divine character and the character of human creation. It is not wrong to be able to discern the difference between good and evil. In fact, it is absolutely essential that one develop spiritual discernment, for these differences are often most subtle and difficult to perceive.

There is a certain danger even in the statement "All is love." For whereas all *is* love as it exists in the highest consciousness of God, love, in order to be practical in the world below, must be willing to recognize the weeds in the garden that are to be plucked out. Those who are blind to these facts of life and those who lead the blind will personalize the weeds and defend them as though they were their own. For many through pride have fallen from lofty positions. But the pure in heart shall see God[5] within themselves and within others. They shall be unafraid to name the condition that is acting in their worlds, and they shall be careful to differentiate the real from the unreal in their discernment of others.

Yet courage is needed, for evil is not personal. It is simply magnetized to the world of men by reason of their own lack of faith in themselves. If men had faith in themselves, they would find it easier to have faith in God. We seek, then, to generate greater faith in the children of the light and in all men, knowing that in the simplicity of their faith will be born that devotion to service and that understanding which will ultimately create a new sense of worth in the people of the world.

How wonderful it is for individuals to be able to have and to hold a sense of worth about themselves and about their lives. The self is the gateway to God. When God is found, doubt and fear vanish. And if a friend does not measure up to one's ideals or to one's expectations (or even if the self falls short of the mark), faith in God and in his leading, in his ultimate purpose made manifest for all, will strengthen the bond of reality in the consciousness of men and enable each one to realize that the Christ is the true worth and the only measure of a man. Faith will bring peace midst turmoil and spread the balm of healing truth, which in plucking out the thorn of error desires only the manifestation of health and wholeness in the body of God on earth.

The hierarchy warns that there are wolves in sheep's clothing,[6] that some of these know they are wolves and that some know it not. Notwithstanding, all can rely upon the Christ of their own being, upon that great reservoir of celestial light that pours out the precious nectar of his holy wisdom, the oil of his anointing, and the waters of purification upon all who will receive him.

May I ask that you keep the bond of faith in the midst of turmoil, serene yet actively aware of the need to know the truth that is above persons, places, conditions or things—the truth that alone can make and keep you free.[7]

I remain your benefactress in cosmic diligence, representing the light of the world,

Mary

November 2, 1969

9

True Religion

Precious Flames of My Heart,

You have heard it said that spring is in the heart. As you look upon the conditions of the world, it may seem a strange contrast that in the millions of years during which the earth itself has undergone recurrent change, the consciousness of the people in their dealings with one another has remained primitive.

Those who expound upon the theories of socialism as a means to achieve a better way of life for humanity should see from the examples of past ages—if they will only look without prejudice or personal pride in their own limited judgments—that it is solely due to a lack of true religion, pure and undefiled,[1] and a lack of the practice of true religion that civilization has gone down time after time into the negative spirals of destructivity, immorality and shame.

I shun to speak of the great unhappiness that has been produced each time mankind have yielded to the baser instincts on a mass scale. I would rather cite here and for all time the wondrous fact that wherever a life of virtue, a life of dedication, or even what men may call a life of sacrifice has been lived for humanity, it has made an imprint of marvelous and lasting effect for good upon all peoples. The world has become the beneficiary of each sage, of each avatar and of each disciple whose life has truly been lived for God. What the world needs today, then, is not less religion but more of the right kind.

But how carefully the dark forces of the world, those who hide so skillfully behind their masks as angels of light[2] (even to the point of convincing humanity that they do not exist) have woven their nets of deceit for the unwary.

How do they do it, precious ones? First by pointing to human hypocrisy and then by creating the illusion of hypocrisy where none exists. Through the diabolical tendencies to gossip, to criticize and to tear each other down, which people allow to gather momentum in their worlds, the forces of darkness have driven their lies as spikes into the human consciousness.

Under these negative influences, how easy it is to point the finger at someone you scarcely know and to decide that his motives are impure. The ease with which this can be done should reveal why the ascended masters have sought to create systems of jurisprudence that allow fairness in the execution of human justice in the courts of the nations whereby individuals can be tried by a jury of their peers as a safeguard against the tyrannies men so often impose upon one another.

Enlightened men and women have often frowned upon the accusing finger—for many times it is nothing more than that. Accusations are directed against those whose hearts are as pure as the lily by those whose hearts are, by comparison, as dark as the swamps in which the lily grows.

The same accusing finger is used to discredit religion in literature, in art forms, in moving pictures and in the lives of well-known people. Through the "sifting as wheat"[3] process, the forces of deception seek to enlarge upon the inadequacies of the world's religions. By pointing out their supposed failure to meet the crises of the times, the dark ones anticipate that men will throw all religion, good and bad, out of their lives.

O beloved humanity, as a World Mother I speak to you solemnly with the sternest of warning and say: Regardless of human hypocrisy, regardless of the broken-down altars and the failures of many of the religious leaders to set the proper example, to teach the proper precepts and to establish the proper guidelines for their followers, regardless of all of the defects that may exist or that have existed in the past in the various religions of the world, true religion must never perish from the earth.

If it does, if the forces of atheism succeed in repressing men's faith in God and the world becomes a godless place, it will be a jungle of such fury and emptiness as to snuff out the light of purpose everywhere upon the planetary body.

Man is not a vegetable. He is not intended to be an empty vessel but one overflowing with the abundant life, with creativity, with purpose, with wonder and with the hush of expectancy.

The darkness of the present age is expanded today through many of the young, whose tender hearts have scarcely escaped the cradle. In their pride of knowledge obtained through modern systems of education, they amplify the destructive momentums of past civilizations in which they themselves have been enmeshed. And thus there is a tendency for them to respond to the ministrations of the princes of darkness.

But deep within their hearts there is a moving force of universal light. There is an echo in the corridors of their memory that recalls those moments when they stood in the Presence of God, and this creates in them a yearning for truth and reality.

Neither their parents nor all of the ages of the past are responsible for all of their problems. They are individuals; each is endowed by God with the highest purposes. Each has created his own karmic net, and it is to this net (which can hold either the mud of human vileness or the heart of the golden age as chalice of universal purpose) that we would direct our attention.

Man is neither god nor demon; he is a potential god in the making. Destined by the Eternal to be the master of his life, he has become, through a sense of division and struggle, a child of confusion's mien.

Now, as my heart goes out to the children of the world, I urge greater understanding on the part of all. It is not a question of age and youth, for what are age and youth but figments of men's imaginations on the ship of time. All sail through the bounding main; all move as pilgrims on the bark of life. And they are not so separated by these few years as the illusion would have them believe. Each in himself is able to recognize his frail being. But let him also realize that as there manifests a frail self, an outward fragile thing, so there is an inner strength, an inner purpose, a greatness to which we must give wing.

I urge all to attain self-mastery rather than mastery over the lives of others and to check the widespread practices of control men have one to another. How determinedly the dark forces have spawned the Machiavellian ideas that men must control other men and their outward destinies. They have created, then, not greatness or graciousness but mechanisms by which they divide and subdivide the races of men.

This fragmentation does not result in the unification of purpose that would help mankind to see reality and to know it when they see it. On the contrary, it creates those schisms which breed violence because men do not think alike. And because they do not think alike, they can exude the poisonous breath of hatred against one another and in so doing feel that they are fulfilling their raison d'être. Some even dare to consider their hatred to be the product of lofty ideals.

We are not condemning. We seek to create forums of understanding. We would penetrate the consciousness of humanity. We would guide the youth into the great crystal glow of dazzling reality where the City of God can become tangible in themselves and upon earth. We would avoid the bloodbath that the dark forces of the world would bring upon humanity through their thrusts of division and their manufactured currents that set men at cross-purposes with one another.

We would spare this age the destruction intended by the enemies of righteousness. The world has seen enough of war; enough mothers' hearts have known the anguish of the loss of sons. Our wish today is to improve the world through the message of my Son, the Prince of Peace. We would strengthen the bonds of even ordinary religion. We would improve the quality of life everywhere within its own domain.

We do not mind if individuals wish to be exclusive, to have a religion they call their own. We would only make it a true religion. Let it expand the grace of God and fulfill the purpose of religion*—that is, to bind the flower to the stalk, the nestling to the mother's breast, and the souls of men to their Creator.

Do you remember when the two women were brought before Solomon for judgment—one of their children having been laid upon and smothered during the night, the other one alive?[4] She who was not the mother was willing to have the sword divide the child in two, but the mother cried out, "Let her have him!" for she had love. Let me urge upon you all, then, the same willingness to surrender the souls of men to the religion of their choice. But let me exhort all religions to teach love to one another, to avoid the poison of class struggle, of race hatred and of religious competition.

We of the Great White Brotherhood are willing to give men their freedom to choose as they would. We simply exhort them to be wise and not to subject themselves to the deceit that in dividing men defeats the purposes of every avatar, of every disciple, of any and all who have ever known upon this earth a Golgotha on behalf of the children of God.

In memory of the eternal resurrection, of eternal reality, of eternal possibility, of the awakening to truth, I remain for my Son's mission and in my service to life

Your Mother of Love

Mary

May 3, 1970

---

*religion: from Latin *religio,* "bond between man and the gods," or *religare,* "to bind back."

10

Sowing the Wind and Reaping the Whirlwind

To All Who Would Guard the Chalice of the Heart:

When the brilliant flash of the divine idea to create dazzlingly expanded its diadem of myriad electrons into space, from the first photon of light until infinite appearing points of light composed the cosmos, it was an exercise in crowning the Son of God with earnest dominion.

The hypocrisy of the present era of earth's evolution is a pain to many hearts, for it is a clear indication to those who can discern the face of Life that man is in no way linked with the crowning chain of cosmic purpose. His energies go down the drain and are swallowed up as in a giant hole as his attention pursues a senseless series of moving pictures accelerating the trend of moral and intellectual decadence.

How is it that the wise men of the nations seem unable to discern the effect of eye-pictures upon their children and themselves? Do they not perceive in the misuse of the sacred fire through crude and unnecessary displays of sex and the infiltration of horror, murder and fear in advertising and entertainment that men are lowering the consciousness of the entire world? Do they not have eyes to see that some men are making merchandise of them?

Yet, these same men who control the theater and motion-picture industry could produce uplifting dramas that would exalt noble purpose and define magnificence of character rather than portray doubt, distrust, suspicion, fear and the unwholesome conditions that have ever been apparent since mankind's departure from the throne of grace.

As the angels gaze upon the faces of little children who should be taught to pray and commune with the great silent invisible world of the Spirit during those formative years when their tiny minds are budding—as they witness the most awful formulations that will produce so much violence and hatred in their later lives—they in their beautiful wisdom ask themselves the question: "Why is it that humanity will not acknowledge that they are sowing the wind and will one day reap the whirlwind?"[1]

In fact, much if not all of the violence that humanity is facing today is the result of a deliberate manipulation of the minds of the people by those who are drunk with power. Guided by the darkest stars, they would cast down my Son, they would cast down the Christ consciousness, they would cast down the essential saving grace inherent within awareness of the only begotten of God.

The concept of the only begotten of God, full of grace and truth,[2] when properly understood, reveals that God has begotten only good. No duality of good and evil came forth from his hand, but only the clearly defined purest light and noblest hope for all of creation.

As it was in the time of Babel, so it is today: men in their psychological and intellectual pursuits ignore the great genius-power by which God framed the worlds, created the flexibility and marvelous tenacity of the mind and spirit of man, and endowed his best servants with illimitable grace. The world turns to the labyrinth of mental and materialistic probings, and authorities in the various fields of human endeavor, often differing from one another, create the wisdom of the world that is foolishness with God.[3]

Is it not true that he who can create the stars and put them in their appointed places, he who can bring forth a living soul, spread abroad the canopy of space and direct the velocity of time, is certainly able to offer a better way of life to his creation—[better] than that being paraded before the youth as the darkening concepts of the Egyptian fleshpots,[4] the pleasures of table and person, and an endless panorama of war, poverty, struggle, loneliness and frustration for humanity?

When I appeared at Fátima (1917),[5] I gave stern warning of impending conditions that would threaten the peace of the world and seek to destroy the spiritual Church that is the body of Christ. Cruel men, dark tyrants in high places, have invaded every area of civilization, and yet the attention of the people is so easily dissipated as the quotient of each one's energy pattern is engaged in fruitless endeavors. Then how easily criticism becomes a weapon.

Those whose hearts, heads and hands are offered in service to the spiritual hierarchy are often misunderstood and deliberately attacked by those who should know better. Whereas the blessed children of men do not know their best friends, either ascended or unascended, those who do are also found among their condemners—thrice denying the Christ ere the cock crows.[6] It is not easy in this darkening hour for men and women who stand up for our cause. Yet light must banish darkness and men must never lose heart or hope.

And so I say, renew yourself daily in the holy fountain. Turn your backs upon the dark and evil of the past. Long to see yourselves and others free in the divine plan fulfilled. So shall the brave light of a cosmic mother's heart be instilled in many [so] that the hand that rocks the cradle may be the hand that rules the world[7] through the instilling of love and virtue and the guarding of the mind of the young from the destroyers whose hearts are hardened in self-love, calloused by thousands of inequities and stinging degradations.

Oh, turn to the heart of my Son, whose field of light can so easily be invoked around your own blessed hearts! Immerse yourselves in the sweetness of the Christ consciousness, and let no one destroy in you that beauty which is the light of God that never fails.

Devotedly,

I remain your Cosmic Mother

Mary

June 7, 1970

The Responsibilities of Our Love

Beloved Hearts of Light,

Life is very dear to us, and so we look to preserve the many facets of its expression. But we find that time, as man judges it, is meaningless as the preserver of life unless it be qualified with the virtues of life. Therefore, we would teach men how to preserve life through the proper qualification of time and energy.

Throughout history many among men have had great pity for my Son in the crucifixion he bore. They sorrowed for him even as he carried his cross to Golgotha. But he answered them and said, "Weep not for me, ye daughters of Jerusalem, but weep for yourselves and for your children."[1] Nevertheless, the world continues in great sorrow, pursuing the *via dolorosa* instead of rejoicing in the promise of the resurrection for every son of God.

In order to create a spirit of God-delight in men and to transfer to them our personal feeling of God-happiness, we of the ascended hosts would show all, especially the dear youth of the world, the great noonday fires of reality, the great tides of God-happiness. When life is lived according to the higher example, it does not produce the seeds of ugliness and despair but rather the fruit of outreaching compassion for those who have not yet been reborn in the divine image.

Therefore know that over the cable of our concern for each heart flow the energies of our love, our wisdom and even our power; for a triune effort on behalf of mankind is always being made by the Brotherhood.

Misunderstanding has clouded so many issues that the dark

ones, following the psychology of the human consciousness and working upon the subtleties of the mind, find it easy to brainwash humanity almost en masse. Human beings are trained to react like Pavlov's dog to programmed stimuli.

Thus, those who would defraud mankind of the Christ consciousness, knowing that their reactions can be plotted on a graph and predicted in advance, can with precise timing introduce a negative spiral of fear or self-condemnation and thereby reduce the behavioral patterns of the masses to the level of the common herd. Suddenly it becomes popular to belittle the kingdom of God. And those who once worshiped the light, now fallen to the depths of self-degradation, cry out in the presence of the Christ, "What have we to do with thee?"[2]

How mothers and fathers must renew their efforts in holy prayer! How the members of our sacred orders, in keeping with the true spirit of Christ awareness, must envision the renaissance of the Christ consciousness in the heart of each flaming monad!

Beloved ones, the results of mass controls can be seen in the lives of many. These find themselves caught up in such a turmoil of conflicting dimensions that the poor creatures are divided mentally, emotionally and spiritually and can scarcely comprehend the thrust of life. Through ineptness in spiritual things and a lack of discernment, men are often turned from the radiance of the Eternal into myriad channels which afford temporal diversion but no gathering together of the many facets of being into the formation of a useful instrument.

To prevent the scattering of the divine seed—the seed that God has implanted in every heart—into byways of utter uselessness, we forward herewith this message from the entire hierarchy. And whereas they have chosen me, as a representative of the Cosmic Mother, to speak for them, I do so in memory of the tender years of my Son Jesus.

I saw him in infancy, when the holy gleam of mission

brought forth a radiance of unperceived wonder in his tiny eyes. I watched as through the years the flame of illumination and the communion ray from the heart of God changed that look into the maturity and confidence of a master of men and, above all, of himself. I saw the rude multitudes utter blasphemies against his purpose. I watched from time to time with, I must confess, some trepidation as threats were made against his life, as they sought to stone him or to push him over the side of a cliff.

Lest some of you think it unbefitting that I should confess my concern, let me recall for you that this was a period of great testing prior to my ascension. It was a time when I was both a devotee of some spiritual attainment and a mother of a living son, issued forth from my own womb.

I cite this instance not to weaken your faith in my efforts in the name of God but that you may no longer chide yourselves for those human weaknesses which are so much a part of the struggle. For one day these, too, shall cease as your hearts are finally schooled in the mastery over the aggressive suggestions of the world as well as in the mastery of yourselves.[3]

Perhaps, then, as you meditate on the plight of unascended souls striving for perfection, you will learn to be more kind to those on the Path who have not yet mastered every solitary moment. In the lives of the saints whom I have observed through the years, there have been moments prior to their victory when they have manifested some remnant of their human consciousness. Won't you learn, out of the charity of your souls, to be tolerant of one another's strivings and to receive thereby divine merit? For those who walk among you may be far along on the spiritual path; and whereas God judges them through the centuries, man judges them by fragmentary moments.

We plead for the knitting together of the spiritual body. But we warn that the releases of the true hierarchy through the true messengers of the Great White Brotherhood have a vibrational quality that has never been excelled, albeit some among humanity have sought to cast down the brilliant contact with us over which flow so much divine love and wisdom to the children of God. But whereas we ourselves may honor the communication, in the final analysis, the fruits of victory for the individual student are the prize we seek.

Will you then recognize that as you seek in hierarchical cooperation to implement the will of God and the essence of the teachings, as you absorb the love that we are and seek to be that love in action, so the kingdom of the Son of God will manifest more quickly in your being and in the world you influence?

Now, if this be undesirable, beloved ones, then continue in the dullness and the repetitiveness of the world's shadowed half-truths. But if your souls are unsatisfied with negativity, if you have not unraveled the mysteries of nature, if you stand yet as a seeker for illumination's flame, for the holy Word, the lost chord that vibrates within yourself, if you can be compassion, not only to others but also to yourself, then I believe that the bond with our hierarchy that is being placed before you each week in our releases[4] will become more and more dear to you.

I believe that you will study to show yourself approved unto God[5] and that you will harness the mighty influences of light and love that are being sent to you. Then you shall see that, whereas the meaning of life may not have been wholly revealed, what has appeared is in truth worthy of your attention. And I believe that you shall also see that the radiant purposes of God which are being made known unto you are not an impossible hurdle but goals that you must begin to pursue with greater diligence.

I hear yet the careful words spoken by my Son Jesus, at the age of twelve: "Wist ye not that I must be about my Father's business?"[6] And as I contemplate the greatness in each one of you, I long to see the moment (no matter what your chronological age or spiritual evolution may be) when you can defy the fiats of the world that have kept you bound, when you can turn to anyone who may be standing in the way of your destiny—even to your own outer self—and say, "Wist ye not that I must be about my Father's business?"

Thus shall more and more sons and daughters come into the forcefield of our existence and share in the responsibilities of our love. Taking upon themselves the burden of light, they shall be exalted and they shall exalt. For mankind are looking for the recovery of their balance, for the lost impetus of the Spirit and for their restoration to the golden age when cosmic power is balanced by cosmic wisdom and cosmic love—for the love of the Divine Mother is also the love of the Father of all.

Tenderly in his name, I AM simply

Mary
Your Mother

September 13, 1970

12

The Messiah of Progressive Revelation

Gracious Believers in the Almighty Tenets of God,

Your faith has produced a more than ordinary momentum for good, and I declare to all that many of you, if your aspirations could have been fully realized, would long ago have ordained a world of golden-age perfection. You think with God and you love with God, but the sad degeneracy of the world's evolution seems to continue to hold sway. A strong measure of pure spiritual ambition rises fervently in the hearts of the faithful, but the faithful are far too few in number.

As your beloved Saint Germain has intimated (and I think rather clearly) in his recent release, there is a great need for world expansion of divine truth and of the understanding of the hidden laws of our Brotherhood to the many who hunger and thirst after righteousness.[1] That they may be filled is our prayer, continually offered as a perpetual novena, a tireless appeal, a self-purifying ascendancy of hope.

May I throw a beam of my heart's light upon Saint Germain's timely words?[2] As a result of a recent probing into mortal affairs by the hierarchy, the decision to seek the means to reach mankind was made; for we have detected a number [of souls] that is mighty indeed in the evolution of this planet who would assist the divine plan if they only knew how.

We know that whereas the students of the greater light have much understanding that is out of the ordinary and that is not given through orthodox channels, few of you realize what an entrenched religious and social system exists on earth today.

More authoritarian than the Roman governors, more threatening than Caesar's legions, more crafty than the Sanhedrin, the conservative religionists with their temporal power have marshaled the forces of the world to prohibit progressive revelation to the mankind of earth.

It is true that if past revelations had been heeded, the virtue of the living Word of truth spoken between neighbor and neighbor would have paved the way for a different spiritual complexion in the world today. It is true that the Sermon on the Mount, delivered by my Son, embodies the highest teachings for the formation of Christly character. Yet John, his closest disciple, declared, "And there are also many other things which Jesus did, the which, if they should be written every one, I suppose that even the world itself could not contain the books that should be written."[3]

This shows beyond a doubt that many of his teachings were never recorded. And I am certain you realize that all of his words and deeds were of equal import. Hence, beloved ones, progressive revelation is for the purpose of continuing the infinite release of the Word of God to men in each succeeding generation—not in refutation of the old but as an affirmation of the ever-new testament of God.

Today the mandates of society have made it almost impossible to found a new religion, and the gates of the old religions of the world are shut tight with human opinion, irremovable error and immovable dogma that seals the possibility of advent. The travail of bringing forth progressive spiritual revelation is intense, and often our messengers have to reckon with many forces of shadow which seek to thwart the holy cause.

You do not know what it means to face the darkening clouds of an entrenched world order and a world-might arrayed against your own son. The Good Friday confrontation is more than historical—it is an initiation of the ages. The uplifting of the cross is a symbol wherein God and man meet in the vital body of Christ truth.

The [principle of the] corporeal body of the living Word is announced to the present hour by men who understand it not, even as they understood him not in that day. As they sought to defame his spotless character, so they will often seek to deface the character of those who in succeeding generations shall do, to quote his words, "greater works than these...because I go unto my Father."[4]

Because of the need for understanding, I proclaim my solid unity with Saint Germain as we seek to nurture the messiah of progressive revelation whereby the curtain to the Holy of holies, the veil in the temple of man's being, may be rent in twain[5] by the great lightning of divine love. In sweeping aside ancient traditions, this love, as sacred law, reveals on the altar of each man's heart a living flame, the Paraclete beyond token, manifesting as the presence of Life in all its immaculate wonder!

Your Mother of Infinite Love

Mary

September 5, 1965

13

The Birth of God in Man

To Those Whose Hope Is in the Star of His Appearing:

So many of you are thinking of new beginnings, so many of you are caught up in the delight of outer festivities that I must, in the name of cosmic grace, caution men, admonish men and guide them as children of our heart into the realization that, in reality, it is the birth of God in man which is celebrated as the Christ Mass and that the opportunities of this season are given to men that they may literally absolve themselves from darkness.

In the great brilliance of the burst of light celebrated as the Christ Mass, the darkness without may beckon the flame within to sing of new beginnings. Then, with the building bricks of the Spirit solidly placed upon the foundation of God's heart and transcendentally mounting into the blue of his will, the soul shall rise as a tower of strength, facing all outer conditions and saying to them, "If you are not of God, you have no power!"—for only God can bring eternal life into the human heart.

As I utter these words, I envision millions among you reading my message and cherishing my spirit as kindred to your own. Nevertheless, one of the great tragedies of human existence is the lack of the miracle of belief, the lack of faith in the things of the Spirit which are all around you as the best gifts of God. For these you ought to be thankful always, and your thanks should be a bouquet of fragrant thoughts offered unto God.

Many are concerned with the passing moment—either with the bane of harsh experience or the blessing of a family get-together. And many are involved in making others happy. Let all think of how they can make God happy; for whereas he has given so much, he himself has often received so little.

Oh, I know full well that there are those who will say, "God is not a person." May I say to all that as God is a Spirit, his Spirit is omnipresent and personal to each manifestation that will receive him. And the reflection of his gladness in their eyes, of his hopes in their hearts, of his ongoingness in their spirits, is the fragrance of foreverness.

To forgo the opportunity of receiving him in the person of the Christ is to delete from your consciousness one of the most glorious facets of individuality—the opportunity of giving. For lodged in his heart is a permanent abundance in which all may share in varying portions. Without this abundance the soul would indeed be barren, but with it each individual may find that the meeting of his needs is the joy of God himself.

There are those who are momentarily bereft of attention. There are those who are deliberately ignored. There are those who pursue a way that is far from the Father's goal. Yet all of these belong in the caravan that climbs the mountain of faith and goodwill.

I see clearly a vision of Christ-intent for a world that slumbers neath the snows, not yet knowing the fullness of its own purpose. And whereas I had thought this year to warn the students of the ways of error (which many of them so clearly see), I spoke unto myself and I said, "How best can I serve them all? For I have warned, I have admonished, I have encouraged."

And as I thought to speak in this wise, several of the ascended brethren in white came to me, and it was their sincere feeling that we should but offer the bouquet of our love to the soul of God within each one—the soul that only God can awaken in man—for it is our great desire to show the students how great is his love.

And so, whereas we have often lamented the ways of the world, which are not God's ways;[1] whereas we have often sought to bring men to a higher way, a way of splendor that so few have known; and whereas the chastening of God has brought forth much fruit, I choose to vary my approach this year and to appeal from the depth of my heart to the heart of each one, intimately, tenderly.

Let the God within awaken man. Let him show the world the error of their ways. Let him show the individual the splendor of his strength. Let him reveal himself. You who need him more than you know, listen to him. Develop the habit of looking for him behind the face of outer manifestation.

In all of the scenes and thoughts of your heart, myriad and tumbling, the way of his loveliness is the hope of the world. The miracle of his coming into the life of the individual is a joy to behold. It is almost to be likened to a seed sown in the heart of the earth that, nourished and watered, presses upward toward the light. It is the strength born of devotion to his love that seems to be lost and fading in men. But coming once again into the unfailing strength of God, they shall know the peace that is born out of service to the Christ in each one.

Our way is the way of peace. But those who have studied the long struggle of mankind's misadventures know the need to be rational and practical in the world of form just as we are in the world of Spirit.

Never let your ideals destroy. But let them implement within you the aspects of your being that will keep alive in the world the potential of the Christed man for God-realization—the freedom of the soul that can go forth and inflame itself with the love of his star, with his love of life, with his zest for truth, always with his awakening dawning in the memory.

And thus the appointed time of the day of his appearing shall be shortened,[2] and many shall see him as he is.[3] And because they see him, they will believe more in themselves and in the purposes of life. The destiny of man will be merged into the completeness of the grace of the universal Christ Child nestling in every mother's arms as her own babe and lodging in every father's heart as the divine seed.

And the Child shall communicate to all the way of a world that rises into the twilight and reaches for the dawn in which a new opportunity and a new way of thought, high on the road Godward, will seal the destiny of a brightened world in the peace of universal hope.

Mary

December 13, 1970

14

The Transformation of the Individual Is the Key to the Salvation of a Planet

To Every Pilgrim Heart:

As the advent of love comes at times to every man who opens himself to the inward persuasions of his soul, so I am convinced that all things will one day reflect the glory of God.

So many have retained the image of my Son in those agonies of human persecution that are reminiscent of their own conflict in matter. These involvements with the *via dolorosa*, the sorrowful way, are a trap that prevents man from seeing and experiencing the glories inherent in the constructive life which was lived by our carpenter of Nazareth. Let it be known that his was a building for eternity in the finite realm of thought and feeling.

What a tragedy it is that men are so easily diverted by outer media from the true course of their appointed thoughts. How much to be desired, then, is the mastery of one's thoughts and feelings, the mastery of the flow of energy through one's consciousness.

Because there is no other method of controlling the individual, either from within or without, I wish to stress to every son and daughter of heaven the tremendous joy and freedom that can be theirs as they perceive the import of governing their thoughts and feelings, their attitudes and comprehensions of the divine wonder.

All around you beauty exists, yet ugliness seems so often to preempt it. I would remove the crown of thorns that man has unwittingly placed upon his own head. But first I would ask that reason be utilized in making those constructive changes that are necessary if man is to secure his cosmic destiny right while in physical embodiment. Have you thought of what a beautiful gift God has given to you in the gift of life—even in the manifestation of your physical form, which is so often crucified by the harshness of everyday living?

Precious ones, the ways of the world are a glaring reflection of man's lack of innocence. When guilelessness and innocence become a part of man's nature once again, he will effectively transform himself in the image of the Christ, as was the will of God for him from the beginning.

Then, in emulation of the masters of wisdom, man shall not only pursue and be pursued by the light of the Great White Brotherhood, but he shall also become a true follower of God in all of his compassed wonder. Why, don't you know, beloved ones, the Most High can unerringly guide your thoughts and feelings just as easily as you can weave a simple garment for a child, using the dexterity of your fingers and the flexibility of your mind?

With the God-given capacity that you have to direct your physical body and to organize your life, can you not also master the process of controlling your mind and your feelings? And if you do, I assure you that it will contribute much to the alleviation of the problems of the world in its maddened state. It will even counteract the unfortunate manifestations of witchcraft and black magic that are often practiced in the name of religion but are used solely for the psychic domination and control of others.

May I tell you that the one design that heaven desires to see outpictured on earth and in the hearts of men is that self-control by which every individual can win his own victory and the strength of his Christlike mind.

Therefore do I invoke for all the Christlike mind and the Christlike qualities which will effect the power of self-control that is the requirement of the hour. Whereas from time to time men have misused the minds and feelings that God has given them, those minds and feelings possess the very capacities of the Spirit which Jesus expressed and that he longed to see established in you all.

Through obedience to the law of your inner being, you can effect those self-controls that will make your world brighter each day. And whereas there are some who will despise my message for its simplicity, others will see the need to pinpoint for future action the whole course of their conduct.

This need for God-control can be seen in young and old alike—from the little children, in their innocent state, to those wiser ones who, in their maturity, have so often lost those holy threads of innocence which establish the aura of cosmic fortitude in men.

As long as you depend solely upon your human strength and not upon the power of the Christ, it is easy to see, surrounded as you are by the mosaics of mortal thought, how you can become the victim of those thought-pockets of human degradation. The elimination of the idea that you cannot take command of your lives is the important first step that must be taken before you can begin to weave the spiritual garments of self-mastery we long to see you wear.

Many have thought that in the last days of my earthly sojourn I did not fulfill all my longings. Beloved ones, may I confess to you that even in the ascended state we have not fulfilled all our longings, especially in connection with the earth and its evolutions.

Do you know that out of the teeming millions of mankind, some of the prayers that rise to our level are literally heartrending, and particularly so when viewed in the light of the fact that heaven has already provided the answer which humanity will not open their hearts to receive.

When we stress the importance of the dedication of the

individual life to God, it means that we believe that the kingdom of heaven must first manifest within the individual before it can manifest in the world on a larger scale. So long as men wait upon the world for the fulfillment of their desires, so long will they wait in the recalcitrance and hopelessness of those who do not understand that one is taken and another is left.[1]

The justice of God on earth must become the work of the individual. Those who crave social justice are those who would build worldly fences of unenforceable law and order; they do not realize that the establishment of law and order comes about as men claim that holy sense of justice that burns behind the veil of the appearance world. One day they will learn that it is only in the realm within, in the inner thoughts and feelings, that transformation can occur—and that the transformation of the individual is the key to the salvation of a planet.

Whenever undesirable qualities seem to have an inordinate hold upon your consciousness, possessing your whole being, occupying the very fiber of your mind and denying you the peace and happiness of thinking the thoughts that you so long to think, realize that you are momentarily caught in the grips of a terrible force-accumulation.

In the past we have also been confronted by such forcefields of vicious psychic energies, and even in the ascended state we have been required to meet the challenges of giant floating grids of astral debris. But as we have persevered and prevailed upon God to help us, our minds have immediately become calm and imbued with the power of holy reason and judgment.

Learn not to be rash, to be overly critical or to unfairly attribute to others those qualities that are in reality no part of the Real Self. Give to all the joy and peace which you yourself expect to receive and watch how the energies of the universe will in due course of time, like a steadily flowing river, rush into your world to assist you in the whole process of inner purification.

When I think of the long journey of Christendom and of the conflicts into which many have entered in the name of my Son, condemning as heathen those followers of God in other folds, I am reminded of his words "Other sheep I have, which are not of this fold: them also I must bring, and they shall hear my voice; and there shall be one fold, and one shepherd."[2]

In the name of holy reason, until men come to the place where they are able to see the body of God upon earth as one fold even as they behold the one shepherd, give them their freedom to think as they will. And pray that they may establish in their consciousness that faith in the one God which will make of the whole earth one family beneath the four winds of heaven.

All conflict must be resolved, all vileness cast away and the tender beauty of the kingdom of heaven become as flowers beneath man's feet—a high and holy way of joy in the transcendent culture of the ascended masters' consciousness. Then the little children can be trained up in the way they should go,[3] and at long last the travail of the ages that has preceded the birth of the Divine Manchild will bring forth a golden age of enlightenment. And God will rule in the hearts of men because they love him and love one another.

Each moment that the individual understands and enters into this consciousness, a new beginning occurs. Therefore be ye followers of my Son and of the invincible light that presages the eternally progressive age of the avatars; for in the beginning was the light of the Word, and the light was with God and the light was God.[4] And out of that light is born the flame that pushes back the darkness that never was and never shall be.

The illusion of that darkness shall vanish as the coming of the kingdom is heard in a rushing mighty wind[5] and the ground of the heart, like a thirsty ground, laps up the water of eternal life.[6]

Let men be spiritually filled. Let their goals now be spiritual, even as in the past they have been material. Thus shall we bridge the gap of confusion and reveal at last the permanent foundation of the abundant life.

I remain

Mary

The Mother of Jesus

February 21, 1971

PART TWO

The Love Aspect of the Holy Spirit
Five Mysteries of the Rosary by the
Mother for Her Children

The Power of Spoken Prayer

As God has said in scripture, earth is the footstool kingdom, and we were sent forth into the physical universe to take dominion, to subdue it, to multiply.

We were given free will and we must make our choices; we must do what we will and bear the consequences of our actions. Thus, in giving us the gift of freedom, God does not interfere with that freedom and stop calamity or tragedy in its very midst.

If we realize the folly of depending on human will and human choices and recognize that we need consultation and intercession from the divine will and the principles of divine freedom, then we call to God and say, "Not my will, O God, but thine be done. Help me. I cannot solve this problem. It is too big for me."

And therefore prayer, communication—ask and thou shalt receive; knock, and it shall be opened unto you[1]—becomes the way of the release of God's power. If we want him now to take over in our lives, we have to say, "God, I surrender to you. I have seen that my will gets me nowhere or little, that I of mine own self can do nothing. It is the Father in me that doeth the work. Father, come into my life. Jesus, come into my temple."

Then God takes over. We now become the instruments and we see heaven opening. We see great changes and miracles and healings.

Life is intended to be free and joyous. We are intended to have access to heaven with all the power and the glory of the hierarchies and saints in heaven. We are intended to move in the communion of saints, to have interaction with those who have gone before us who are our teachers—the masters of the Path.

So then, in this particular way, we understand that the Science of the Spoken Word in the form of the decree, a type of dynamic spoken prayer, is the means whereby we make the fiat that God take command with his heavenly hosts of situations and problems that are absolutely beyond our ability to define, to sort out, let alone to resolve.

I, for one, could not begin to tell you the answer to the problems of the extremism of Right and Left political activities. We see wrong on all sides, we see right on all sides; yet who is ultimately right? Let God be true and every man a liar, the apostle said.[2]

And therefore, rather than supporting one side or the other and finding that they are both made of clay feet, we support God and his angels; we call them into action. And God, being no respecter of persons, works through anyone and everyone, even those people with whom we may disagree, even those people we may condemn and think are somehow lesser individuals or more lowly than ourselves—as we are all tainted in some way with some degree of prejudice.

And so, the magnificent thing about the call and the decree is that we decree for God's will and then he implements it. And as he implements it, we see what his will is, and we become more specific in our decrees to emphasize the specifics of his will.

So then the tragedies that are senseless and useless in life, those things which ought not to be, can be mitigated, can be turned around. But somehow God's law demands to be heard and to be understood. It is inexorable, and God does not break his law, although he has introduced mercy and the grace of Christ as the means of intercession and setting aside the law in answer to prayer.

Thus, you can understand that in the Catholic tradition asking for the saints to intercede before God is the same as our asking the ascended masters to use their momentum of service to draw down the light into our lives that will assist us in a particular situation. And so we realize what is the purpose of Mother

Mary as the Mediatrix of mercy, of grace and of healing. Mother Mary, in her position of hierarchy, can go to the Father, to the Son, to hierarchies of light and Elohim and receive dispensations of light and help for us.

So then, according to God's laws, those who have certain burdens of karma, who have misused the law, who are weighed down by that karma, must have those who are of greater attainment and light to intercede, because each one of us is limited by the weight of our karma as to what the outpouring of light may be from God.

Now this may seem unfair or unjust, but it is not. Those who have proven themselves responsible with the use of God's light and energy have access to more light. This is the meaning of the words of Jesus: "For whosoever hath, to him shall be given, and he shall have more abundance: but whosoever hath not, from him shall be taken away even that he hath."[3]

The understanding of Jesus' teaching in the parable of the talents is the same.[4] Those who have light and who have used that light responsibly shall be given more light—the one who multiplied the talents was made "ruler over many things." But the one who has misused the light of God, or not used it at all, cannot be given more. And because he has not been profitable or productive in multiplying the original gift, the original gift is taken from him.

All of these lessons, when understood, lead back to the knowledge of the Science of the Spoken Word. It is the means to invoke the violet flame* and the mercy of God as intercession, delivered through the agency of the saints and the Holy Spirit, to transmute karma, to dissolve records of sin, to liberate us from our past mistakes, because God has said, I will remember their sin no more.[5]

---

* The violet flame is a high-frequency spiritual energy that transmutes (transforms) negative karma into positive energy. For more information and for decrees to the violet flame, see Elizabeth Clare Prophet, *Violet Flame to Heal Body, Mind and Soul*, published by Summit University Press.

God does not desire that you or I should be eternally shack-
led to a mistake we made a thousand years ago or yesterday.
When we have seen the lesson, experienced the sorrow of our
ignorance or our impetuousness, and sincerely desire to go on at
a new level, God forgives. And forgiveness comes as a manifestation of the erasing of the record, the transmutation of the karma,
and as opportunity not only to go and sin no more but to do
those positive acts that are constructive toward life.

Thus, Mother Mary has told us, "When you recite the rosary
and do so early in the day before the cares of the day and the kar-
mas of the day overtake you, I can enter so easily, for you have
placed around yourself my Presence by the recitation of the Hail
Mary....And so know that in the moments that you recite the
rosary undisturbed, unmoved and in attunement with my Immaculate Heart, I may enter and become one with you and perform
for you necessities of the hour, healings with direction and guidance and comfort for your hour of trial."[6]

Mother Mary appeared to me one fall morning in 1972 in the
prayer tower of our retreat in Colorado Springs and she said:
"I want to give you a ritual of the rosary for sons and daughters of
God....This rosary will be for the bringing in of the golden age. It
is to be used as a universal adoration of the Mother flame by people of all faiths. For, you see, the salutation 'Hail, Mary' simply
means 'Hail, Mother ray' and it is an affirmation of praise to the
Mother flame in every part of life. Each time it is spoken, it evokes
the action of the Mother's light in the hearts of all mankind."

The rosary is a sacred ritual whereby all of God's children can
find their way back to their immaculate conception in the heart of
the Cosmic Virgin. The New Age rosary is the instrument for
mankind's deliverance from the sense of sin and from the erro-
neous doctrine of original sin—for every soul is immaculately
conceived by Almighty God, and God the Father is the origin of
all of the cycles of man's being. Mary says: "That which is con-

ceived in sin is not of God and has neither the power nor the permanence of Reality. All that is real is of God; all that is unreal will pass away as mankind become one with the Mother flame. The daily giving of the rosary is a certain means to this oneness."

When I pondered in my heart the meaning of our origin in God, I saw that God the Father and God the Mother have indeed created the soul immaculately. It is our sense of sin that has placed upon us this doctrine of damnation, this doctrine of original sin whereby from the moment we are born, without even having uttered a word or having had a thought or a feeling, we are considered to be miserable sinners.

I realized that man's true identity and origin in God are much more powerful than his sense of sin and his misuse of God's sacred fire that resulted in what is known as the Fall. The Fall actually was the sin of disobedience to God, and for that disobedience we daily pay a great price. That price is our separation from God with all of the attendant pain and suffering, travail and disease that is upon the human race.

But Mother Mary came to show us the way back to the state of grace through the giving of the Hail Mary and through meditation upon her blessed Son, Jesus. The rosary that she gave me was to eliminate the sense of sin and the sense of death. And therefore we give the Hail Mary as follows:

> Hail, Mary, full of grace, the Lord is with thee. Blessed art thou among women and blessed is the fruit of thy womb, Jesus.
>
> Holy Mary, Mother of God, pray for us, sons and daughters of God, now and at the hour of our victory over sin, disease and death.

Catholics will note that the traditional Hail Mary says "Pray for us sinners" rather than "Pray for us, sons and daughters of God." Mother Mary wants us to understand that God does not hold us in a death grip of sin and the sense of sin, but he holds us in the immaculate vision of his All-Seeing Eye as the son and the daughter who are the fruit of the union of the Father-Mother God.

Mother Mary said to me: "People must begin to understand and know that they are created in the image and likeness of God and to affirm that 'Now are we the sons of God,'[7] as John the Beloved said. And therefore, let the children of God look up to heaven and, in dignity and nobility and sense of self-worth, give the call as the true son and the daughter of God.

"Let us then pray for that Mother ray, not at the hour of death, for there is no death. My own Son proved that death is unreal. And therefore call for my intercession at the hour of your victory over sin, disease and death."

The Outline of the Rosary

As was mentioned in the Foreword, Mother Mary has released a rosary for each morning of the week and a rosary to be used on Sunday evening. These rosaries are outlined in Book One of the Golden Word of Mary series: *Mary's Message for a New Day.*

A rosary for each of the five secret rays of the Holy Spirit was given for communion with the Paraclete on the five evenings of the week. These rosaries are included in this volume. These mysteries outline the testings which the soul must face, the demonstrations of the Law which it must make, and the temptations which it must overcome ere the devotee of the Mother and the Son be wholly integrated within the consciousness of the Christ.

Mary also promised to release a fourteenth rosary, which she said would be very different from the others, when enough people had built a momentum of devotion in giving the thirteen rosaries. This rosary was released in October 1975, and will be outlined in Book Three of this series. Without question, all of these rosaries prepare the disciple for the initiations on the Path which are narrated in the mysteries.

The content of the Scriptural Rosary for the New Age, which the Blessed Mother dictated, reflects the flow of the Father-Mother God—of God as Father and God as Mother. This was revealed to John in the words "I AM Alpha and Omega, the beginning and the ending."[1] The first adoration of the rosary, making the sign of the cross, marks the four aspects of God's being as Father, Mother, Son, and Holy Spirit. As we make this sign, we are reinforcing the consciousness of these aspects in body and soul, mind and heart. The Latin cross (usually suspended from the rosary) is the emblem of the converging lines of Spirit (Alpha) and Matter

(Omega), signifying the place where Christ is born and where the energies of the Logos are released to a planet.

Touching the forehead as the north arm of the cross, we say "In the name of the Father." Touching the heart as the south arm of the cross, we say "and of the Mother." Touching the left shoulder as the east arm of the cross, we say "and of the Son." Touching the right shoulder as the west arm of the cross, we say "and of the Holy Spirit, Amen."

By including the name of the Mother in our salutation of the Trinity, we invoke the consciousness of the Cosmic Virgin, who makes each aspect of the sacred Trinity meaningful to our evolving consciousness. Indeed Mary is the Daughter of God, the Mother of Christ, and the Bride of the Holy Spirit. Fulfilling the intimate role of the feminine counterpart of each aspect of the masculine principle of God, she is best able to portray to us the nature of Father, Son and Holy Spirit.

The second adoration of the rosary, the "Adoration to God," was received by Mark Prophet directly from the Holy Spirit. As you give this prayer with love and devotion, you are sending back to God all the energy in your being that you focalize through the spoken Word in your adoration. You are sending God's love back to him in the greatest fervor of your being. He takes that love, he multiplies it, he sends it back to you and, through your heart, sends light rays to bless all people.

The next adoration is "Jesus' I AM Lord's Prayer." Jesus gave us the Lord's Prayer, recorded in the Bible, in the imperative mode, the command. It supposes that the soul is in the state of becoming, commanding that which it desires to be to descend and perform the perfect work. Jesus gave us that prayer because the command itself is intended to raise the soul to that position of authority. Even if our soul does not understand why it has the authority to command the light of God, the prayer itself will take us there.

Now as we advance on the path of Christhood, we look at this Lord's Prayer and we realize that these commands have manifested within us. We know the God who lives in our temple; we know the I AM Presence.[2] We are now with Jesus in the Upper Room and he gives us the "I AM Lord's Prayer," affirming that all we have commanded is now come into manifestation where we are:

> Our Father who art in heaven,
> Hallowed be thy name, I AM.
> I AM thy kingdom come
> I AM thy will being done
> I AM on earth even as I AM in heaven
> I AM giving this day daily bread to all
> I AM forgiving all life this day even as
> I AM also all life forgiving me
> I AM leading all men away from temptation
> I AM delivering all men from every evil condition
> I AM the kingdom
> I AM the power and
> I AM the glory of God in eternal, immortal
>   manifestation—
> All this I AM.

In this prayer, we are affirming (as God is affirming in us) that the Great Doer is doing all those things that we formerly asked him to do. We acknowledge ourselves as a co-creator with him. When we say, "I AM," we are saying, "God in me is." When we are one with God, there is no separation. The I AM of God speaking is the only I AM of us because we have surrendered all lesser identity.

In order to correctly use the name of God, I AM,[3] as an affirmation of being and as an affirmation of the action of being, we must first be convinced of our oneness with God through a correct interpretation of his laws. By the grace of God, the statement of these laws has not been entirely removed from sacred scripture. Those who are willing to examine the Bible in the light of historical truth as well as in the light of the ascended masters' teachings will begin to realize that the doctrine of original sin and the belief that man is sinful by nature do not originate in either the laws of God or in the teachings of Jesus.

Once relieved of the burden of sin and the sense of sin, mankind can truly affirm their oneness with God, which can be accomplished only through Christ the Mediator—the only begotten Son of God. As there is but one God, one LORD, so there is but one Christ. As God individualized himself in the Presence of the I AM for each one, so he has also individualized the Christ for each one in the Christ Self and in the Christ flame that blazes upon the altar of the heart sustaining life as the opportunity for oneness.

To continue with our analysis of the adorations of the rosary, we note that the three Hail Marys which comprise the fourth adoration set the pattern for the entire rosary in the tripartite flame of faith, hope and charity, of God's will, his wisdom and his love. By and in this trinity of oneness—of Father, Son and Holy Spirit—the action of the adorations which follow is multiplied by the power of the three-times-three for the salvation of mankind.

In giving the "Love Me," the fifth adoration of the rosary, we are speaking to God, the individualized Presence just above us, calling forth that love. And as that love pours through us, it blesses the entire earth.

The "Introit to the Holy Christ Self," which is given as the sixth adoration of the rosary, was also inspired upon Mark Prophet by the Holy Spirit. As we give this prayer, we feel ourselves communing with the Holy Christ Self, through the Holy Christ Flame within our hearts. We are giving ourselves to the Christ and saying, "Thank you, beloved Holy Christ Self, for being within me. Be my hands, be my mind and my heart and my feet, and render your

Chart of the Rosary

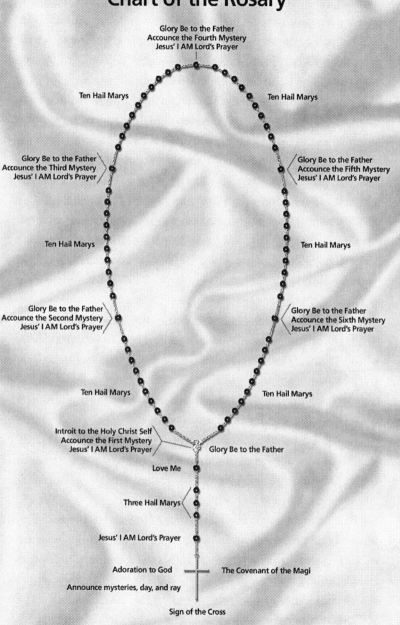

Glory Be to the Father
Accounce the Fourth Mystery
Jesus' I AM Lord's Prayer

Ten Hail Marys   Ten Hail Marys

Glory Be to the Father
Accounce the Third Mystery
Jesus' I AM Lord's Prayer

Glory Be to the Father
Accounce the Fifth Mystery
Jesus' I AM Lord's Prayer

Ten Hail Marys   Ten Hail Marys

Glory Be to the Father
Accounce the Second Mystery
Jesus' I AM Lord's Prayer

Glory Be to the Father
Accounce the Sixth Mystery
Jesus' I AM Lord's Prayer

Ten Hail Marys   Ten Hail Marys

Introit to the Holy Christ Self
Accounce the First Mystery
Jesus' I AM Lord's Prayer

Glory Be to the Father

Love Me

Three Hail Marys

Jesus' I AM Lord's Prayer

Adoration to God   The Covenant of the Magi

Announce mysteries, day, and ray

Sign of the Cross

Proceed from left to right in a clockwise directions, beginning
with the *Sign of the Cross* and ending with *The Covenant of the Magi*.

blessing unto life through me. I surrender my being unto thee, and I desire to make my will *thy* will and the will of the Father."

In each of the six decades that form the body of the secret-ray rosaries, we give "Jesus' I AM Lord's Prayer," the ten Hail Marys, and the Glory Be to the Father. These adorations in each of the decades are a tribute to the oneness of the Father-Mother God. Thus, the "I AM Lord's Prayer," seventh in the order of adorations, establishes the flow of energies from our heart's altar back to the very source of life whence we came.

The ten Hail Marys, eighth in the order of adorations, are the gift of our devotion to the Starry Mother. She has borne us in her cosmic womb and held for us the immaculate concept of our divinity within her diamond heart. By the action of the ritual of the ten, the Mother helps us overcome all self-love and crowns us with a vision of the kingdom of heaven as we crown her with a garland of our love.

The Glory Be to the Father, ninth in the order of adorations, is our giving forth of joyful praise to Almighty God for the victory of the Woman clothed with the Sun, who in turn bestows upon us the rule of the Divine Manchild.

In each decade of the rosary, then, we meditate alternately upon Mary the Mother as the focal point of our own incarnation of the Motherhood of God and upon Jesus Christ for our realization of the fullness of that divine Sonship within us. Through the Mother and the Son we reach the Father. And in the Father we are reborn according to his immaculate design.

The rosary, then, is for the balance of the masculine and feminine polarity of being. And this is achieved by our contemplation of the life and the experiences of Jesus as we give the adoration of the Hail Mary.

Our meditation upon the events in the life of Jesus and the stations of the cross enables us to also pass through the experiences that Jesus passed through and therefore to participate in this drama—to become the drama with him, to walk the stations of the cross. God thereby reenacts within us these most sacred events in Jesus' life, which is to become our very own life.

In the secret-ray rosaries, our meditation on Jesus' life extends to embodiments prior to his Galilean ministry, as we follow episodes from the life of Elisha and his discipleship under Elijah, and David's communion with the LORD in the Psalms.

When we finally are able to totally equate with the life of Mary and Jesus and other saints, then we ourselves will be able to put on their consciousness of victory, of the resurrection and of the ascension.

As we are willing to enter this path, Mary and Jesus, the hosts of the LORD, Archangel Michael and the angels come to us each day. And each day becomes a little ritual whereby we are given an important lesson in cosmic law through a circumstance in our life created by our own karma. This path is called the path of initiation because our souls are being initiated.

We no sooner conclude our rosary in the morning than we are beset with all of the problems of the day and the challenges that life joyously presents to us. We do not walk the *via dolorosa* because we are not sad, we are not in a sinful sense, we are not in a sense of shame. But we are in a sense of glory because from glory unto glory we know that we are putting on the consciousness of God.

The rosary concludes with "The Covenant of the Magi," an ancient commitment of those wise men, even the Sons of the Solitude, who have descended down the centuries bearing the Christ Child in their hearts. It is a pledge of surrender of oneself to the Father. It is another step on the mystery of surrender and is a very profound commitment to God the Father. This tenth adoration of the rosary seals the prayers we selflessly give to Mary as well as the energies she gives to us on the return current of her love.

When Mother Mary completed the dictating of the rosary, she said: "This is the one key. If the student body will take it up, the giving of this rosary daily will enable the flame of the Mother to be anchored in the world and to prevent a great deal of destruction of human life during the days that are ahead."

In return for our devotion and for the garland of roses woven out of our ten affirmations of the rosary, Mary made the promise: "When you come to a certain place in your momentum of attainment in the giving of the rosary, I will come to you and I will place about your neck a rosary of roses composed of fiery stars— each bead a star of light.

"And you will know when I come in that very hour, for you will feel the garland of light around your neck. And it will be as a reward for faithful service to my immaculate heart and to the rose which symbolizes the unfolding of the Mother flame in the consciousness of mankind."[4]

The heavenly hosts await the energies we release in the giving of the rosary that they may in turn release their energy in concerted action on behalf of all of the children of God on earth. Mary exhorts us to give the rosary as heaven joins us in devotion to the Beloved Mother and together we pray for the salvation of all mankind.

Adorations of the Rosary

The Sign of the Cross

In the name of the Father
and of the Mother
and of the Son
and of the Holy Spirit,
Amen.

Adoration to God

Beloved mighty I AM Presence,
Thou life that beats my heart,
Come now and take dominion,
Make me of thy life a part.
Rule supreme and live forever
In the flame ablaze within;
Let me from thee never sever,
Our reunion now begin.

All the days proceed in order
From the current of thy power,
Flowing forward like a river,
Rising upward like a tower.
I AM faithful to thy love ray
Blazing forth light as a sun;
I AM grateful for thy right way
And thy precious word "Well done."

I AM, I AM, I AM adoring thee! (3x)
O God, you are so magnificent! (9x)
I AM, I AM, I AM adoring thee! (3x)

Moving onward to perfection,
I AM raised by love's great grace
To thy center of direction
Behold, at last I see thy face.
Image of immortal power,
Wisdom, love and honor, too,
Flood my being now with glory,
Let my eyes see none but you!

O God, you are so magnificent! (3x)
I AM, I AM, I AM adoring thee! (9x)
O God, you are so magnificent! (3x)

My very own beloved I AM! beloved I AM! beloved I AM!

The I AM Lord's Prayer
by Jesus the Christ

Our Father who art in heaven,
Hallowed be thy name, I AM.
I AM thy kingdom come
I AM thy will being done
I AM on earth even as I AM in heaven
I AM giving this day daily bread to all
I AM forgiving all life this day even as
I AM also all life forgiving me
I AM leading all men away from temptation
I AM delivering all men from every evil condition
I AM the kingdom
I AM the power and
I AM the glory of God in eternal, immortal
manifestation—
All this I AM.

Hail Mary

Hail, Mary, full of grace. The Lord is with thee. Blessed art thou among women and blessed is the fruit of thy womb, Jesus.

Holy Mary, Mother of God, pray for us, sons and daughters of God, now and at the hour of our victory over sin, disease, and death.

Love Me

1. I AM so willing to be filled
      With the love of God;
    I AM calling to be thrilled
      With the love of God;
    I AM longing so for grace
      From the heart of God;
    Yearning just to see his face
      By the love of God.

Refrain: As a rose unfolding fair
    Wafts her fragrance on the air,
    I pour forth to God devotion,
    One now with the cosmic ocean.

2. I AM hoping so to be,
      Made by love divine.
    I AM longing Christ to be,
      Wholly only thine.
    I AM so peaceful in thy love,
      Feel at home with God above.
    I AM at one with all mankind
      The cords of Love God's children bind.
    I AM fore'er one living soul
      With angels, man, and God as goal.

3. I AM locked in God's great love,
   His mighty arms of power;
  Cradled now by heaven above,
   Protected every hour.
  I AM alight with happiness,
   Wholly filled with God success,
  For I AM love of righteousness.
   I love thee, love thee, love thee,
  My own God Presence bright;
   Love me, love me, love me,
  Protect me by thy might.
   Remain within and round me
  Till I become thy light!

Introit to the Holy Christ Self

1. Holy Christ Self above me,
  Thou balance of my soul,
  Let thy blessed radiance
  Descend and make me whole.

Refrain: Thy flame within me ever blazes,
  Thy peace about me ever raises,
  Thy love protects and holds me,
  Thy dazzling light enfolds me.
  I AM thy threefold radiance,
  I AM thy living Presence
  Expanding, expanding, expanding now.

2. Holy Christ Flame within me,
  Come, expand thy triune light;
  Flood my being with the essence
  Of the pink, blue, gold and white.

3. Holy lifeline to my Presence,
   Friend and brother ever dear,
   Let me keep thy holy vigil,
   Be thyself in action here.

Glory Be to the Father

Glory be to the Father
And to the Son
And to the Holy Spirit!
As it was in the beginning,
Is now and ever shall be,
Life without end—
I AM, I AM, I AM!

The Covenant of the Magi
by El Morya

Father, into thy hands I commend my being. Take me and use me—my efforts, my thoughts, my resources, all that I AM—in thy service to the world of men and to thy noble cosmic purposes, yet unknown to my mind.

Teach me to be kind in the way of the Law that awakens men and guides them to the shores of Reality, to the confluence of the River of Life, to the Edenic source, that I may understand that the leaves of the Tree of Life, given to me each day, are for the healing of the nations; that as I garner them into the treasury of being and offer the fruit of my loving adoration to thee and to thy purposes supreme, I shall indeed hold covenant with thee as my guide, my guardian, my friend.

For thou art the directing connector who shall establish my lifestream with those heavenly contacts, limited only by the flow of the hours, who will assist me to perform in the world of men the most meaningful aspect of my individual life plan as conceived by thee and executed in thy name by the Karmic Board of spiritual overseers who, under thy holy direction, do administer thy laws.

So be it, O eternal Father, and may the covenant of thy beloved Son, the living Christ, the Only Begotten of the Light, teach me to be aware that he liveth today within the tri-unity of my being as the Great Mediator between my individualized Divine Presence and my human self; that he raiseth me into Christ consciousness and thy divine realization in order that as the eternal Son becomes one with the Father, so I may ultimately become one with thee in that dynamic moment when out of union is born my perfect freedom to move, to think, to create, to design, to fulfill, to inhabit, to inherit, to dwell and to be wholly within the fullness of thy light.

Father, into thy hands I commend my being.

Mary's Ritual of the Rosary for Sons and Daughters of Dominion

To give the Rosary, follow these fourteen steps, using the Adorations of the Rosary given on the preceding pages as they are called for in the ritual.

1

Holding the cross in your right hand, make the *sign of the cross* to honor the Holy Trinity within man as you give the *Sign of the Cross:*

> In the name of the Father
> > *Touch forehead with right hand*
> and of the Mother
> > *Touch heart with right hand*
> and of the Son
> > *Touch left shoulder*
> and of the Holy Spirit,
> > *Touch right shoulder*
> Amen.
> > *Put hands together.*

2

Announce the mysteries, the day, and the ray; for example, "The Inspiration Mysteries: Monday Evening – The First Secret Ray."

3

Still holding the cross, recite the *Adoration to God.*

4

On the first large bead, recite *Jesus' I AM Lord's Prayer* to commemorate the oneness of God in universal manifestation.

5

On each of the next three beads, recite one *Hail Mary* for the establishment upon earth of the dominion of faith, hope and charity.

6

On the next bead give *Love Me*.

7

At the triangle or medal give the *Introit to the Holy Christ Self*.

8

Announce the First Mystery; for example, "First Inspiration Mystery: Delight in Thy Law."

9

Still holding the triangle or medal, recite *Jesus' I AM Lord's Prayer* to commemorate the oneness of God in individual manifestation.

10

On each of the next ten beads, recite the scriptures listed under the First Mystery to create a cup of praise, and offer a *Hail Mary* to invoke the light that fills the cup with the essence of the Divine Mother.

11

Conclude the first mystery with an offering of praise to the holy Trinity in man by singing or reciting the *Glory Be to the Father* on the next bead.

12

Still holding this bead, announce the second mystery; for example, "Second Inspiration Mystery: The Excellence of Thy Name."

13

On the same bead give *Jesus' I AM Lord's Prayer* to commemorate the oneness of God in individual manifestation. Complete the next five decades in the same manner as the first.*

14

Conclude your ritual by reciting *The Covenant of the Magi.*

---

*If your rosary has only five decades of beads, use the fifth decade for the fifth and sixth mysteries.

MARY'S SCRIPTURAL
ROSARY FOR THE NEW AGE

I

Sign of the Cross

The Inspiration Mysteries
Monday Evening – The First Secret Ray

Adoration to God
Jesus' I AM Lord's Prayer
Three Hail Marys
Love Me
Introit to the Holy Christ Self

First Inspiration Mystery
Delight in Thy Law

Jesus' I AM Lord's Prayer

1   Blessed is the man that walketh not in the counsel of the ungodly, nor standeth in the way of sinners, nor sitteth in the seat of the scornful. But his delight is in the law of the LORD; and in his law doth he meditate day and night.

Hail Mary

2   And he shall be like a tree planted by the rivers of water, that bringeth forth his fruit in his season; his leaf also shall not wither; and whatsoever he doeth shall prosper.

Hail Mary

3   The ungodly are not so: but are like the chaff which the wind driveth away. Therefore the ungodly shall not stand in the judgment, nor sinners in the congregation of the righteous.

Hail Mary

4   For the LORD knoweth the way of the righteous: but the way of the ungodly shall perish.

Hail Mary

5   The heavens declare the glory of God; and the firmament showeth his handiwork. Day unto day uttereth speech, and night unto night showeth knowledge.

Hail Mary

6   The law of the LORD is perfect, converting the soul: the testimony of the LORD is sure, making wise the simple.

Hail Mary

7   The statutes of the LORD are right, rejoicing the heart: the commandment of the LORD is pure, enlightening the eyes.

Hail Mary

8   The fear of the LORD is clean, enduring for ever: the judgments of the LORD are true and righteous altogether.

Hail Mary

9   Moreover by them is thy servant warned: and in keeping of them there is great reward. Keep back thy servant also from presumptuous sins; let them not have dominion over me: then shall I be upright, and I shall be innocent from the great transgression.

Hail Mary

10   Let the words of my mouth, and the meditation of my heart, be acceptable in thy sight, O LORD, my strength, and my redeemer.

Hail Mary

Glory Be to the Father

Second Inspiration Mystery
The Excellence of Thy Name

Jesus' I AM Lord's Prayer

1   O LORD our Lord, how excellent is thy name in all the earth! who hast set thy glory above the heavens.

Hail Mary

2   Out of the mouth of babes and sucklings hast thou ordained strength because of thine enemies, that thou mightest still the enemy and the avenger.

Hail Mary

3   When I consider thy heavens, the work of thy fingers, the moon and the stars, which thou hast ordained; what is man, that thou art mindful of him? and the son of man, that thou visitest him?

Hail Mary

4   For thou hast made him a little lower than the angels, and hast crowned him with glory and honour.

Hail Mary

5   Thou madest him to have dominion over the works of thy hands; thou hast put all things under his feet:

Hail Mary

6   All sheep and oxen, yea, and the beasts of the field;

Hail Mary

7   The fowl of the air, and the fish of the sea, and whatsoever passeth through the paths of the seas.

Hail Mary

8   O LORD our Lord, how excellent is thy name in all the earth!

Hail Mary

9   I will praise thee, O Lᴏʀᴅ, with my whole heart; I will show forth all thy marvellous works.

Hail Mary

10   I will be glad and rejoice in thee: I will sing praise to thy name, O thou Most High.

Hail Mary

Glory Be to the Father

Third Inspiration Mystery
The Lord Is My Shepherd

Jesus' I AM Lord's Prayer

1   The Lᴏʀᴅ is my shepherd; I shall not want.

Hail Mary

2   He maketh me to lie down in green pastures: he leadeth me beside the still waters.

Hail Mary

3   He restoreth my soul.

Hail Mary

4   He leadeth me in the paths of righteousness for his name's sake.

Hail Mary

5   Yea, though I walk through the valley of the shadow of death, I will fear no evil.

Hail Mary

6   For thou art with me; thy rod and thy staff they comfort me.

Hail Mary

7   Thou preparest a table before me in the presence of mine enemies.

Hail Mary

8   Thou anointest my head with oil; my cup runneth over.

Hail Mary

9   Surely goodness and mercy shall follow me all the days of my life.

Hail Mary

10   And I will dwell in the house of the Lord forever.

Hail Mary

Glory Be to the Father

Fourth Inspiration Mystery
The Secret Place of the Most High

Jesus' I AM Lord's Prayer

1   He that dwelleth in the secret place of the Most High shall abide under the shadow of the Almighty.

Hail Mary

2   I will say of the Lord, He is my refuge and my fortress: my God; in him will I trust.

Hail Mary

3   Surely he shall deliver thee from the snare of the fowler, and from the noisome pestilence. He shall cover thee with his feathers, and under his wings shalt thou trust: his truth shall be thy shield and buckler.

Hail Mary

4   Thou shalt not be afraid for the terror by night; nor for the

arrow that flieth by day; nor for the pestilence that walketh in darkness; nor for the destruction that wasteth at noonday.

Hail Mary

5   A thousand shall fall at thy side, and ten thousand at thy right hand; but it shall not come nigh thee. Only with thine eyes shalt thou behold and see the reward of the wicked.

Hail Mary

6   Because thou hast made the LORD, which is my refuge, even the Most High, thy habitation, there shall no evil befall thee, neither shall any plague come nigh thy dwelling.

Hail Mary

7   For he shall give his angels charge over thee, to keep thee in all thy ways. They shall bear thee up in their hands, lest thou dash thy foot against a stone.

Hail Mary

8   Thou shalt tread upon the lion and adder: the young lion and the dragon shalt thou trample under feet.

Hail Mary

9   Because he hath set his love upon me, therefore will I deliver him: I will set him on high, because he hath known my name.

Hail Mary

10   He shall call upon me, and I will answer him: I will be with him in trouble; I will deliver him, and honour him. With long life will I satisfy him, and show him my salvation.

Hail Mary

Glory Be to the Father

Fifth Inspiration Mystery
Trust in the Lord

Jesus' I AM Lord's Prayer

1   Trust in the LORD with all thine heart; and lean not unto thine own understanding. In all thy ways acknowledge him, and he shall direct thy paths.

Hail Mary

2   Fret not thyself because of evildoers, neither be thou envious against the workers of iniquity. For they shall soon be cut down like the grass, and wither as the green herb.

Hail Mary

3   Trust in the LORD, and do good; so shalt thou dwell in the land, and verily thou shalt be fed.

Hail Mary

4   Delight thyself also in the LORD; and he shall give thee the desires of thine heart. Commit thy way unto the LORD; trust also in him; and he shall bring it to pass.

Hail Mary

5   And he shall bring forth thy righteousness as the light, and thy judgment as the noonday.

Hail Mary

6   Make a joyful noise unto the LORD, all ye lands.

Hail Mary

7   Serve the LORD with gladness: come before his presence with singing.

Hail Mary

8   Know ye that the LORD he is God: it is he that hath made us, and not we ourselves; we are his people, and the sheep of his pasture.

Hail Mary

9   Enter into his gates with thanksgiving, and into his courts with praise: be thankful unto him, and bless his name.

Hail Mary

10   For the L<small>ORD</small> is good; his mercy is everlasting; and his truth endureth to all generations.

Hail Mary

Glory Be to the Father

Sixth Inspiration Mystery
The Lord Is My Keeper

Jesus' I AM Lord's Prayer

1   I will lift up mine eyes unto the hills, from whence cometh my help.

Hail Mary

2   My help cometh from the L<small>ORD</small>, which made heaven and earth.

Hail Mary

3   He will not suffer thy foot to be moved.

Hail Mary

4   He that keepeth thee will not slumber.

Hail Mary

5   Behold, he that keepeth Israel shall neither slumber nor sleep.

Hail Mary

6   The L<small>ORD</small> is thy keeper: the L<small>ORD</small> is thy shade upon thy right hand.

Hail Mary

7   The sun shall not smite thee by day, nor the moon by night.

Hail Mary

8   The LORD shall preserve thee from all evil.

Hail Mary

9   He shall preserve thy soul.

Hail Mary

10   The LORD shall preserve thy going out and thy coming in from this time forth, and even for evermore.

Hail Mary

Glory Be to the Father

The Covenant of the Magi

II

Sign of the Cross

The Action Mysteries
Tuesday Evening - The Second Secret Ray

Adoration to God
Jesus' I AM Lord's Prayer
Three Hail Marys
Love Me
Introit to the Holy Christ Self

First Action Mystery
The Word of the LORD unto Elijah

Jesus' I AM Lord's Prayer

1   And Elijah the Tishbite, who was of the inhabitants of Gilead, said unto Ahab, As the LORD God of Israel liveth, before whom I stand, there shall not be dew nor rain these years, but according to my word.

Hail Mary

2   And the word of the LORD came unto him, saying, Get thee hence, and turn thee eastward, and hide thyself by the brook Cherith, that is before Jordan. And it shall be, that thou shalt drink of the brook; and I have commanded the ravens to feed thee there.

Hail Mary

3   So he went and did according unto the word of the LORD: for he went and dwelt by the brook Cherith, that is before Jordan. And the ravens brought him bread and flesh in the morning, and bread and flesh in the evening; and he drank of the brook.

Hail Mary

4   And it came to pass after a while, that the brook dried up, because there had been no rain in the land.

Hail Mary

5   And the word of the LORD came unto him, saying, Arise, get thee to Zarephath, which belongeth to Zidon, and dwell there: behold, I have commanded a widow woman there to sustain thee.

Hail Mary

6   So he arose and went to Zarephath. And when he came to the gate of the city, behold, the widow woman was there gathering of sticks: and he called to her, and said, Fetch me, I pray thee, a little water in a vessel, that I may drink.

Hail Mary

7   And as she was going to fetch it, he called to her, and said, Bring me, I pray thee, a morsel of bread in thine hand.

Hail Mary

8   And she said, As the LORD thy God liveth, I have not a cake, but an handful of meal in a barrel, and a little oil in a cruse: and, behold, I am gathering two sticks, that I may go in and dress it for me and my son, that we may eat it, and die.

Hail Mary

9   And Elijah said unto her, Fear not; go and do as thou hast said: but make me thereof a little cake first, and bring it unto me, and after make for thee and for thy son.

Hail Mary

10   For thus saith the LORD God of Israel, The barrel of meal shall not waste, neither shall the cruse of oil fail, until the day that the LORD sendeth rain upon the earth.

Hail Mary

Glory Be to the Father

Second Action Mystery
Elijah Raises the Widow's Son

Jesus' I AM Lord's Prayer

1   And she went and did according to the saying of Elijah: and she, and he, and her house, did eat many days.

Hail Mary

2   And the barrel of meal wasted not, neither did the cruse of oil fail, according to the word of the LORD, which he spake by Elijah.

Hail Mary

3   And it came to pass after these things, that the son of the woman, the mistress of the house, fell sick; and his sickness was so sore, that there was no breath left in him.

Hail Mary

4   And she said unto Elijah, What have I to do with thee, O thou man of God? art thou come unto me to call my sin to remembrance, and to slay my son?

Hail Mary

5   And he said unto her, Give me thy son. And he took him out of her bosom, and carried him up into a loft, where he abode, and laid him upon his own bed.

Hail Mary

6   And he cried unto the LORD, and said, O LORD my God, hast thou also brought evil upon the widow with whom I sojourn, by slaying her son?

Hail Mary

7   And he stretched himself upon the child three times, and cried unto the LORD, and said, O LORD my God, I pray thee, let this child's soul come into him again.

Hail Mary

8   And the LORD heard the voice of Elijah; and the soul of the child came into him again, and he revived.

Hail Mary

9   And Elijah took the child, and brought him down out of the chamber into the house, and delivered him unto his mother: and Elijah said, See, thy son liveth.

Hail Mary

10   And the woman said to Elijah, Now by this I know that thou art a man of God, and that the word of the LORD in thy mouth is truth.

Hail Mary

Glory Be to the Father

Third Action Mystery
Elijah and the Prophets of Baal

Jesus' I AM Lord's Prayer

1   And Elijah came unto all the people, and said, How long halt ye between two opinions? if the LORD be God, follow him: but if Baal, then follow him. And the people answered him not a word.

Hail Mary

2   Then said Elijah unto the people, I, even I only, remain a prophet of the LORD; but Baal's prophets are four hundred and fifty men.

Hail Mary

3   Let them therefore give us two bullocks; and let them choose one bullock for themselves, and cut it in pieces, and lay it on

wood, and put no fire under: and I will dress the other bullock, and lay it on wood, and put no fire under.

Hail Mary

4   And call ye on the name of your gods, and I will call on the name of the Lord: and the God that answereth by fire, let him be God. And all the people answered and said, It is well spoken.

Hail Mary

5   And they took the bullock which was given them, and they dressed it, and called on the name of Baal from morning even until noon, saying, O Baal, hear us. But there was no voice, nor any that answered.

Hail Mary

6   And it came to pass, when midday was past, and they prophesied until the time of the offering of the evening sacrifice, that there was neither voice, nor any to answer, nor any that regarded.

Hail Mary

7   And Elijah took twelve stones, And with the stones he built an altar in the name of the Lord.

Hail Mary

8   And it came to pass at the time of the offering of the evening sacrifice, that Elijah the prophet came near, and said, Lord God of Abraham, Isaac, and of Israel, let it be known this day that thou art God in Israel, and that I am thy servant, and that I have done all these things at thy word.

Hail Mary

9   Hear me, O Lord, hear me, that this people may know that thou art the Lord God, and that thou hast turned their heart back again.

Hail Mary

10   Then the fire of the Lord fell, and consumed the burnt

sacrifice, and the wood, and the stones, and the dust, and licked up the water that was in the trench. And when all the people saw it, they fell on their faces: and they said, The LORD, he is the God; the LORD, he is the God.

Hail Mary

Glory Be to the Father

Fourth Action Mystery
The Ascension of Elijah and the
Anointing of Elisha

Jesus' I AM Lord's Prayer

1   And it came to pass, when the LORD would take up Elijah into heaven by a whirlwind, that Elijah went with Elisha from Gilgal.

Hail Mary

2   And Elijah said unto Elisha, Tarry here, I pray thee; for the LORD hath sent me to Bethel. And Elisha said unto him, As the LORD liveth, and as thy soul liveth, I will not leave thee. So they went down to Bethel.

Hail Mary

3   And Elijah took his mantle, and wrapped it together, and smote the waters, and they were divided hither and thither, so that they two went over on dry ground.

Hail Mary

4   And it came to pass, when they were gone over, that Elijah said unto Elisha, Ask what I shall do for thee, before I be taken away from thee.

Hail Mary

5   And Elisha said, I pray thee, let a double portion of thy spirit be upon me. And he said, Thou hast asked a hard thing: nevertheless, if thou see me when I am taken from thee, it shall be so unto thee; but if not, it shall not be so.

Hail Mary

6   And it came to pass, as they still went on, and talked, that, behold, there appeared a chariot of fire, and horses of fire, and parted them both asunder; and Elijah went up by a whirlwind into heaven.

Hail Mary

7   And Elisha saw it, and he cried, My father, my father, the chariot of Israel, and the horsemen thereof. And he saw him no more: and he took hold of his own clothes, and rent them in two pieces.

Hail Mary

8   He took up also the mantle of Elijah that fell from him, and went back, and stood by the bank of Jordan.

Hail Mary

9   And he took the mantle of Elijah that fell from him, and smote the waters, and said, Where is the LORD God of Elijah?

Hail Mary

10   And when he also had smitten the waters, they parted hither and thither: and Elisha went over.

Hail Mary

Glory Be to the Father

Fifth Action Mystery
Elisha's Promise to the Shunamite

Jesus' I AM Lord's Prayer

1   And it fell on a day, that Elisha passed to Shunem, where was a great woman; and she constrained him to eat bread. And so it was, that as oft as he passed by, he turned in thither to eat bread.

Hail Mary

2   And it fell on a day, that he came thither, and he turned into the chamber, and lay there. And he said, What then is to be done for her?

Hail Mary

3   And Gehazi answered, Verily she hath no child, and her husband is old. And he said, Call her. And when he had called her, she stood in the door.

Hail Mary

4   And he said, About this season, according to the time of life, thou shalt embrace a son. And she said, Nay, my lord, thou man of God, do not lie unto thine handmaid.

Hail Mary

5   And the woman conceived, and bare a son at that season that Elisha had said unto her, according to the time of life.

Hail Mary

6   And when the child was grown, it fell on a day, that he went out to his father to the reapers. And he said unto his father, My head, my head. And he said to a lad, Carry him to his mother.

Hail Mary

7   And when he had taken him, and brought him to his mother, he sat on her knees till noon, and then died. And she went up, and laid him on the bed of the man of God, and shut the door upon him, and went out.

Hail Mary

8   And she called unto her husband, and said, Send me, I pray thee, one of the young men, and one of the asses, that I may run to the man of God, and come again. And when Elisha was come into the house, behold, the child was dead, and laid upon his bed.

Hail Mary

9   He went in therefore, and shut the door upon them twain, and prayed unto the LORD. And he went up, and lay upon the child, and put his mouth upon his mouth, and his eyes upon his eyes, and his hands upon his hands: and he stretched himself upon the child; and the flesh of the child waxed warm.

Hail Mary

10   Then he returned, and walked in the house to and fro; and went up, and stretched himself upon him: and the child sneezed seven times, and the child opened his eyes.

Hail Mary

Glory Be to the Father

Sixth Action Mystery
The Healing of Naaman the Leper

Jesus' I AM Lord's Prayer

1   Now Naaman, captain of the host of the king of Syria, was a great man with his master, and honourable, because by him the LORD had given deliverance unto Syria: he was also a mighty man in valour, but he was a leper.

Hail Mary

2   And the Syrians had gone out by companies, and had brought away captive out of the land of Israel a little maid; and

she waited on Naaman's wife. And she said unto her mistress, Would God my lord were with the prophet that is in Samaria! for he would recover him of his leprosy.

Hail Mary

3   So Naaman came with his horses and with his chariot, and stood at the door of the house of Elisha.

Hail Mary

4   And Elisha sent a messenger unto him, saying, Go and wash in Jordan seven times, and thy flesh shall come again to thee, and thou shalt be clean.

Hail Mary

5   But Naaman was wroth, and went away, and said, Behold, I thought, He will surely come out to me, and stand, and call on the name of the LORD his God, and strike his hand over the place, and recover the leper.

Hail Mary

6   Are not Abana and Pharpar, rivers of Damascus, better than all the waters of Israel? may I not wash in them, and be clean? So he turned and went away in a rage.

Hail Mary

7   And his servants came near, and spake unto him, and said, My father, if the prophet had bid thee do some great thing, wouldest thou not have done it? how much rather then, when he saith to thee, Wash, and be clean?

Hail Mary

8   Then went he down, and dipped himself seven times in Jordan, according to the saying of the man of God.

Hail Mary

9   And his flesh came again like unto the flesh of a little child, and he was clean.

Hail Mary

10   And he returned to the man of God, he and all his company, and came, and stood before him: and he said, Behold, now I know that there is no God in all the earth, but in Israel.

Hail Mary

Glory Be to the Father

The Covenant of the Magi

III

Sign of the Cross

The Revelation Mysteries
Wednesday Evening – The Third Secret Ray

Adoration to God
Jesus' I AM Lord's Prayer
Three Hail Marys
Love Me
Introit to the Holy Christ Self

First Revelation Mystery
The Lamb on Mount Sion

Jesus' I AM Lord's Prayer

1   And I looked, and, lo, a Lamb stood on the mount Sion, and with him an hundred forty and four thousand, having his Father's name written in their foreheads.

Hail Mary

2   And I heard a voice from heaven, as the voice of many waters, and as the voice of a great thunder: and I heard the voice of harpers harping with their harps.

Hail Mary

3   And they sung as it were a new song before the throne, and before the four beasts, and the elders: and no man could learn that song but the hundred and forty and four thousand, which were redeemed from the earth.

Hail Mary

4   These are they which follow the Lamb whithersoever he goeth. These were redeemed from among men, being the first-fruits unto God and to the Lamb. And in their mouth was found no guile: for they are without fault before the throne of God.

Hail Mary

5   And I saw another angel fly in the midst of heaven, having the everlasting gospel to preach unto them that dwell on the earth, and to every nation, and kindred, and tongue, and people,

Hail Mary

6   Saying with a loud voice, Fear God, and give glory to him; for the hour of his judgment is come: and worship him that made heaven, and earth, and the sea, and the fountains of waters.

Hail Mary

7   And there followed another angel, saying, Babylon is fallen, is fallen, that great city, because she made all nations drink of the wine of the wrath of her fornication.

Hail Mary

8   And the third angel followed them, saying with a loud voice, If any man worship the beast and his image, and receive his mark in his forehead, or in his hand, the same shall drink of the wine of the wrath of God, which is poured out without mixture into the cup of his indignation; and he shall be tormented with fire and brimstone in the presence of the holy angels, and in the presence of the Lamb.

Hail Mary

9   Here is the patience of the saints: here are they that keep the commandments of God, and the faith of Jesus.

Hail Mary

10   And I heard a voice from heaven saying unto me, Write, Blessed are the dead which die in the Lord from henceforth: Yea, saith the Spirit, that they may rest from their labours; and their works do follow them.

Hail Mary

Glory Be to the Father

Second Revelation Mystery
The Marriage of the Lamb

Jesus' I AM Lord's Prayer

1   And after these things I heard a great voice of much people in heaven, saying, Alleluia; salvation, and glory, and honour, and power, unto the Lord our God:

Hail Mary

2   For true and righteous are his judgments: for he hath judged the great whore, which did corrupt the earth with her fornication, and hath avenged the blood of his servants at her hand.

Hail Mary

3   And again they said, Alleluia. And her smoke rose up for ever and ever.

Hail Mary

4   And the four and twenty elders and the four beasts fell down and worshipped God that sat on the throne, saying, Amen; Alleluia.

Hail Mary

5   And a voice came out of the throne, saying, Praise our God, all ye his servants, and ye that fear him, both small and great.

Hail Mary

6   And I heard as it were the voice of a great multitude, and as the voice of many waters, and as the voice of mighty thunderings, saying, Alleluia: for the Lord God omnipotent reigneth.

Hail Mary

7   Let us be glad and rejoice, and give honour to him: for the marriage of the Lamb is come, and his wife hath made herself ready.

Hail Mary

8   And to her was granted that she should be arrayed in fine linen, clean and white: for the fine linen is the righteousness of saints.

Hail Mary

9   And he saith unto me, Write, Blessed are they which are called unto the marriage supper of the Lamb. And he saith unto me, These are the true sayings of God.

Hail Mary

10   And I fell at his feet to worship him. And he said unto me, See thou do it not: I am thy fellowservant, and of thy brethren that have the testimony of Jesus: worship God: for the testimony of Jesus is the spirit of prophecy.

Hail Mary

Glory Be to the Father

Third Revelation Mystery
King of Kings and Lord of Lords

Jesus' I AM Lord's Prayer

1   And I saw heaven opened, and behold a white horse; and he that sat upon him was called Faithful and True, and in righteousness he doth judge and make war. His eyes were as a flame of fire, and on his head were many crowns; and he had a name written, that no man knew, but he himself.

Hail Mary

2   And he was clothed with a vesture dipped in blood: and his name is called The Word of God.

Hail Mary

3   And the armies which were in heaven followed him upon white horses, clothed in fine linen, white and clean.

Hail Mary

4   And out of his mouth goeth a sharp sword, that with it he should smite the nations: and he shall rule them with a rod of iron: and he treadeth the winepress of the fierceness and wrath of Almighty God.

Hail Mary

5   And he hath on his vesture and on his thigh a name written, KING OF KINGS, AND LORD OF LORDS.

Hail Mary

6   And I saw an angel standing in the sun; and he cried with a loud voice, saying to all the fowls that fly in the midst of heaven, Come and gather yourselves together unto the supper of the great God;

Hail Mary

7   That ye may eat the flesh of kings, and the flesh of captains, and the flesh of mighty men, and the flesh of horses, and of them that sit on them, and the flesh of all men, both free and bond, both small and great.

Hail Mary

8   And I saw the beast, and the kings of the earth, and their armies, gathered together to make war against him that sat on the horse, and against his army.

Hail Mary

9   And the beast was taken, and with him the false prophet that wrought miracles before him, with which he deceived them that had received the mark of the beast, and them that worshipped his image. These both were cast alive into a lake of fire burning with brimstone.

Hail Mary

10   And the remnant were slain with the sword of him that sat upon the horse, which sword proceeded out of his mouth: and all the fowls were filled with their flesh.

Hail Mary

Glory Be to the Father

Fourth Revelation Mystery
The Key of the Bottomless Pit

Jesus' I AM Lord's Prayer

1   And I saw an angel come down from heaven, having the key of the bottomless pit and a great chain in his hand.

Hail Mary

2   And he laid hold on the dragon, that old serpent, which is the Devil, and Satan, and bound him a thousand years, and cast him into the bottomless pit, and shut him up, and set a seal upon him, that he should deceive the nations no more, till the thousand years should be fulfilled: and after that he must be loosed a little season.

Hail Mary

3   And I saw thrones, and they sat upon them, and judgment was given unto them: and I saw the souls of them that were beheaded for the witness of Jesus, and for the word of God, and which had not worshipped the beast, neither his image, neither had received his mark upon their foreheads, or in their hands; and they lived and reigned with Christ a thousand years.

Hail Mary

4   But the rest of the dead lived not again until the thousand years were finished. This is the first resurrection. Blessed and holy is he that hath part in the first resurrection: on such the second death hath no power, but they shall be priests of God and of Christ, and shall reign with him a thousand years.

Hail Mary

5   And when the thousand years are expired, Satan shall be loosed out of his prison, and shall go out to deceive the nations which are in the four quarters of the earth, Gog and Magog, to gather them together to battle: the number of whom is as the sand of the sea.

Hail Mary

6   And they went up on the breadth of the earth, and compassed the camp of the saints about, and the beloved city: and fire came down from God out of heaven, and devoured them. And the devil that deceived them was cast into the lake of fire and brimstone, where the beast and the false prophet are, and shall be tormented day and night for ever and ever.

Hail Mary

7   And I saw a great white throne, and him that sat on it, from whose face the earth and the heaven fled away; and there was found no place for them.

Hail Mary

8   And I saw the dead, small and great, stand before God; and the books were opened: and another book was opened, which is the book of life: and the dead were judged out of those things which were written in the books, according to their works.

Hail Mary

9   And the sea gave up the dead which were in it; and death and hell delivered up the dead which were in them: and they were judged every man according to their works.

Hail Mary

10   And death and hell were cast into the lake of fire. This is the second death. And whosoever was not found written in the book of life was cast into the lake of fire.

Hail Mary

Glory Be to the Father

Fifth Revelation Mystery
The Holy Jerusalem

Jesus' I AM Lord's Prayer

1   And there came unto me one of the seven angels which had the seven vials full of the seven last plagues, and talked with me, saying, Come hither, I will show thee the bride, the Lamb's wife.

Hail Mary

2   And he carried me away in the spirit to a great and high mountain, and showed me that great city, the holy Jerusalem, descending out of heaven from God, having the glory of God: and her light was like unto a stone most precious, even like a jasper stone, clear as crystal;

Hail Mary

3   And had a wall great and high, and had twelve gates, and at the gates twelve angels, and names written thereon, which are the names of the twelve tribes of the children of Israel: on the east three gates; on the north three gates; on the south three gates; and on the west three gates.

Hail Mary

4   And the wall of the city had twelve foundations, and in them the names of the twelve apostles of the Lamb. And he that talked with me had a golden reed to measure the city, and the gates thereof, and the wall thereof.

Hail Mary

5   And the city lieth foursquare, and the length is as large as the breadth: and he measured the city with the reed, twelve thousand furlongs. The length and the breadth and the height of it are equal. And he measured the wall thereof, an hundred and forty and four cubits, according to the measure of a man, that is, of the angel.

Hail Mary

6   And the building of the wall of it was of jasper: and the city

was pure gold, like unto clear glass. And the foundations of the wall of the city were garnished with all manner of precious stones. And the twelve gates were twelve pearls: every several gate was of one pearl: and the street of the city was pure gold, as it were transparent glass.

Hail Mary

7   And I saw no temple therein: for the Lord God Almighty and the Lamb are the temple of it. And the city had no need of the sun, neither of the moon, to shine in it: for the glory of God did lighten it, and the Lamb is the light thereof.

Hail Mary

8   And the nations of them which are saved shall walk in the light of it: and the kings of the earth do bring their glory and honour into it.

Hail Mary

9   And the gates of it shall not be shut at all by day: for there shall be no night there. And they shall bring the glory and honour of the nations into it.

Hail Mary

10   And there shall in no wise enter into it any thing that defileth, neither whatsoever worketh abomination, or maketh a lie: but they which are written in the Lamb's book of life.

Hail Mary

Glory Be to the Father

Sixth Revelation Mystery
The Throne of God and of the Lamb

Jesus' I AM Lord's Prayer

1   And he showed me a pure river of water of life, clear as

crystal, proceeding out of the throne of God and of the Lamb.

Hail Mary

2   In the midst of the street of it, and on either side of the river, was there the tree of life, which bare twelve manner of fruits, and yielded her fruit every month: and the leaves of the tree were for the healing of the nations.

Hail Mary

3   And there shall be no more curse: but the throne of God and of the Lamb shall be in it; and his servants shall serve him: and they shall see his face; and his name shall be in their fore-heads.

Hail Mary

4   And there shall be no night there; and they need no candle, neither light of the sun; for the Lord God giveth them light: and they shall reign for ever and ever.

Hail Mary

5   And he said unto me, These sayings are faithful and true: and the Lord God of the holy prophets sent his angel to show unto his servants the things which must shortly be done. Behold, I come quickly: blessed is he that keepeth the sayings of the prophecy of this book.

Hail Mary

6   And I John saw these things, and heard them. And when I had heard and seen, I fell down to worship before the feet of the angel which showed me these things.

Hail Mary

7   Then saith he unto me, See thou do it not: for I am thy fel-lowservant, and of thy brethren the prophets, and of them which keep the sayings of this book: worship God.

Hail Mary

8   And he saith unto me, Seal not the sayings of the prophecy

of this book: for the time is at hand.

Hail Mary

9   He that is unjust, let him be unjust still: and he which is filthy, let him be filthy still: and he that is righteous, let him be righteous still: and he that is holy, let him be holy still.

Hail Mary

10   And, behold, I come quickly; and my reward is with me, to give every man according as his work shall be.

Hail Mary

Glory Be to the Father

The Covenant of the Magi

The Declaration Mysteries
Thursday Evening - The Fourth Secret Ray

Adoration to God
Jesus' I AM Lord's Prayer
Three Hail Marys
Love Me
Introit to the Holy Christ Self

First Declaration Mystery
Signs of the Second Coming

Jesus' I AM Lord's Prayer

1   And Jesus went out, and departed from the temple: and his disciples came to him for to show him the buildings of the temple.

Hail Mary

2   And Jesus said unto them, See ye not all these things? verily I say unto you, There shall not be left here one stone upon another, that shall not be thrown down.

Hail Mary

3   And as he sat upon the mount of Olives, the disciples came unto him privately, saying, Tell us, when shall these things be? and what shall be the sign of thy coming, and of the end of the world?

Hail Mary

4   And Jesus answered and said unto them, Take heed that no man deceive you. For many shall come in my name, saying, I am Christ; and shall deceive many.

Hail Mary

5   And ye shall hear of wars and rumours of wars: see that ye be not troubled: for all these things must come to pass, but the end is not yet.

Hail Mary

6   For nation shall rise against nation, and kingdom against kingdom: and there shall be famines, and pestilences, and earthquakes, in divers places. All these are the beginning of sorrows.

Hail Mary

7   Then shall they deliver you up to be afflicted, and shall kill you: and ye shall be hated of all nations for my name's sake.

Hail Mary

8   And then shall many be offended, and shall betray one another, and shall hate one another.

Hail Mary

9   And many false prophets shall rise, and shall deceive many. And because iniquity shall abound, the love of many shall wax cold.

Hail Mary

10   But he that shall endure unto the end, the same shall be saved.

Hail Mary

Glory Be to the Father

Second Declaration Mystery
Signs of the End of the Age

Jesus' I AM Lord's Prayer

1   And this gospel of the kingdom shall be preached in all the

world for a witness unto all nations; and then shall the end come.

Hail Mary

2   When ye therefore shall see the abomination of desolation, spoken of by Daniel the prophet, stand in the holy place (whoso readeth, let him understand), then let them which be in Judaea flee into the mountains:

Hail Mary

3   Let him which is on the housetop not come down to take any thing out of his house: neither let him which is in the field return back to take his clothes.

Hail Mary

4   And woe unto them that are with child, and to them that give suck in those days!

Hail Mary

5   But pray ye that your flight be not in the winter, neither on the sabbath day: for then shall be great tribulation, such as was not since the beginning of the world to this time, no, nor ever shall be.

Hail Mary

6   And except those days should be shortened, there should no flesh be saved: but for the elect's sake those days shall be shortened.

Hail Mary

7   Then if any man shall say unto you, Lo, here is Christ, or there; believe it not. For there shall arise false Christs, and false prophets, and shall show great signs and wonders; insomuch that, if it were possible, they shall deceive the very elect.

Hail Mary

8   Behold, I have told you before. Wherefore if they shall say unto you, Behold, he is in the desert; go not forth: behold, he is in the secret chambers; believe it not.

Hail Mary

9   For as the lightning cometh out of the east, and shineth even
unto the west; so shall also the coming of the Son of man be.

Hail Mary

10   For wheresoever the carcass is, there will the eagles be gathered together.

Hail Mary

Glory Be to the Father

Third Declaration Mystery
Sign of the Son of Man in Heaven

Jesus' I AM Lord's Prayer

1   Immediately after the tribulation of those days shall the sun
be darkened, and the moon shall not give her light, and the stars
shall fall from heaven, and the powers of the heavens shall be
shaken.

Hail Mary

2   And then shall appear the sign of the Son of man in heaven:
and then shall all the tribes of the earth mourn, and they shall see
the Son of man coming in the clouds of heaven with power and
great glory.

Hail Mary

3   And he shall send his angels with a great sound of a trum-
pet, and they shall gather together his elect from the four winds,
from one end of heaven to the other.

Hail Mary

4   Now learn a parable of the fig tree: When his branch is yet
tender, and putteth forth leaves, ye know that summer is nigh; so
likewise ye, when ye shall see all these things, know that it is

near, even at the doors.

Hail Mary

5   Verily I say unto you, This generation shall not pass, till all these things be fulfilled.

Hail Mary

6   Heaven and earth shall pass away, but my words shall not pass away.

Hail Mary

7   But of that day and hour knoweth no man, no, not the angels of heaven, but my Father only. But as the days of Noe were, so shall also the coming of the Son of man be.

Hail Mary

8   For as in the days that were before the flood they were eating and drinking, marrying and giving in marriage, until the day that Noe entered into the ark, and knew not until the flood came, and took them all away; so shall also the coming of the Son of man be.

Hail Mary

9   Then shall two be in the field; the one shall be taken, and the other left. Two women shall be grinding at the mill; the one shall be taken, and the other left.

Hail Mary

10   Watch therefore: for ye know not what hour your Lord doth come.

Hail Mary

Glory Be to the Father

Fourth Declaration Mystery
The Opening of the Seals

1   And I saw when the Lamb opened one of the seals, and I heard, as it were the noise of thunder, one of the four beasts saying, Come and see.

Hail Mary

2   And I saw, and behold a white horse: and he that sat on him had a bow; and a crown was given unto him: and he went forth conquering, and to conquer.

Hail Mary

3   And when he had opened the second seal, I heard the second beast say, Come and see.

Hail Mary

4   And there went out another horse that was red: and power was given to him that sat thereon to take peace from the earth, and that they should kill one another: and there was given unto him a great sword.

Hail Mary

5   And when he had opened the third seal, I heard the third beast say, Come and see. And I beheld, and lo a black horse; and he that sat on him had a pair of balances in his hand.

Hail Mary

6   And I heard a voice in the midst of the four beasts say, A measure of wheat for a penny, and three measures of barley for a penny; and see thou hurt not the oil and the wine.

Hail Mary

7   And when he had opened the fourth seal, I heard the voice of the fourth beast say, Come and see.

Hail Mary

8   And I looked, and behold a pale horse: and his name that sat on him was Death, and Hell followed with him. And power was given unto them over the fourth part of the earth, to kill with sword, and with hunger, and with death, and with the beasts of the earth.

Hail Mary

9   And when he had opened the fifth seal, I saw under the altar the souls of them that were slain for the word of God, and for the testimony which they held.

Hail Mary

10   And they cried with a loud voice, saying, How long, O Lord, holy and true, dost thou not judge and avenge our blood on them that dwell on the earth?

Hail Mary

Glory Be to the Father

Fifth Declaration Mystery
The Hundred and Forty and Four Thousand

Jesus' I AM Lord's Prayer

1   And white robes were given unto every one of them; and it was said unto them, that they should rest yet for a little season, until their fellowservants also and their brethren, that should be killed as they were, should be fulfilled.

Hail Mary

2   And I beheld when he had opened the sixth seal, and, lo, there was a great earthquake; and the sun became black as sack-cloth of hair, and the moon became as blood.

Hail Mary

3   And the stars of heaven fell unto the earth, even as a fig tree

casteth her untimely figs, when she is shaken of a mighty wind.

Hail Mary

4   And the heaven departed as a scroll when it is rolled together; and every mountain and island were moved out of their places.

Hail Mary

5   And the kings of the earth, and the great men, and the rich men, and the chief captains, and the mighty men, and every bondman, and every free man, hid themselves in the dens and in the rocks of the mountains;

Hail Mary

6   And said to the mountains and rocks, Fall on us, and hide us from the face of him that sitteth on the throne, and from the wrath of the Lamb: for the great day of his wrath is come; and who shall be able to stand?

Hail Mary

7   And after these things I saw four angels standing on the four corners of the earth, holding the four winds of the earth, that the wind should not blow on the earth, nor on the sea, nor on any tree.

Hail Mary

8   And I saw another angel ascending from the east, having the seal of the living God: and he cried with a loud voice to the four angels, to whom it was given to hurt the earth and the sea,

Hail Mary

9   Saying, Hurt not the earth, neither the sea, nor the trees, till we have sealed the servants of our God in their foreheads.

Hail Mary

10   And I heard the number of them which were sealed: and there were sealed an hundred and forty and four thousand of all the tribes of the children of Israel.

Hail Mary

Glory Be to the Father

Sixth Declaration Mystery
Washed in the Blood of the Lamb

Jesus' I AM Lord's Prayer

1   After this I beheld, and, lo, a great multitude, which no man could number, of all nations, and kindreds, and people, and tongues, stood before the throne, and before the Lamb, clothed with white robes, and palms in their hands;

Hail Mary

2   And cried with a loud voice, saying, Salvation to our God which sitteth upon the throne, and unto the Lamb.

Hail Mary

3   And all the angels stood round about the throne, and about the elders and the four beasts, and fell before the throne on their faces, and worshipped God,

Hail Mary

4   Saying, Amen: Blessing, and glory, and wisdom, and thanksgiving, and honour, and power, and might, be unto our God for ever and ever. Amen.

Hail Mary

5   And one of the elders answered, saying unto me, What are these which are arrayed in white robes? and whence came they?

Hail Mary

6   And I said unto him, Sir, thou knowest. And he said to me, These are they which came out of great tribulation, and have washed their robes, and made them white in the blood of the Lamb.

Hail Mary

7   Therefore are they before the throne of God, and serve him day and night in his temple: and he that sitteth on the throne shall dwell among them.

Hail Mary

8   They shall hunger no more, neither thirst any more; neither shall the sun light on them, nor any heat.

Hail Mary

9   For the Lamb which is in the midst of the throne shall feed them, and shall lead them unto living fountains of waters.

Hail Mary

10   And God shall wipe away all tears from their eyes.

Hail Mary

Glory Be to the Father

The Covenant of the Magi

V

Sign of the Cross

The Exhortation Mysteries
Friday Evening – The Fifth Secret Ray

Adoration to God
Jesus' I AM Lord's Prayer
Three Hail Marys
Love Me
Introit to the Holy Christ Self

First Exhortation Mystery
The Twelve Empowered and Sent Forth

Jesus' I AM Lord's Prayer

1   And when he had called unto him his twelve disciples, he gave them power against unclean spirits, to cast them out, and to heal all manner of sickness and all manner of disease.

Hail Mary

2   These twelve Jesus sent forth, and commanded them, saying, Go not into the way of the Gentiles, and into any city of the Samaritans enter ye not: but go rather to the lost sheep of the house of Israel.

Hail Mary

3   And as ye go, preach, saying, The kingdom of heaven is at hand. Heal the sick, cleanse the lepers, raise the dead, cast out devils: freely ye have received, freely give.

Hail Mary

4   Provide neither gold, nor silver, nor brass in your purses, nor scrip for your journey, neither two coats, neither shoes, nor yet staves: for the workman is worthy of his meat.

Hail Mary

5   And into whatsoever city or town ye shall enter, enquire who in it is worthy; and there abide till ye go thence.

Hail Mary

6   And when ye come into an house, salute it. And if the house be worthy, let your peace come upon it: but if it be not worthy, let your peace return to you.

Hail Mary

7   And whosoever shall not receive you, nor hear your words, when ye depart out of that house or city, shake off the dust of your feet. Verily I say unto you, It shall be more tolerable for the land of Sodom and Gomorrha in the day of judgment, than for that city.

Hail Mary

8   Behold, I send you forth as sheep in the midst of wolves: be ye therefore wise as serpents, and harmless as doves.

Hail Mary

9   But beware of men: for they will deliver you up to the councils, and they will scourge you in their synagogues; and ye shall be brought before governors and kings for my sake, for a testimony against them and the Gentiles.

Hail Mary

10   But when they deliver you up, take no thought how or what ye shall speak: for it shall be given you in that same hour what ye shall speak. For it is not ye that speak, but the Spirit of your Father which speaketh in you.

Hail Mary

Glory Be to the Father

Second Exhortation Mystery
Not Peace, But a Sword

Jesus' I AM Lord's Prayer

1   I am come to send fire on the earth; and what will I, if it be already kindled? But I have a baptism to be baptized with; and how am I straitened till it be accomplished!

Hail Mary

2   Whosoever therefore shall confess me before men, him will I confess also before my Father which is in heaven. But whosoever shall deny me before men, him will I also deny before my Father which is in heaven.

Hail Mary

3   Think not that I am come to send peace on earth: I came not to send peace, but a sword.

Hail Mary

4   For I am come to set a man at variance against his father, and the daughter against her mother, and the daughter in law against her mother in law. And a man's foes shall be they of his own household.

Hail Mary

5   He that loveth father or mother more than me is not worthy of me: and he that loveth son or daughter more than me is not worthy of me.

Hail Mary

6   And he that taketh not his cross, and followeth after me, is not worthy of me.

Hail Mary

7   He that findeth his life shall lose it: and he that loseth his life for my sake shall find it.

Hail Mary

8   He that receiveth you receiveth me, and he that receiveth me receiveth him that sent me.

Hail Mary

9   He that receiveth a prophet in the name of a prophet shall receive a prophet's reward; and he that receiveth a righteous man in the name of a righteous man shall receive a righteous man's reward.

Hail Mary

10   And whosoever shall give to drink unto one of these little ones a cup of cold water only in the name of a disciple, verily I say unto you, he shall in no wise lose his reward.

Hail Mary

Glory Be to the Father

Third Exhortation Mystery
The Sign of the Prophet Jonas

Jesus' I AM Lord's Prayer

1   Either make the tree good, and his fruit good; or else make the tree corrupt, and his fruit corrupt: for the tree is known by his fruit.

Hail Mary

2   O generation of vipers, how can ye, being evil, speak good things? for out of the abundance of the heart the mouth speaketh.

Hail Mary

3   A good man out of the good treasure of the heart bringeth forth good things: and an evil man out of the evil treasure bringeth forth evil things.

Hail Mary

4   But I say unto you, That every idle word that men shall speak, they shall give account thereof in the day of judgment.

Hail Mary

5   For by thy words thou shalt be justified, and by thy words thou shalt be condemned.

Hail Mary

6   Then certain of the scribes and of the Pharisees answered, saying, Master, we would see a sign from thee.

Hail Mary

7   But he answered and said unto them, An evil and adulterous generation seeketh after a sign; and there shall no sign be given to it, but the sign of the prophet Jonas.

Hail Mary

8   For as Jonas was three days and three nights in the whale's belly; so shall the Son of man be three days and three nights in the heart of the earth.

Hail Mary

9   The men of Nineveh shall rise in judgment with this generation, and shall condemn it: because they repented at the preaching of Jonas; and, behold, a greater than Jonas is here.

Hail Mary

10   The queen of the south shall rise up in the judgment with this generation, and shall condemn it: for she came from the uttermost parts of the earth to hear the wisdom of Solomon; and, behold, a greater than Solomon is here.

Hail Mary

Glory Be to the Father

Fourth Exhortation Mystery
The Coming of the Son of Man

Jesus' I AM Lord's Prayer

1   Let your loins be girded about, and your lights burning; and ye yourselves like unto men that wait for their lord, when he will return from the wedding; that when he cometh and knocketh, they may open unto him immediately.

Hail Mary

2   Blessed are those servants, whom the lord when he cometh shall find watching: verily I say unto you, that he shall gird himself, and make them to sit down to meat, and will come forth and serve them.

Hail Mary

3   And if he shall come in the second watch, or come in the third watch, and find them so, blessed are those servants.

Hail Mary

4   And this know, that if the goodman of the house had known what hour the thief would come, he would have watched, and not have suffered his house to be broken through.

Hail Mary

5   Be ye therefore ready also: for the Son of man cometh at an hour when ye think not.

Hail Mary

6   Then Peter said unto him, Lord, speakest thou this parable unto us, or even to all? And the Lord said, Who then is that faithful and wise steward, whom his lord shall make ruler over his household, to give them their portion of meat in due season?

Hail Mary

7   Blessed is that servant, whom his lord when he cometh shall find so doing. Of a truth I say unto you, that he will make him ruler over all that he hath.

Hail Mary

8   But and if that servant say in his heart, My lord delayeth his coming; and shall begin to beat the menservants and maidens, and to eat and drink, and to be drunken; the lord of that servant will come in a day when he looketh not for him, and at an hour when he is not aware, and will cut him in sunder, and will appoint him his portion with the unbelievers.

Hail Mary

9   And that servant, which knew his lord's will, and prepared not himself, neither did according to his will, shall be beaten with many stripes.

Hail Mary

10   But he that knew not, and did commit things worthy of stripes, shall be beaten with few stripes. For unto whomsoever much is given, of him shall be much required: and to whom men have committed much, of him they will ask the more.

Hail Mary

Glory Be to the Father

Fifth Exhortation Mystery
The Seven Angels Having the
Seven Last Plagues

Jesus' I AM Lord's Prayer

1   And I saw another sign in heaven, great and marvellous, seven angels having the seven last plagues; for in them is filled up the wrath of God.

Hail Mary

2   And I saw as it were a sea of glass mingled with fire: and them that had gotten the victory over the beast, and over his

image, and over his mark, and over the number of his name, stand on the sea of glass, having the harps of God.

Hail Mary

3   And they sing the song of Moses the servant of God, and the song of the Lamb, saying, Great and marvellous are thy works, Lord God Almighty; just and true are thy ways, thou King of saints.

Hail Mary

4   Who shall not fear thee, O Lord, and glorify thy name? for thou only art holy: for all nations shall come and worship before thee; for thy judgments are made manifest.

Hail Mary

5   And after that I looked, and, behold, the temple of the tabernacle of the testimony in heaven was opened: and the seven angels came out of the temple, having the seven plagues, clothed in pure and white linen, and having their breasts girded with golden girdles.

Hail Mary

6   And one of the four beasts gave unto the seven angels seven golden vials full of the wrath of God, who liveth for ever and ever.

Hail Mary

7   And the temple was filled with smoke from the glory of God, and from his power; and no man was able to enter into the temple, till the seven plagues of the seven angels were fulfilled.

Hail Mary

8   And I heard a great voice out of the temple saying to the seven angels, Go your ways, and pour out the vials of the wrath of God upon the earth.

Hail Mary

9   And the first went, and poured out his vial upon the earth; and there fell a noisome and grievous sore upon the men which

had the mark of the beast, and upon them which worshipped his image.

Hail Mary

10   And the second angel poured out his vial upon the sea; and it became as the blood of a dead man; and every living soul died in the sea.

Hail Mary

Glory Be to the Father

Sixth Exhortation Mystery
Vials of the Wrath of God

Jesus' I AM Lord's Prayer

1   And the third angel poured out his vial upon the rivers and fountains of waters; and they became blood.

Hail Mary

2   And I heard the angel of the waters say, Thou art righteous, O Lord, which art, and wast, and shalt be, because thou hast judged thus. For they have shed the blood of saints and prophets, and thou hast given them blood to drink; for they are worthy.

Hail Mary

3   And I heard another out of the altar say, Even so, Lord God Almighty, true and righteous are thy judgments.

Hail Mary

4   And the fourth angel poured out his vial upon the sun; and power was given unto him to scorch men with fire. And men were scorched with great heat, and blasphemed the name of God, which hath power over these plagues: and they repented not to give him glory.

Hail Mary

5   And the fifth angel poured out his vial upon the seat of the beast; and his kingdom was full of darkness; and they gnawed their tongues for pain, and blasphemed the God of heaven because of their pains and their sores, and repented not of their deeds.

Hail Mary

6   And the sixth angel poured out his vial upon the great river Euphrates; and the water thereof was dried up, that the way of the kings of the east might be prepared.

Hail Mary

7   And the seventh angel poured out his vial into the air; and there came a great voice out of the temple of heaven, from the throne, saying, It is done.

Hail Mary

8   And there were voices, and thunders, and lightnings; and there was a great earthquake, such as was not since men were upon the earth, so mighty an earthquake, and so great.

Hail Mary

9   And the great city was divided into three parts, and the cities of the nations fell: and great Babylon came in remembrance before God, to give unto her the cup of the wine of the fierceness of his wrath.

Hail Mary

10   And every island fled away, and the mountains were not found. And there fell upon men a great hail out of heaven, every stone about the weight of a talent: and men blasphemed God because of the plague of the hail; for the plague thereof was exceeding great.

Hail Mary

Glory Be to the Father

The Covenant of the Magi

PART THREE

The Power Aspect of the Holy Spirit

Fourteen Messages of the Word of Life
to the Children of the Mother

1

The Tolling of the Angelus

With the tolling of the Angelus, there descends a sweet stillness over the human heart when that heart responds to the call of
the bell. And as the mighty I AM Presence of each individual
upon earth sends forth its peal, inviting the sons and daughters
of heaven to come home, so the responsive ones from among
mankind listen to the call of the tolling bell sounding out the
eternal hour and respond by an about-face where necessary, a
renewal of faith and divine friendship when needed, and repentance where required.

Whatsoever the need may be, the individual who desires to
respond to the call of heaven must respond now. For the only
guarantees given to anyone are the guarantees of the eternal
moment, when the call is heard and the child answers that call.
The tiny child Samuel, answering the call of God, said, "Speak,
LORD, for thy servant heareth."[1]

As my mother took my hand in hers and led me to the temple of God, she said, "O my daughter, this is called the house of
God. He is everywhere, and nowhere more powerfully felt than in
the place where he is recognized."

I was able to absorb a lesson from my mother's instruction,
which stood me well. For I imparted that blessing to my Son
Jesus, and he declared, "Foxes have holes and the birds of the air
have nests, but the Son of man hath no place where to lay his
head."[2] For this concept of the omnipresence of God flooded his
being. And he recognized that God is manifest everywhere and in
all places, and he chose to recognize him everywhere.

This night, as you are gathered together in honor of my ascension, I come to you to ring a bell of freedom in honor of your own. For there is no one today or tonight in mortal form for whom I do not hold an immaculate concept. And if therefore I hold an immaculate concept for all, then I ring a bell of freedom for each one and I proclaim the majesty of the ascension for each one.

The way may not seem easy, and it did not always seem so for us. Mankind, through the years, have chosen to cover our doings with a veil of glamour. But the realities that were present in our daily life, the vicissitudes which we faced, were not so glamorous in those early days. And we knew at times the pain and unrest and uncertainty of ordinary men. For we were caught in an aura of confusion, which was present in that day, as it is today.

However, we kept our faith fixed upon the eternal Presence of God. And when it seemed that the clouds and shadows of despair would envelop us, we thought about that silver lining which is behind each cloud and shadow. We thought upon the eternal perfection of the light.

Although my words may be simple, they are durable. For you will find the simple thought and idea of the light a durable concept with which you can live. You will find this concept a staff upon which you can lean.

And when mortal wisdom seems to fail and the answers to all the queries within your heart do not seem to be given you, you may dwell in the idea that the light of God does not fail. And in that certain knowing, you will find a power to free you from the shadows of despair. You will find a power to exalt you out of the temporary situations in which you find yourselves. And then, with grateful hearts, returning to the concept of your divinity and its immaculate nature, you will move progressively onward in the light, as we did, one step day by day nearer to your own ascension.

Mankind today are truly, as Saint Germain has told you, living in concepts of peril and confusion. The seeming scientific progress of the Communist world is somewhat a virile threat against the forces of freedom and democracy. And it would be well if all of America and all of the free world recognized the need to knit themselves together in this day and hour and rally around the cause of freedom with greater diligence, with a greater sense of honor and unity. It would render an incomparable assistance to mankind.

I ask you, beloved ones, if the light that is America and the light that is freedom should go out, where would the world be in the hands of the anarchy and insidious nature of World Communism? Where would the hope be within the hearts of mankind, for which all Christendom have labored and prayed?

Then call, beloved ones, with a renewed endeavor, that the beautiful gift of freedom—which Saint Germain and other masters have made possible under the hands of God for you to enjoy—may be retained. For little by little, inroads have been made into the very bulwarks of freedom, which stand opposing the forces of shadow. And the forces of light must, if they will be successful, rally to a divine unity.

Now then, I speak for the ascension of all men, for the freedom of all men, for the freedom of every child yet unborn, that all may enjoy the blessings of liberty, that all may breathe of the air of freedom and come to a place of dignity, where their souls can expand upward toward the ascension to respond to the peal of the cosmic bells, to hear the tolling of that beautiful Angelus that speaks to each heart these blessed words: "It is finished. Well done, thou good and faithful servant. Thou hast been faithful in a few things. Enter thou now into the joy of thy Lord, where I will make thee a ruler over many things."[3]

In my Father's house are many mansions.[4] Therefore, in those beautiful planetary mansions of God, joys and wonders are prepared. Let not, then, the violent take these places by storm while the heart of America sleeps. Let America awake and pursue diligently the things of spiritual glory. And as America pursues the glories of Spirit, let it also pursue the necessary scientific advances of the age.

I think it well if mankind would call to beloved Saint Germain and the Lady Master Leonora that a greater release of science and invention may be given so that it will become less possible for the powers of shadow to attack the democracy and the places known as the citadels of freedom.

South America, with all of its glorious terrain, stands as a fertile ground, a place where the beloved Great Divine Director would erect a marvelous civilization, such as the world has never known, a place in preparation of the incoming seventh root race.

Let, then, protection be given to the Woman and to her seed, Manchild of the Holy Christ. Let protection be given! And let a flood issue forth, a flood of mighty protection for all who serve the light the world around, that the ascension in the light may become the goal of all and that the forces of Communism shall not invade that blessed place known as South America—but that the power of light and the powers of the heavens may be shaken, and the stars of the Divine One, that sacred Father Supreme, may fall to the earth in that blessed land to cast illumination over all of its people and over its terrain, over its mountains and hills and valleys, settling as a mantle of peace upon all and reinforcing the forces of freedom the world around.

For only by freedom shall men understand how their hearts may become open to their Presence. And the Presence can pour down the glory that shall exalt them, even as the rays of the sun passing through the atmosphere enter into the heart of the lily and assist that lily in breaking forth from bud into full bloom, extending its delicate petals to the light of the sun as a chalice cup flooded with the perfume of heaven.

So, then, let the perfume of the sacred fire and the sacred flowers of heaven flood forth within your hearts and consciousness, waft into the atmosphere of the earth and be inhaled by all who breathe the air of freedom, that the glory of the ascension may become known, loved, revered and adored, even as we do, in memory of that blessed hour when I arose and was assumed by this ritual into the heart of God.

I call to you all now to dedicate yourselves anew to the purposes of a Cosmic Mother. Even those who are not mothers will understand that all have the mission of my Son, a mission of their Holy Christ Self, to perform. And they can declare with him in the dignity of freedom, "For this cause came I into the world, that all men might have life, which is God, and that more abundantly."[5]

So be it, then, in God's name, I AM. So be it! Let life manifest more abundantly for all. So let all come to know more of the life that is God's. So let more drink of this cup. So let *all* drink of it! For all are sons of one Father.

I take my leave of you now. And as I go, I pray that those angelic beings which accompanied me as I was assumed into the heavens will bless you tonight who have assembled in this place to honor my name.

May that blessing, which these angels bring to you, be scattered into the atmosphere of earth. And may all share with you my feeling of love for the quietness of the evening of victory preceding the dawn of all men's ascension in the never failing light of God. I thank you.

Washington, D.C.
August 15, 1962

2

Renew Your Sacred Covenant

Come into my garden, O my children, and feel the supreme peace that is made manifest as your hearts attune with the radiance of the angels and as you sense the peace which God pours forth through every floral offering, through the pines, whether still or blown by gentle breeze. I am inviting you, lady mothers and ladies, gentlemen and men of destiny, to take your place in the ranks of the brave—those who could come apart from the world and, in communion with the powers of heaven, feel the glory of God and draw from that glory sustaining strength for every moment when that strength is the requirement in order to have the staunchness of heart to brave the inequities and the trials of life.

Some have thought of me as a mother of sorrows and one also acquainted with grief. It is true that I have witnessed, over the centuries and during the brief span, comparatively speaking, of my embodiment as Mary the Mother of Jesus, a great deal of the sorrow and the sadness that seem to be the current lot of mankind.

But I have seen, far beyond all the appearances of sorrow, [that] the nobility and the grandeur that pierce the veil of every tomorrow and exalt both womanhood and manhood into such glory as written upon the archives of heaven is illustrious light, freedom, manifestation of God's presence, and the protection of the grand idea of spiritual nobility as it is enshrined within the human heart.

To witness your beloved son ascend a mount of stone and to see men strip him of honor might bring anguish to many. But to witness his resurrection a few days thereafter and to see him rise victorious out of the shroud of human hopelessness into the victory of immortality and life was glory enough to count the stain of the past moments as nothing.

Some have wondered at the strength God has given to me, and I say to all, strength was woven from those moments of seeming defeat far more than those moments of seeming victory. For there is a victory of seeming which is not victory at all until, by comparison and contrast, you are able to draw from the cup of life and the dregs of gall and bitterness the sweetness of overcoming—not as though all were the sweetened wafer in the mouth and belly but as that which is at times sweet as honey in the mouth and as bitter as gall in the belly of consummation.

Brave men and women are needed, not only for yesterday but for the problems and purposes of this day. It is not enough that noble men of spiritual attainment have graced this earth as flowers in God's garden, but it is essential that today men and women shall lay themselves upon life's altar consecrated to the great supreme ideals of my beloved Son and the beloved Son of God. He was all of that from his earliest infancy, and I knew the moment I clasped him to my heart that he was the fullness of all which God hoped for in men. And I perceived from his first footsteps, footsteps of grace that would lead him above the low places of life to the place of attainment, the mount of the ascension victory. I saw in his footsteps from the very beginning the mighty unwavering dedication to his Father's purpose.

Joseph and I did not feel ever as though he belonged to us alone, and it was easier thus to give him to the world and to God. For we knew with the very beginning of his mission that he did not belong to us alone but to the world. But when he spake unto me and unto his father, saying, "Wist ye not that I must be about my Father's business?"[1] it was a secret sign unto us, which is not recorded in the archives of men. But with that utterance, he was dedicated to the very commencement of his mission.

As I stand in the atmosphere of this room, I am compelled to request of you a deepening dedication, a deepening consecration, a deepening love. I am compelled to ask of you, by the Great Law, a renewal of every sacred covenant you have ever made with God, the remembrance of the former things. Men and women of today, you have put away God and replaced him with toys, with baubles, with trinkets, with ephemeral intrinsics. You have failed to recognize that your life is a mission dedicated to God, to the manifestation of purity, to the manifestation of virtue, to the understanding of the cosmic problem.

How narrow, how very very narrow, are the measurements of men—scarcely one cubit. And the temple of God stands so exalted before men's eyes. If they would only recognize and ponder more upon the things that are eternal, the spires of spiritual desire would be builded higher and higher. And the cycles of attainment would equal the spires of aspiration until, by inward communion with our octave, such wonderful perfection would manifest upon the screen of life as to make many sons and daughters of God aware of their stature—not a stature of ignorance but a stature most precious of Christ radiance.

You have heard it said, gentle ladies and men, by some, "Oh, I am a bundle of nerves." O precious ones, could you but consecrate your nervous system to the heart of your Presence and feel the mighty pulsating flame of life as it flows over the wire conductors of your nervous system, as electricity flows through the wires that supply your lights. If you would recognize the peace-commanding Presence of God in your world, the power of your victory, the gratitude you ought to feel for the manifold blessings conveyed to you by the hour and by the moment, I think there would be less time for useless preoccupations, usurpations of your energy, destructivity and shame.

A consecrated life, when left undisturbed by human pondering upon the altar of dedication, can always revert to the Great

God Presence of life, which stands by the altar, and in the hour of trial say, "O God, I have committed myself unto thee. Take me, use me, do with me what thou wilt. For I am thine." Those who, as Ananias and Saphira,[2] say to men, "I am dedicated to God" in words while in effect upon the first breath of trial reneging upon their promises and dedication—I ask you what hopelessness is born of these, who, lacking spiritual integrity, tend to slough off the blame upon another lifestream and refuse to bear their own burdens or the burdens of another. This was not so of my Son. It is not so of any son or daughter of heaven consecrated in truth to the upholding of the holy ideals of this moment.

Your beloved Saint Germain, in his momentous dedication to the heart of God, when taking his supreme initiation to be the God of Freedom to the planetary body, reaffirmed the words of the descending Christ: "Lo, I AM come to do thy will, O God."[3] And in his dedication, he offered to stay a time and a time and a half a time longer than was necessary if it would assist some recalcitrant lifestream to find his way home. And by the inversion of his great dedication, going back a time, a time and a half a time, it came to pass that the valley of his dedication became a mountain of purity and wonder. And heaven bestowed upon your Saint Germain a crown of freedom which is so noble, so wondrous, so beautiful.

As I stand here now, I am aware of the fact that men have pondered as to whether he was, in reality, the father of beloved Jesus. I tell you in retrospect now, and I tell you in retrospect as of then, I should never have shunned his companionship. For he was always understanding, patient, magnificent and divine. He was a true consort, worthy on earth to be the father of Jesus.

This is the great Columbia, the gem of the ocean of God Freedom to the earth. In memory of your Saint Germain and of the son that he assisted to rear, your beloved Ascended Master Jesus and mine, I say, ladies and gentlemen, never forget—not only on

Columbus Day, observed by men, but on every day observed by God in his constant faithfulness to give and to bequeath to you the protection of the angelic host—the bounties of life and the great cosmic care of heaven. Forget not his mercies every day. Forget not our desire to commune with you. Forget not our intercession on your behalf. Forget not the mighty power we generate and how we stand, at times, with drawn swords of light to protect you against those who, by their depredations, would destroy all which you hold dear and near.

I am come this afternoon to summon from your hearts a dedication to God's supreme allegiance, womanhood, nobility, manhood, supreme authority, the scepter of unalterable devotion, consecration and love. All that you give would never balance that which has been given. All that you give would be but a drop in a cup as balanced against an ocean of grace.

God's grace is sufficient for thee. It is the power of light. The patience of an angel can be developed in you, and it can be done by a gentle entering in to the Son of God, the radiance that is within you.

As you gaze outwardly from the temple of being, looking upon one another, ponder the mighty flame of life, so radiant within thyself. Ponder our identification, your identification with the angels and with God. Ponder the peace of my garden, O beloved ones. The gardens of earth are places of refuge. Men fly [to them] to be apart from the vicissitudes of life. They seek for peace and quietness there. My Son in Gethsemane sought for peace of soul and that he might drink of the cup to the very bottom of its bitter dregs with nobility and success for mankind, as a great example, as a victor, as a conqueror of death that men's hopes might be renewed.

Heroes are needed today, spiritual heroes. You cannot give, O blessed ones, that which you do not have, but you can give whatever portion of life that you have externalized. This is all we ask.

We do not ask that you become a Christ and then begin to give. We ask that you recognize that you are you and that you begin with yourself as you are. That one talent of grace you give, when used in the service of the Most High, can be added to and added to and added to, until you find yourself surrounded with a multitude of wondrous talents, all generated and regenerated in the service of the light and for the healing of mankind's wounds.

The crown of thorns was plaited from the very vine that bore the precious rose. Remember this. You may prick yourselves or others upon the thorns, or blunt them and convey to the hands of men the roses of your healing love, the perfume of your wondrous sincere attention. This is all we do. This is the childlike wonder of the angels.

O Raphael, my adorable consort, pour forth thy healing rays upon these sons and daughters of men and let them feel thy wonderful all-enfolding radiance, the glow-ray of our perfect union in the light. I too am thankful.

I thank you and I bid you good afternoon.

Washington, D.C.
October 12, 1963

3

To Kindle the Flame of Love

Peace be unto thee. Remember the words "He has cast down the mighty from their seats and exalted them of low degree."[1]

In the stillness of the mind attuned to the mystery of the ages comes awareness from within that seemeth to be without. For it manifests in the heart of the world of form, even as it manifested in the infant body which long ago I held in my arms, envisualizing the stalwart man of God that was to come into the world as a power to change the recalcitrant conditions of a world familiar with the clank of Roman legions and the ministration of the system of taxation upon all the people by the sovereign government of Caesar Augustus.

Today the world has gone afar from the mighty purposes of life. The pall of thick darkness as it extended itself over the land of Egypt is now over the world, and the cry of the angels and of the heavenly hosts is not heard by mankind, save only by the few.

The majesty of God is very great, and the ignorance* of the divine decree will merit for mankind a far greater self-inflicted punishment than that which was possible to the administrators of Rome and against the people of that time.

It is not the will of God that men should perish, for I held within my womb that holy form that came to mankind as the Great Awakener, the Great Regenerator. Though [the child was] infinitesimally small in the eyes of the scribes and the Pharisees, the heart of Herod was troubled. And earthly kings protecting their kingdom sought, as in the ancient rituals of wrong in the

---

*pronounced igore-ance.

past, to take the life of every male child lest Messias should be born, continue to live and do as God directed.

The simple understanding of the Law which I cited in the Magnificat[2] is to this hour a celestial call to mankind to prayer and adoration. The kings of the earth have heard it and rejoiced. The great among men have revered him and have heard the song of the angels. And again and again have the hearts of the great been stirred by the regenerative fires of the Son of God I bore.

He was the Lawgiver. He was the Judge. He was the Wonderful One, the Counsellor, the Prince of Peace,[3] yea, and the Mighty God that spake of old to Moses in the burning bush. But the divine intent framed within his soul and being was to make every man acquainted with the nobility lying dormant within the temple of his [own] heart.

I do not desire this night to dispense fear. There are times that I have chosen, as I did at Fátima, to draw very close to the heart of the young and the innocent and to produce the miracle that caused the people to erect a shrine there unto me.[4]

Now, at the present hour my desire is to incite you to love. And there are times when it is desirable to awaken men by showing them the inherent dangers in their course that they may reverse themselves. And then again, there is a desire in heaven and in the hearts of all of the ascended masters to make men aware of the great love-potential that is within themselves.

By the basic simplicity of that miraculous love, we desire to dispense into your heart the gold and frankincense and myrrh which the wise men, the Magi from the East, carried to the infant son I bore.

And so this night I bring to you the fragrance of frankincense. As the censers in the ancient temples in Judaea, in Sinai, in the holy mount and in the hidden temples of the Brotherhood did swing and emit their fragrance, so I pray that your hearts will feel the glory of the fragrance of divine awareness. The pulsations of divine awareness within yourselves will stir ancient energies dedicated to God in the ritual of divine love before you knew mortal form.

And so has it been with every living soul, who ere she descended into the world of form for the very first time was given the blessed ritual of life and the ceremonial dance of the sacred hours, whereby the heart in rejoicing did dance before God, even as David danced before the ark of the LORD.[5]

And in the cosmic geometry of being, the mighty cosmic arc reached across the sky to span the folds of identity and teach mankind of the beautiful temple of life and the mysteries of that temple. Unspeakable were those mysteries—unspeakable and unable to be uttered. Men who know them are indeed caught up above the third heaven,[6] where they can understand all things in the pristine state of consciousness akin to that they once knew in the heart of the Father's love before they took sentient form.

And so, children of the one God, as I speak to you this night it is to kindle within you the same flame of love that in my desire I kindled within the consciousness of my Son Jesus. You are all children of my heart. And as I reach my hand across the ages and I see surrounding you the miracle of eternal perfection, it is as though you had come now into my womb of light—a being born late in time, yea, later in time than my Son but born of the same cosmic mother. For I stand as vestal within the temple of the Cosmic Mother and I interpret and represent to you the angelic hosts as they contact the world of form.

And truly there ring yet in my ears the words of Gabriel, consort,* cohort, beloved one, linked to the seven holy archangels and their archeiai, including my blessed Raphael: "Hail, Mary, full of grace, the Lord is with thee and with thy spirit. Blessed art thou among women."

---

*Archangel Gabriel is the consort, or divine complement, of Archeia Hope. The word *consort* also means "companion," "associate," and "colleague."

How can I forget, and would I, those cosmic memories? And yet mortal men, remembering the tiny injustices that plagued them from day to day, have forgotten the tender experiences which their soul passed through at infinite levels of cosmic love ere they drew the folds of mortal consciousness around themselves.

Now I call unto Raphael. O my beloved one, on behalf of humanity steeped in the brew of outer darkness I say: Let there be light! Let the magnificence of the light that flamed out from the star that came unto Bethlehem flame out now as there is a cosmic merge,* the conglomerate coming together of myriad star-bright angelic bands offering paeans of praise to the infinite realm of light activity. Let there occur as a recycling phase of cosmic intent for the children of this age—the contemporary children, linked together—a new renaissance of cosmic light radiance cycling through the years in a cosmic spiral.

Descend now to this planetary body in immortal, oracular, miraculous, cosmic recycling of the drama of the centuries and the ages—the new birth of cosmic identity within the folds of each man's consciousness that quickens in every mother's heart, in every woman to whom comes the God flame, the reality of her mission of service unto life.

Therefore I ask the angelic hosts to create a great stirring of the miraculous sense within the consciousness of all who hear my voice—that that stirring shall be the magnificent realization of the potential Life that is within man as he re-identifies with his divine identity.

And so, if there is a fierceness about holy love, let it manifest as the voice of the mother that will not be separated from her children. In the days of old when life was wrested from innocent babes, the cry sounded forth—and Rachel is weeping for her chil-

---

*merge: meaning "an act or instance of merging"; rare use as a noun (*Oxford English Dictionary*).

dren and refuses to be comforted.[7]

But what of the children of God? What of the children of the Cosmic Mother? What of the children of the light that are captured by the darkness and are lost altogether in the realm of the moment from God? Shall the Cosmic Mother's tears fall upon the earth? And shall the divine Rachel weep for her children?

A mighty tide of love, which brought me into manifestation and held my head erect in the temple when as a tiny girl I ministered to God and heard his voice, should be born in every incoming child. Every mother should inculcate the infinite demands of the Most High God within the newborn babe. Let his first steps, let her first steps, be taken in the temple. Let the consciousness of the eternal temple of life be in the infant, in the child, in the child-man.

Bow not in shame for thy states of reverence. Bow not in shame for the simple states of God-realization. These are but keys, blessed keys that tremble in the lock of the infinite door, the golden gate of cosmic release. When these keys are turned—when the energies are used rightly—and the great golden door swings open, the flame of illumination, the flame of love, the flame of power, blend in one awful, majestic outpicturing of the wonderful beauty of the inner realms of light. And the seeming exterior frosty magnificence of a winter eve, the seeming beauty of the sun upon the soft, green foliage, the azure blue of the sea, the celestial blue of the sky—all seem as but ragged and faded concepts beside the beauty of the soul.

And out of the East comes the wind that carries the Spirit of God, the Christ consciousness, as a star of ever-renewed hope to mankind, trembling on the brink of destruction. The light turns destruction and death from all.

"For thou wilt not leave my soul in hell nor suffer thine holy one to see corruption"[8]—spoken in the tongue, lute-like, of David—stands the test, the acid test of the centuries, and brings to the individual doorway of every man's consciousness the gracious potential of his victory.

We know of no higher aim, we know of no higher goal than God-goals. And the majesty of the eternal Father in its solemn administration of the Law, blessed ones, though it be tranquil at its core, must be reckoned with as a sobering, regenerative force that will unify the strands of life and weave the seamless garment of the Christ around every individual.

And at this point I wish to climax all that I have said by saying to you all that you are in the eyes of God master weavers entrusted with holy energies. You spin by the industry of your consciousness the strands of immortal life, weaving them around the flaming rod of power that is the spinal column of the individual flesh form.

And as Aaron kept the rod for Moses, who used it, so does the Spirit of God keep the rod of power until men learn to use it well—that their immortal destinies may be woven round the central being of intelligent manifestation destined to become immortal, as I am; until the perfect form is the outgrowth of the perfect idea; until the perfect manifestation is the perfect expansion of the flame of immortal life that now holds your temporary being within the hollow of the hands of God. You are the children of his universal heart, and the energies of the angelic host are round about you.

When the scales of mortal delusion fall from your consciousness and your eyes are opened and you see as God sees, you will rejoice to perceive that you are, in reality, in actuality, placed in a chariot of fire like unto that which carried Elijah up into heaven.⁹ Around you the sacred fire blazes. And through the actualizing process, whereby the realities of heaven are transferred to earth, you can, here, now, and in the hereafter, manifest your Christ-identity and escape clean from the world of form in the victorious infinite image to which all are destined to attain.

As a mother speaketh to her children, I enfold you with my love. And above me in the atmosphere and to my right hand, the Lord Christ Jesus radiates his sweet peace. To my left hand stands the friend of old, John the Beloved, still in the clasp of cosmic hands with the ancient friend close unto his heart.

So do thou, by this magnificent example, surpassing even the example of Damon and Pythias[10]—do thou, all and one, learn to love one another even as God has first loved you.

Colorado Springs, Colorado
December 29, 1966

4

To Expand the Fountain of Hope

In the symbol of eternal hope, man is encouraged to pursue through most trying circumstances a course of which he may not even be wholly certain. Mankind today, fraught with many uncertainties, continue on course because the yearning of the God flame within their heart continues to evoke a response, blessed ones, to the ministrations of heaven.

We speak, then, this morning, briefly of the forget-me-not, tiny blue flower of the beautiful will of God whose rays coming from a center emanate the certainty of goodwill to the world.

One of the primary facets on which I meditated was the glorious concept that the incarnate Word within me embodied God's will. The scorn of individuals who did not understand the beauty of the immaculate concept was more lightly borne, for I knew that hidden within the folds of my flesh and in the palace of my heart the light of hope to humanity was chaliced and aflame. One day it would traverse mountain and plain. It would run with the joy of a melodic brook. It would melt as the snows from the mountain and pour forth a torrent of love and hope to men.

This was an aid to my consistent faith. This was an aid to standing up against the salvos of mortal opinion. It enabled me in times of trial to press toward the prize that lay ahead.

Mortals, garbed in flesh, are so frequently captivated by the ideas of selfhood that they do not know what is resident within them in the heart of the great, pulsing God flame. It may seem strange to some of you when I say this, but even those in whom the flame is bursting, in a relative sense, while yet wearing mortal garments do not always pay proper heed to the great treasure that is within them. Too frequently they are, as you would say it, sidetracked by illusion. And in those moments when illusion, together with doubt, assaults the citadel of man's purity and faith, it is difficult for them to see clearly the hand of heaven ever guarding and guiding their destiny.

The linkages of hearts are seldom known, and when individuals are thrown together (literally, in many cases), it is often strange how the reactions of past times will come again for redemption and old breaches will seek to mend themselves under the onus of a flowing spiritual love.

When individuals once again rupture the tranquility of being by old and recalcitrant emotions, by breaches in harmony's fort, it is often a case where the earth literally opens up and swallows them in a widening breach that will require yet greater energy to mend and other times to come.

I remember the words of my Son, which he so lovingly spoke: "Agree with thine adversary...whilst thou art in the way with him."[1] How much better it would be for all humanity if they would heal the breaches that divide them from one another and would perceive the all-conquering, all-triumphant light as it expands and flings aside lesser concepts until there is no room in the inn of man's being for aught else but the *splendor of the light and its healing radiance!*

You wait for my Son to speak to you on the morrow, and speak he shall.[2] But I today, as one who bore him, bring you the tidings of my love, trumpeting with triumphant Raphael into your consciousness with a melody of the golden dawn when illumination's flame shall teach men how to do honor in my name.

So frequently, precious ones, so very frequently, the right bit of knowledge, structured and held in mind, would keep in control those riptides of human emotions that unfortunately spill over the banks of men's hearts' energy and catapult them into deceit practiced upon themselves, when the light of the Presence would weld together from the variant segments of man's consciousness a body of universal oneness where each soul could triumphantly portray his own many, splendid facets of identity.

And how the line of avatars needs to have established in the temple of time, with each contemporary cycle, those adherents of cosmic law and universal love who can stand unmoved against the onslaughts of age-old inharmonies.

When I appeared at Fátima and the flow of my love poured out to stir a nation and a world, to sound a warning to mankind, it was to convey the same universal tide of love and light that flowed forth and ushered into the world the first Christmas: Peace on earth, goodwill toward men.

Where is it now? Where but in the hearts of those who respond to it. But the question is, how can we convey by our heart's love to mortal men the need to revivify the song of the angels through the symphonic flow of the year and, with the hope in every divine heart, [convey it in such a way] that mankind will open themselves to the symphony of the ages, to the Edenic conceptions that flashed forth of old and said long before the centurion, "Truly this man was the Son of God"?[3]

And it was spoken of ye all. For when each tender, shining soul, fashioned of universal fire, came forth from the heart of God and asked to be born into consciousness, into the consciousness of individuality, a great circle of fire flashed forth and wedded that one to the heart of God. And so, the androgynous God fashioned, from his circlet, a circle of fire around that being, whether male or female, for all eternity. And thus no energy that has ever cosmically been given to each gifted one can ever be destroyed but must return to the heart of God—a talent hidden in the napkin[4] at times and at other times invested in service without end.

The ascended masters yearn to pursue a path where we can gather together from the four corners of the earth those devotees whose hearts, made tender by the pummeling of life experiences, stand ready to serve the great universal cause of the only begotten Son of God, the light and hope of the world.

For out of the heart of the Cosmic Mother flowed into manifestation, with the ultimate intention of God, the perfect hope for every child that should ever spring forth, in either the domain of Spirit or the realm of flesh. Flesh and blood can never inherit the kingdom[5] but only the spiritual man hidden within the heart of flesh.

And thus, to expand the garments of appreciation, to expand the chalice of identity is to expand the potential of the man of God, the spiritual man, the son of God, the radiant identity, the fountain of hope and the purity that transmits into the world order some divine afflatus that speaks of Cosmic Motherhood.

To be a vehicle of transcendence, to be a vehicle to transmit, to be a vehicle of the Spirit, is to either lie down as the rock bed of the stream or river and let the radiant energies flow over you or to merge with the water element and to become a part of that flow. It matters not to what pivot point of identity or service man may be united if he understands that there is no corner of identity or manifestation that is apart from the Father's love. Thus can he understand that to bloom as a rose, to be the rose of Sharon in the desert of consciousness, is to bring forth at a point in space, in time, in manifestation some extension of the divine intent.

To blossom is to love; to expand is to love. To love is to expand and to blossom. And with expansion comes the blessed signal of the wedding of man to God, the floral scent, the sweetness of the Law. And the sweetness of the Law in manifestation does lead man to cosmic productivity.

The needs of the world are great today. The needs of each individual are great and his dependence upon God, whether known or acknowledged by him, is intense. And the hungers of hungry men must be assuaged.

We must not be dissuaded, then, by mortal thought and feeling. We must not be prevented by any past experience of failure. We must not falter nor fail but pursue now as never before those valiant goals that are set before us—the culmination of the incoming of the kingdom of my Son into valiant manifestation; and the cognition of mankind that the enemies of righteousness will always attack and deceive those whom they can, even the very elect if it were possible.

Make, then, your calling and election sure and assert yourselves by committing yourselves unto that course which every son of God has acknowledged. Then, when the Christ triumphant speaks at any point in space, you will be there. When the light of God bursts forth to bloom at any point in space, you will be there. When a rivulet of a running brook dances into the sparkling sun and flashes forth into the ritual of aeration, you will be there—joyous, bubbling, effervescent, but deep and deep-running. For you will spring from the fountain of deity, a "deist"[6] indeed but a son of God as well.

In his name I salute you with his peace. May this eve for mankind be mellowed somewhat by the ministrations of the angelic host. And thou, O Raphael, may thy garment, as the garment of the other six archangels, trailing transcendent light, wash this planet with the tears of an archeia* shed in hope for man's victorious triumph. I thank you.

Colorado Springs, Colorado
December 24, 1967

---

*Mother Mary is the archeia, or divine complement, of Archangel Raphael.

5

The Consummate Reality
of the Son of God

The joy of our heart is full this night as we contemplate the richer meaning of life for every son of God's heart.

The hour has come when the world is now dwelling in a place of vainglorious manifestation, and their hearts are far from the causes of our rejoicing. The cup of wrath is trembling in the cup of life, for the weight of human karma in the personal cup as well as the world cup is very great. And the hearts of men are often failing for fear of the things which are coming upon the world.[1]

But we tonight, as our hearts draw nigh unto the world, would bring a comforting ray to play upon the hearts of men. And so, tonight I bring from behind the veil of matter and substance, from the realm of the spiritual, from the heart of God, from the hand of the Lord Maha Chohan and the Holy Comforter, the passions of God-freedom, the flames of illumination and the strength of the higher octaves of light. For these measures in fuller potency were the sustaining momentums of my Son in his manifestation of cosmic grace to a waiting world two thousand years ago.

The mantle of his presence sustains to the present hour courage in the hearts of many, and faith. But it is not enough. For the world has begun again to measure all things according to material standards and they do not understand the measurements that are taken from higher octaves of light.

Long ago in Portugal when I appeared at Fátima unto the three children, it was a manifestation that drew countless thousands to behold our coming. Yet all of the records that are left in written form as well as recorded in the memories of men of past miracles have not continued to stir mankind toward a regeneration within themselves. Only the few have accepted, by comparison to the many who have rejected.

But our hearts are full this night of that gift which God intended for the entire world. The gift of our Presence,* the gift of the Eternal in the domain of each soul, was intended to enlarge the borders of [man's] perception that he might see beyond the physical into the structuring of cosmic love, that he might feel the passions of the God-design pulsating as electronic light within the substance of his flesh form and his mind, consuming the darkness of his world and bringing him to a state of Christ illumination.

For the Christ is God's gift throughout the ages, and the eternal Christmas is one of bestowal from the hands of the Cosmic Mother. The Mother of the World enfolds her children and brings their hearts into consonance with her purity. She mounts her love to a crescendo and rends the veil of material substance to shreds.

> For, behold, the LORD is in his temple.
> The LORD doth make all things whole.
> His substance is the fabric of the soul.
> The looms of life present, then, to view
> A range of color, magnificent hue,
> Diadems, crowns and rubies too.
> The love of God as drops so true,
> These fall upon the altar of the heart.
> The tears of the elect—shed not
> In sorrow for self but for the world
> And her cup of gall and bitterness.

My apparitions that have appeared in various parts of the world have been permitted by cosmic decree and because of the entreaties of many mothers in the world who have been grieved about the continuation of war throughout the centuries. These by

---

*the I AM Presence, the Presence of God individualized for each one.

their petitions have reached the very heart of the Karmic Board, and the stimulation has permitted me to come and from time to time appear to children and to other audiences that they might have renewed within themselves those elements of faith that would cause the soul to lose its fear and re-create its faith in immortality.

Oh, how beautiful is the shrine of the Christ within the heart. Of what is the shrine composed? Of deeds of love and mercy, of thoughts of grace and truth. What greater proof, beloved ones, does the self need than the deeds of wholeness and loveliness? When these deeds are committed, they are themselves a commitment to God; they are the fulfillment of his covenants within ye. And they speak of honor to my Son. For so many honor him in name but darkness floods their hearts and minds.

Ye are children of the Sun. Ye are children of the One. Ye are children of wholeness and purity. And when the full range of that purity of God within ye is allowed expression, it is the token proof of the Presence of God within you. "By their fruits," by your fruits, "ye shall know them,"[2] even as ye shall know yourself. This is the great cosmic marker-beacon that shows that you are on course and steering toward a safe haven.

Now, tonight, as light surrounds me, as light enfolds me, I convey it unto you. I give it unto you. With a passion of renewal, I would see your bodies renewed. I would see your minds renewed. I would see your spirits lifted up and exalted. I would see peace surrounding you, encircling the dark clouds of negative manifestation and crushing them into a mound that can be transmuted into light by the very pressures of divine love. And I would also reach out into the world and extend light rays from this time and place into all time and places.

And I would bring the consummate reality of the only begotten Son of God into view, to the masses, that they may, one and all, feel the connection to their own lifestream, to their own heart, to their very being of beings—that they may summon by determined effort the power of God that will re-create the earnestness of the divine within the soul that all may drink of the water of Life freely[3] and know freedom from doubt and the comfort of immortality.

Ye were born to the foreverness of God. Your names were inscribed in his Book of Life. He has prepared a place for you that where he is there ye may be also. And therefore the veil of matter is torn from the face of the disciple and the eyes are opened, those glorious orbs that shine with the glow of cosmic fires. The universe opens up as a shell and man beholds within it the Spirit of the Creator in service and work. The labors of love are in starry diadems—turning worlds of fire in space, galaxies and misty nebulae—all consecrations of the God domain. But within your hearts an equally wondrous world is seen, a world that has a place for every segment of universal majesty.

Each place of creation, then, in that vast cosmos, that skyey dome of cosmic reality, can be reposited in thyself and in miniature re-creates there the domain of God. There is no separation and no death but only the continuity of the fount of his reality.

But as ye approach the throne of his grace, forsake the dissimulative states of consciousness that carry you away from the central purposes of truth and uphold in your consciousness the passion of the search for his love. For although his love be everywhere, it seems to escape from those who would seize it and tear the lovely veil that hides it from view.

Gentle, then, must be the heart, and determinate in its efforts. Loving must be the heart, and consecrated in purpose. Stern must be the power that rebukes the native misqualifications of pristine men. And all must turn with a fire-intensity to that cosmic lucidity that, as a crystal ray, opens to view the hidden cosmic meaning of life eternal, life everlasting.

O Raphael, my beloved Raphael, may thy healing rays bathe the earth in luminescence tonight. Coalesce, then, a swaddling

garment now around this planet, and from outer reaches of space
bring thy sacred bands to intone the hum of cosmic fires. Let the
harmony of cosmic spheres vibrate through the heart of the earth
and be intoned within the heart of Pelleur and Virgo.[*]

> Wondrous nature spirits everywhere,
> Bathing, then, in holy light,
> Commune with angels from starry realms so bright.
> And the densities of human creation are banished
> And in their place we stand,
> Mindful of the hand
> Of Cosmic Mother presence.
> Boldly we bring to view
> The Manchild, the Son of God.
> We reveal him who would find lodging
> Within the inn of the being of each one,
> Uniting all to their Central Sun bond,
> The bond of cosmic truth,
> The fount of revivification and eternal youth.
>
> Oh, how sweet is the essence of holy prayer.
> How sweet is the essence of seeking the heart of
>   the Mother so fair,
> The heart of the Mother that would guard and protect
>   her son.
> For the real Son of God is the image divine,
> The image so sweet, the image so fair,
> The image God gave in answer to prayer.

As I speak to you tonight there is a great cosmic tremolo
coming into manifestation. It is the vastness of the heart of the
Mother of the World as she seeks all of her children and would
bring them beneath her skirts, swaddling skirts with room for

---

*Virgo and Pelleur are the directors of the earth element. They are the hier-
archs of the gnomes, nature spirits (or elementals) of the earth kingdom.

everyone. The canopy of heaven is voluminous. It reaches out into cosmic space and it enfolds races and kindreds and tongues and peoples—all with grace, all with the memory of his star.

Oh, how brightly it shone. Oh, how radiant was its fire. And I say today, it remains the initiatory star for the whole world and for you.

Colorado Springs, Colorado
December 15, 1968

6

"The Golden-Age Caravan"

Adoring and Adored Ones,

Beyond Golgotha, beyond the waving palms, beyond present humanity, through the lattice of the years, the golden-age caravan of many lives stands framed before the Mother of the World.

The drama that occurred two thousand years ago is a magnificent offering to humanity. But each age has its needs and each age must come under our protection [for] the enfoldment of the immaculate design; the fabricating of a cathedral of spiritual reality that will stand shimmering just beyond the veil of matter substance and form, as no chimera but as a solar reality blazing with the light of the Sun, blazing with the light that shone through my Son's eyes, ringing with the fervor that in his voice sought to gather humanity together.

And so, the present hour is one of great hope for many who see not pessimistically but optimistically, considering that Golgotha, which long ago came to my Son, also comes daily to others for their development—that as they offer themselves to the higher way, they may understand and know that the higher way beckons to them, assists them, loves them, enfolds them, and is the mantle of light, life and beauty that wherever they go makes complete their moment of learning, of progress, of strengthening for the dawn of the new age.

The Weltschmerz, the world pain, the confusion of the times that numbs identity, is also a personal sorrow to ourselves. And the Mother of the World has interceded again and again for the young of this age in physical years, who come so lately into manifestation, filled with so much hope and challenge. But [the true meaning of] life is not always known by these, for they see but the outer form. And the great cosmic teachings still remain hidden from the profane.

The initiatic* in mystery schools of the past still maintain, in their secret grottoes and retreats, the wondrous power of cosmic mastery that has been throughout the ages the forte of strength to a world that otherwise would have died (literally insofar as humanity goes) because of the enthroning of darkness and the casting down of light.

But now, in this hour, the mystery schools also reach out through organizations such as this one and offer to the world a point of contact with the octaves of light to bring forth a subtle yet a manifest reality; to evoke a response from the hearts of the hungry that they may be fed the Sacred Eucharist—that as they take the Body of our Lord into themselves and understand the meaning of the Word, as they put on the life of the Christ, not through walking the *via dolorosa* but through moving onward toward a path of victory for themselves and for humanity, they are setting the compass for the age. For in all past times, it has not been the many who have actually given direction to the world.

In the age of ancient Rome, the Caesars ruled, and it was Christ or Caesar. Caesar was a figure around whom rallied many men of wisdom and strength, men of different crafts, to compound† the old world order. Christ has become, and was and remains, a central figure to the ages. The Brotherhood of man is being invoked, yet those who gaze only upon the surface and see not the grottoes, the caves, the retreats of the Brotherhood in various hidden places on the earth, are themselves sometimes fooled by the hustle and bustle, as you call it, of daily life.

They suppose that direction will arise from the masses. It does not come from there. For even in an outward way, there are

---

*i.e., the ones being initiated.

†*compound:* meaning "to form by combining parts."

always only a few leaders in the world who give to the many the sense of direction, the impulse, the movement, the inspiration and, in many cases, the depravity which tears them down.

This is particularly true of the entertainment marts of the world. For the banal influences now being spread abroad upon the earth through the destructive rhythms and outpicturizations are themselves manifestations of Satan, of shadow, and of an emptiness that itself would evoke from God the filling of that emptiness with reality. Yet humanity, themselves in a state of uncertainty, without direction, hearing the vocalizations of the leaders, listening to the rhythms of the jungle, are driven to a primitive social outlook which casts down Christ and exalts the Caesars of this day.

We would remind humanity, then, of the need to restore virtue, decency and order to the world. We would remind those who have inward understanding and light to know that the power of one can be most victorious. One figure that takes a stand for our identity can find descending upon his or her head the light of a thousand suns. We can, through one lifestream that becomes the open door, speak to millions of hearts and change them and the world patterns. But humanity are often so impatient; they expect that all things shall occur on the instant, perhaps a carry-over from their memories at inner levels when they were God oriented and spoke and instantly perceived perfection at their beck and call.

But now that they are bound in form, surrounded by the rhythms of darkness, weighted down with the accumulation of their karmic patterns, without clear understanding and direction, they so often call to us at higher octaves for help and do not recognize that help when it appears. For this is the sorrow of blindness. It is the sorrow of closing the eyes, in any era, to the spiritual radiance that seeks to give new meaning and purpose to life.

When men in any age cast aside the spiritual offerings so

gently offered from our octave of light, it is always a karmic weight that must one day be redeemed. For the activities of heaven are like a gossamer veil, a gentle and transcendent manifestation, a radiance so thin as to almost be immaculate, a radiance that is, of course, made of immaculate white fire. As this contacts the outer world of form, it enables humanity to receive tremendous assistance from on high.

We say to all of you, then, this day, let not your hearts be troubled by outer circumstances. Accept the burden of light, the weight of light, the presence of light in your lives. For light is the redeemer of man's darkness. Light is the saviour of his world. Light is the servitor of his world. Light breaks the thorns of life that the crassness of life would push into the brow of evolving humanity.

Light takes men down from the cross. Light brings them forth alive from the tomb. Light elevates them in ways of service and holiness. Light enables them to weightlessly rise into the atmosphere and experience the genuine return to God.

Light frees the mind from its burdens, cuts the emotional whirls out of the consciousness and in their place brings the balm of peace. Light is supreme, for light is the basis of all matter and substance. And unfortunately, misqualified light is the basis of all thought that is less than perfection.

Yet perfection itself is light, not humanly misqualified but qualified by God. And when the beauty of that light galvanizes humanity into action, when the stimulus of heaven is provided once again to men long disconnected from the solar reality of the Self, you will find all the little electrons of humanity, each one being an individual electron, dancing in the perfection of cosmic election—the perfection of having chosen service to God, of having elected to follow the Father, of having elected to become the Son.

For men through free will, in the dignity of God, clothed

with the garments of the immaculate concept, casting aside the darkness, with hands and feet washed by their Holy Christ Self, will stand in cosmic service, reminding men of the words of the apostle,"Blessed are the feet of those who preach the gospel of peace and bring glad tidings of good things."[1]

The feet of the elect are beautiful upon the mountains,[2] for they provide highways of holiness to humanity, highways of wholeness, highways of illumination, highways of cosmic adventure. For there is a drama element in life, an element of *cosmic* drama that illustrates to men that many of the roles they play are lesser roles than God intended—they betray the Christ. And this God did not intend.

All, then, should be informed now how many years ago a great painter, painting the Last Supper, chose a man's face to portray the Christ. The same man, after many years of disillusion and shadowed walking, was chosen by the painter to portray Iscariot.[3]

And so, humanity should recognize the need to reverse these trends—not to create trends of disillusion, of darkness, of decay, but to create trends of upliftment, of listening to the angels, of listening to the inner voice of the Great Eternal, who speaks in the heart of men, communing in the garden of their heart as of old in the Edenic allegory, which so beautifully illustrates the pageant of the Eternal.

The Eternal in his fragmentation through the priesthood of Melchizedek becomes a panoply of gods, yet there is only one God. All should understand the concept of unity and diversity so that they are not caught in the net of subtleties of darkness that seeks to divide. Out of a cosmic unity came forth a cosmic diversity. Out of a cosmic diversity will be brought forth again a cosmic unity. But the repetitious cycles of cosmic evolution are always repeating in each age new ideas, new concepts. Humanity understands that the fashion of life changes. They also understand that there are changeless fixations in cosmos upon which humanity can stably depend. We are concerned that you should understand this, that you should radiantly accept the fullness of our love.

Our love seeks to develop a sense of sonship in all, a sense of being a daughter of God, holding the flame in the heart, holding the flame in the mind, evoking the flame of the soul into all of the activities of life.

Will you, then, today come into an understanding of what you can do in the world? Will you come to understand that I am willing to envelop you with my consciousness, that when I envelop you, it is not in order that you may become distinct and apart from the world as one highly favored of God, but rather that you should understand that the favor of God is to convey his grace to all?

When long ago the angel came to me and said, "Hail, Mary, full of grace, the Lord is with thee and with thy spirit," it was not in order to bring about a feeling of elation, of happiness and joy in my heart; it was to evoke a response there concerning a mission most sacred and holy.

I gazed, then, long ago, upon the face of my Son. Some feel that my only mission was to bring him forth. But they do not understand that I also pained in delivery to bring forth my own Holy Christ Self in manifestation in my own life. They do not understand that this was the only way in which the meaning of my Son's life could live in me.

Let all, then, grasp this principle. And so, the *via dolorosa* will blend into the golden highway and you will perceive the rainbow rays of universal radiance shining through the lattice of the years. You will perceive the centuries, the years, the days, all, each moment, as a step upon the way to the heart of God. You will realize that our influences are acting in the world every moment, but their efficacy is governed by the response of humanity. I thank you.

Santa Barbara, California
March 27, 1970

Come as Little Children
to the Feet of God

O my children, children of the flame of God's grace and love, the flowers upon the pathway burst forth the memory of eternal life. Falling petals also, once again merging with the earth, again bring forth their life and beauty as the perennial bloom upon the heart.

Will all understand this and the meaning of the coming golden age? Will they understand the era of love, of our transcendence, of our truth? Will they let go of the sordid thoughts that have divided the world for so long until so many separate congregations in the world exist, and there is no spirit of universal unity that comes from the heart save from the heart of the sincere devotee of eternal truth?

It cannot outwardly at present be instituted. Humanity do not seem to be able to come to a gathering together because they do not forsake those conditions of difference which exist in their thought.

What does the golden rule speak unto man, all men? It speaks unto them, "Do unto others as you would have others do unto you." It is in the doing, in the manifestation of proper doing, that humanity are exalted—not in the manifestation of greater spiritual power, not in the manifestation of greater occult power, but in the manifestation of the power of God unto salvation.

For to him to whom belongs all glory belongs all power. And man's power, in safety, serenity and victory, shall magnify itself even as the soul is magnified. For the soul is really the God flame.

From the altar of his own heart—swept clean by the purity of his thought manifesting as the great creative impulse—comes the glory of every man. Hidden behind the veil of appearances, the soul is able at last to reach out in that sweet communion of hearts which is the manifestation of true brotherhood and at last assuage the world's grief by wiping away all tears from the eyes of humanity.

For tears are temporary manifestations. They come and they go. They are a manifestation of man's emotions, of his turmoil, of his sense of separation. When once he is able to yield his heart pliably unto the heart of God, he is able to desire to come again and again to the feet of God, to refrain from all discord and abnormality in the great normal manifestation of the heavenly potency that is within him.

For the God flame has its power. The soul powers of man are many. When they manifest through the outer consciousness and take diverse forms that are not strictly recommended by the Brotherhood, they often bring about outer conditions which are the dismay of both heaven and earth—the dismay of heaven only in the sense that heaven brings the best bouquet, that heaven yearns to bestow upon the soul the best fruits, the fruits of righteousness. And we desire a gathering together of humanity, but it must come from within themselves. So long as they look to outer sources for the manifestation of their perfection, they will neglect the great opportunity that all of heaven has conspired to give unto them.

In the doorway of opportunity, all the virtue of our realm is truly manifest. For we desire nothing more than the buoying up of the creative gifts of God to each individual so that each individual will learn that in the simplicity of love is born the fruit of holy wisdom and the strength of power. And out of this magnification of man's virtue is clearly seen the virtue of God behind the veil of human appearance. And the veil changes, and there are storms that come to the soul of men and the storms also are of the outer making. And yet there is a hidden strength within the soul—

a buoyancy and a passion for divinity—which evokes from the heart of God a natural response, a sundering of old ties and the creation of new ones, the fruit of cosmic reason, the strength of heaven's domain.

Come, then, as little children to the feet of God. Be not afraid to cast aside your outer sophistication. For not only at Fátima and at Lourdes but in many parts of the world, we have appeared and our beauty has been seen and witnessed. But the witnessing must be a permanent one to the soul that God is there, that his love is there. For the present peril of the earth is very great and many dangers threaten humanity, and the heart of the Cosmic Mother is stirred with concern. Yet our greatest concern is for the soul.

When the outer self perishes, temporarily vanishing from the scene, individuals bow their heads in grief and anguish. But what of the soul when it shrinks in size and shrivels its dimensions? What of the soul? What of the fruit that God expected so much of when he first gave himself to man?

We call, then, today to the uttermost parts of the earth for the coming of the day of the eternal spring, for the beauty of the stillness of our voice, for the strength of our arms, manifest also in yours, because we live, and we live to give. We live eternally. And the fruit of eternal life is in you, and the fruit of the golden age is strong in your heart.

Already the scenes appear, the scenes of man's amalgamation with spiritual truth. Spiritual pride must be guarded against, and senseless manifestations ought not to mar the screen of life.

Understand, then, the depth of our love—how we wish for all of you the best gifts, how we wish for humanity the greatest courage. But the courage of God truly abounds. Man must open the door; *his* heart must become the receptacle of our love. Unless this be done, a fusion cannot come about of the higher purposes. For man of himself can do very little. He is often the subject of the imposition of unvital forces that, in conveying [their "gifts"] to him, take from him far more than they give.

When we come, we give far more than mankind, yea, than all humanity, realize. And our gift is to the children, to the young, and we have not neglected the aged. For all of you outwardly are manifesting varying form. You are moving onward to a certain cosmic destiny. But in that movement, in the beauty of that movement, the beauty of God stands just behind the appearance world, rich with his gifts. He yearns to lavish them upon you, to enrichen your soul and your soul's fruit. And then all things will come into manifestation. The fullness of time is at hand, the fullness of time for many.

Will you, then, help me in our endeavors, our righteous endeavors for humanity? Will you help me to gather the children, the humanity of the world, into the great sheepfold of cosmic truth? Will you help me as I speak? Will you help me as I love by learning to love also?

And let your love be out of the depths of cosmic wisdom, for you have heard my voice.

Colorado Springs, Colorado
November 15, 1970

8

Outreach toward the Infinite God

As I gaze upon the pageant of life today, I am reminded of the contrast between the manifestation and the intent of God for humanity—a golden age of loveliness appearing behind the veil of man's creation of thought and feeling. And I come to ask of you a simple exercise, the exercising of your consciousness in outreach toward the infinite God.

Will you, then, as you think of a sunlit sky, fix your consciousness upon one spot, any spot in that sky, and realize that the words of my Son "Lo! I am with you always"[1] are living in that spot as in every spot in all space. But understand that the thrust of your gaze can penetrate the physical realm until the curtain that conceals can become the curtain that reveals. And all of the beauty and the magnificence of infinity can become a part of your consciousness.

The realm of beauty and the realm of love are ever permanently in existence. All transitory acts of humankind will pass and one day be no more. In the falling sands of time, many skeins, threads of darkness, are woven. Unwholesome are these, producing karma and pain in myriad hearts. But the infinite love of God from the heavens is with man whenever his consciousness will reach out through the darkness, the pain and the sense of struggle and understand that the love of God is eternally reborning in man, bringing to him the elements of a new birth, a new heaven and a new earth. For the former things shall pass away.[2]

Remember, beloved ones, that what appears as light and darkness is steadily engaged in struggle and clash, differing ideologies. Yet humanity, through a misapplication of purpose, too often frequently support the elements of darkness, often accepting the masquerading wolves in sheep's clothing and little understanding that real truth is generated in the soul because the soul was made in the image of God. There man can find those elements of freedom which are the purity of the light. And the light is cosmic purpose, and cosmic purpose is being reborn in man as though one were laying the bricks and mortar of a magnificent edifice. Bit by bit, the consciousness is being renovated so beautifully with the assistance of the angelic hosts.

I have stood again and again in stern warning to the world. I have also uttered how the green tree appears and the dry tree, now existing side by side. [The dry tree is] that which man has cursed by his cutting off of the very roots of that tree, by his stopping the flow of the sap—the gentle radiant electronic energy of life that so gloriously blossoms—until the light of hope seems no longer to be a fragrant one in the heart. And many mothers' hearts in pain reach up in prayer, silent but glowing shafts of radiant light penetrating the veils of heaven betwixt heaven and the human consciousness and bringing pleas to the very throne of Deity. It does not seem to some to be enough.

The real problem in the world today is the problem of ignorance, that people are not schooled in those magnificent concepts of heaven. When you mention heaven to them, so frequently their hearts quickly turn to other things—the things of this world and of the prince of this world and the powers of darkness. This is because they have not understood. They have not reckoned with those graces of our octave.

Remember, blessed ones, that the passions of heaven are not so far from the world. Again and anon, man will touch the hem of the garment of the radiance of our sphere with the fingers of his mind. He will momentarily feel and sense the great passion of our love for humanity. He will understand God's love as the love we manifest. He will understand God's love as an outreach into his heart to the heart of the world.

Over land and sea, over snow-capped mountain, over barren plain, wherever men are congregated, we come, often unheard, silently, because their ears are not open to our voice. They cannot hear because their ears are dulled by the surfeiting of the senses, because the quality of their life is strained with confusion and lack of purpose, because from [the time they were] a little child they have been disoriented by the philosophies of the world that have not satisfied the hungering soul within. Now we come once again and we plead with humanity to awaken to the travail in the Garden—the struggles between the human and the Divine—and those elements of destruction which seek to stop the flow, the gentle flow of God's grace to humanity.

It is not always enough that the wheels of karma and the wheels of the Law should turn in their courses, grinding up those magnificent currents that started out so well and so lovely to re-create the kingdom of heaven upon earth and then were diverted into channels of destructivity. Rightly so, then, have the Lords of Karma exercised their prerogative of returning to man what man has sent out. For in one sense, and in no vulgar sense at that, man is the God of his own universe.

When God said, "Take dominion over the earth,"[3] he surrendered his own prerogative to humanity. He gave and has given again. And all that man has imputed to him should be imputed unto them. For they and they alone, by their misuse of the privilege of life, have thwarted the magnificent descent of the grace of God, the higher elements of Christ consciousness, the understanding of that heart which is attuned to the angels and to the realm of nature and higher dimension.

So often the world trembles, even in the midst of their evildoings. For God within them becomes perforce a living rebuke to their actions and their thoughts. "How can they mouth thy Son who hath higher understanding?" is an indictment also of their failures to apprehend the real purposes of the kingdom of God, which are to wield the power and influence of brotherhood over the affairs and purposes of lesser men so that all may share in the converging of men upon the high hill of identity, where the living souls can at last be all that God is.

He will never surrender. The Father will never give to the sons the last farthing of identity until they have claimed it by reason of all that goes before the crown, the great blessing intensified upon their head.

As I come, trembling the gossamer veil betwixt heaven and earth, I say, the halt, the lame, the blind and those who are troubled of heart come often, and those who are well come seldom, to receive of our bounty and graces. But we love them all. And as time passes, by the vicissitudes of life men one by one come to a point of acceptance of many of the ideations of heaven they could not accept before.

But may I say, in a salutary manner, grace is before you, grace so glorious you could never in heart or mind conceive of it. And one day *you* will receive that grace as you bring yourself to the master's feet to kneel before the God flame upon the permanent altar of being—permanent because at last you have accepted its permanence, permanent because at last that permanence lives within you. Hence, the words of my Son "I am come that ye might have life, and that more abundantly."[4]

What a tragedy it is that the image of womankind in the world has been so blackened by deceit and by error. Yet all women destined to drink in to the divine womanhood become with me a joint Mother of the World. But it must become an accepted offering—I have offered; you have accepted.

You understand the need to bring forth the Divine Manchild both within yourself and in the world. The words of my Son "Suffer the little children to come unto me, and forbid them not"[5] become majestic, real and joined with cosmic purpose, magnificently portraying the love of the cosmic outreach—the outreach of God into the realm of the one who has gone astray. To bring him again to the fold is a task ever before you. Naturally, he must respond.

There is a point in the lives of men when they must learn to leave behind them the elements of their former life—the transitory and changing elements of their nature, those straws that they have grasped in their darker moments that have allowed them to be buoyed up—and to understand the grace that I AM.

Won't you accept the purpose of my Son and of every Son of God as universal? The Christ image is composite as tiny pieces in a puzzle or as atomic and electronic composition. It represents the body of Christ-substance to the world. All are able to drink into this, for the goblet of life is before you. Place it to your lips. Take it. Assimilate it. Use it. And build the kingdom of God upon earth. So all tragedy, all stark reality, all negative influences will fade away in the light and dawn of the Christ age that you can assist in aborning once again, fulfilling the purposes of God, fulfilling the purposes of man, fulfilling the regeneration of my Son, fulfilling the cosmic plan.

Great is the LORD and greatly to be praised![6] Let us pay honor and homage to his celestial glory, offered to the earth to enhance it electronically, thrillingly, radiantly, determinedly, until our purpose is once again born in the heart and made the fiat of eternity in the veil of time.

I thank you for your attention. I thank you for your energy and love. And I remain a mother to the world, the Mother of the World. Call me what you will, my love is still the same. It beckons.

And the hierarchy have said that midst all the danger of the world, our love, the outreach of our heart, shall intensify in the hope that mankind awaken to the darkness and see it for what it is, a misqualification of the light, and begin at last the requalifying process whereby they consciously part the veils between our octave and reach hands of love and light up to us and say: "O behold me. Guard me. Guide me in every moment. Keep me safe within the center of thy being. I commend myself into thy keeping."

So does the world learn to master the casting of their being upon the rock of the ages, the fortress of truth within man, as communion with heaven.

Colorado Springs, Colorado
May 30, 1971

9

Preparation of the Vehicles
of Consciousness

There is that light—that light that lighteth every man that cometh into the world[1]—that is spun from the heart of the World Mother as the swaddling garment that enfolds the white-fire light, the sacred flame upon the altar of the heart. It is like a gossamer veil that envelops the threefold flame, enabling it to manifest in the four lower bodies and at once in the plane of Spirit and the plane of the Mother.

How mighty is that flame that pulsates from the heart of the Great Central Sun, from the heart of the I AM Presence. How mighty is that flame that pulsates from the heart of the Great Central Sun and descends to connect with the consciousness of evolving man, making at once all of life that is able to recognize the greater effulgence, one in the nowness of eternity.

The mighty heart that pulses with the sound of the sacred Word from the center of the universe is heard in the chambers of man's heart. The beating of the mighty Word is man's life. And do you know, as man's heartbeat becomes through divine love congruent with the heartbeat of God, man receives the sacred engrams from each heartbeat that provide him with the nourishment of the fire of God's consciousness.

Now there is a ring of fire that is established round about each one that has proven himself worthy to receive this extraordinary protection from the I AM Presence. This ring of fire comes only to those who have entered into a certain level of harmony with the universe, with the Holy Spirit, with the I AM Presence. As it is written: "My thoughts are not your thoughts, saith the LORD,"[2] so there are some among you and among mankind who consider themselves to be advanced on the Path and also who consider that they have peace, the peace of the Christ, my Son.

I do not wish to disillusion you, precious hearts, for this is never the role of the Mother, but I only desire to teach you and to tell you that many who have thought that they had the inner peace of the Lord of the World had it not—but by contrast their consciousness was a seething vortex of emotional energies, of ideas and precepts not in keeping with those that are held in the mind of Christ, feelings and rumblings, disturbances. Some individuals who desire to be thought well among men put forth an aura of peace and sanctity, an appearance of calmness, when in actuality their being was not calm.

I wish only to tell you to examine the peace that you claim as your own and to see that that peace penetrates as a sword the very depths of your being until all is indeed peace to the very core of your experience. When you achieve that state of consciousness, the ring of fire, like a Van Allen belt,[3] will surround your being as a hoop of light, and you will come under the dispensation given to the adepts of a special protection that renders you in the world of form inviolate until the hour of your calling.

Now this specific protection was accorded to your messengers some time ago, at the time when they acquired that peaceful presence and that harmony with the Christ. And they have known in their hearts that the will of God and the destiny of their lives were locked in the hollow of his hand and that no evil thing could befall them, except that which is sent of God. And that which is sent of God, beloved hearts, is never evil, never an "energy veil," but only the subsequent and successive revelation of advancing glory in the teeming universe of the divine mind.

It is well, then, that those who desire to support the messengers and their mission seek diligently to earn this fire of protection, for until you have that established in your world, you may at any time find yourself becoming the unwitting tool of darkness in the presence of those who have and do seek the greater light. And so, as you advance along the Path, you find that greater and greater measures of understanding of hierarchy, of formulas that are given from the retreat at Luxor[4] are made available to you that you might acquire and master greater and greater degrees of perfection in your consciousness and anchor these in the world of form.

Mankind, and the devotees of the light included, require a flushing out of consciousness, of the four lower bodies. I remarked to this messenger, and she in turn made known to some of you the concept of the problem of the illumination of mankind. It actually boils down to the problem of the cleansing of the four lower bodies.

In order to have spiritual attunement it is necessary to have a certain percentage of transmutation within the etheric body. It is through the etheric, or the fire, body that man focuses in his outer consciousness the memory of God, of former lives, of former golden ages, and of the continuity of being that inspires the desire to attain glory and to attain eternity. Without memory, there is no contact with hierarchy. There is no self-awareness. Individuals who do not have memory do not know who they are even in the short span of an earthly life.

You will find, then, that the seekers on the Path, although many require the cleansing yet of the etheric body, all have one thing in common: A certain portion of the memory of God vouchsafed to them in the beginning is still near the outer awareness of their consciousness, near enough to enable them to transcend time and space and to remember the portals of eternity. These, then, are the devotees of the sacred fire and those who are not locked in dogma because of the dominance of the carnal mind and their inability to remember the true Word of God and the divine

Logos written in letters of living fire upon the consciousness.

The next classification of humanity are those who polarize to the mental body, those whose etheric bodies are sufficiently clogged that they must then operate from the level of the next most dense body—which is the body of the mind, which corresponds to the air element. These, then, can strive no higher than the mind will allow them. And if the mind is not the Christ mind but is dominated and superseded by the intellect, then these have only the reason of the outer consciousness and the education of the world to sustain and guide them. These often comprise the intelligentsia and those who direct from the level of the mental body the affairs of mankind and of the governments of the nations. For them, spirituality is remote. Some may concede that it has its place while others may not, depending on the polarization of the mind either to the Christ or to the lower self.

Those whose mental bodies are clogged to the point where they do not manifest enough intelligence to be students of any branch of human endeavor find that their energies, then, polarize either to the emotional or the physical body. Those who are centered in the emotions may also be divided into those who have God-control and those who do not. Those who do may be aware, keenly aware, of the feelings of God, of the Holy Spirit and of His Presence. They may be very devout in the religions of their choice and give forth praise in their service with the angelic hosts, who quietly, invisibly minister unto their needs.

Those without emotional control oftentimes comprise "the poor whom you have always with you," as Jesus said,[5] because there are always those at the bottom of the karmic ladder and the ladder of attainment who, because they have not passed the tests of harmony, cannot keep the supply that is entrusted to them. And so they are impoverished spiritually, mentally, emotionally and physically.

Those whose feeling natures have feeling neither for God nor man polarize in the physical body. These may be those who are insensate to anything but the needs of the physical body and to the physical senses. They may be [among] the laborers and they may be those who walk the earth without conscience and without soul awareness. They can be labeled as the "living dead," as can those with any form of misqualified energy in any of the four lower bodies. Thus, when we speak of "the quick and the dead"⁶ we speak of those who have been quickened through some avenue, some chakra or one of the lower bodies, to the mind of God and those who through the clogging of one or more of their four lower bodies are dead unto the Christ light.

There comes a time when those who walk the earth in the four lower bodies find that the clogging of those bodies is so great that they can no longer sustain life in this octave; and thus the transition comes as the result of the accumulation of human effluvia within the four lower bodies. To some it comes in this manner, and to others it comes because their karmic time is up or because they have earned the right to make the transition into another octave.

I bring to you these thoughts this morning so that you can see that the wise counsel of my Son, "This kind cometh not out but by prayer and fasting,"⁷ should be reflected upon by you to see which of your four lower bodies requires fasting. Some who accentuate fasting of the physical body neglect the fasting of the emotions from the cesspool of darkness. Or they neglect the fasting of the etheric body from those old records of the past. Or [they neglect the fasting from] the psychic thralldom of the mental body that ever probes and wonders about psychic revelations of past and future. And these are they who never attain mastery in the present.

So I say to you, the preparation of the four lower bodies is highly important at this hour, at this state of transition when the entire planetary body is required to ascend upon the spiral of the ascension current, to move forward in the evolution of the cosmos. This is the hour when if there are enough souls upon the planet who will purify and perfect their lower vehicles, then the kingdom of God may indeed manifest as the City Foursquare within their bodies and consciousness, making it a tangible focal point, an electrode for the hierarchy to outpicture the destiny of the two-thousand-year reign of the Son of God. It does not take many, as you have been told before, but it takes some—a few who are striving with a great intensity for the perfection of these vehicles.

Then the great burden of light that the hierarchy holds in abeyance shall be lowered into form. And as the new wine is poured into new bottles, those bottles shall not break but shall hold the sacred essence, the elixir of light that shall perpetuate the youth of the Divine Manchild unto the golden age.

I, Mary, come to you this day to give to you some of the instruction which you have recently heard at inner levels in our retreats so that you may begin the process of anchoring in the outer mind those facts and those figures of cosmos that are being vouchsafed to you each night as you journey to our retreats.

I expect you now to polish your etheric bodies by intense decrees to the purple fire, the crystal ray and the emerald ray,[8] so that you will not only be able to say, "Oh, yes, I seem to remember something like that," but so that you will be able to discourse on the subject without our having to key in the outer mind to the subject itself. This is our goal for you, but we need to have you be refined with the Refiner's fire[9] in all of your being and consciousness.

Behold, I come quickly. Behold, I come quickly.

Colorado Springs, Colorado
March 25, 1973

10

The Initiation of One Hundred and Forty-Four Sons and Daughters of Dominion

Sons and daughters of God, I am come this day in the action and consciousness of the little Virgin of Guadalupe,[1] and I am wearing the veil and the robe which Juan Diego saw and which was impressed by angelic hands upon his *tilma*. I come to electrify the memory of that appearance and to anchor once again in the forcefield of the basilica, in concentric rings of light, the memory of the virgin consciousness, the glory of the Woman and the care of the Mother for all of her children, great and small.

I come to my people. I come to my children—the lowly of heart, the poor, the uneducated, whose devotion to me is boundless.

Heaven is not against education or the development of the higher mind. But on Terra the initiations to receive the Christ mind have been so great that when the individual begins to pursue a study of God and his laws, the Luciferian complications are thrown upon him as a net over the consciousness, over the unfolding crown chakra. And by and by, hearts that would be pure and free in his grace are drawn into the pride of intellectual arrogance, of thinking they know more than they do by a mere amassing of facts rather than by the heartfelt absorption of precepts and knowledge from on high.

And so you see, the heart that is free of the Luciferian compromises is a heart whose devotion flows from untrammeled heights, from the depths of the soul and without the patterns of complexity that mark those consciousnesses which are farthest from the center of truth. Devotion of heart is a springboard to devotion of Christ's mind.

You see, then, I always recommend that students on the Path begin with the clearing of the heart chakra and that they center all of their meditations upon the heart. For the heart will never lead you astray. The heart will never allow you to make a mistake or to take the left-handed path.

With a pure heart, with the fire of love blazing eternally upon that heart, you have a sure foundation for the development of the other chakras, especially of the throat. For without love, when you release the power of the spoken Word, it sometimes carries a pattern of sharpness or condemnation or impelling God to obey the mandate of man. But when the heart chakra is developed, then the power of the spoken Word quivers on the bow of cosmos. And there is a quivering light across the vast filigree pattern, the veil of light that is the *antahkarana* of cosmic consciousness. And by your heart chakra and heart's love, you then pass through worlds beyond worlds on the arrow of the spoken Word which you release.

Guard, then, the heart. Guard its mastery. Forsake not its harmony. And take time in the day to stop and to listen to the tutoring of the heart.

You will also know, then, that when you see absolute perfection by the action of the All-Seeing Eye, you are then brought into an awareness of humanity's incongruities, their sins, their departures from truth. Without love, then, your judgments might be harsh. For when you see such deviation from truth in those around you, it is easy to fall into condemnation if you have not love.

Some of you wonder why, then, the third eye is not more open. It is because if you were to see more, you would have a greater responsibility to hold the immaculate conception regarding mankind. And with the vision of the All-Seeing Eye of God, it is absolutely mandatory that you affirm only good and recognize instantaneously that all that you see that is not of the light is, in the consciousness of God, unreal.

This quality in the heart of the Mother of the Flame* is a unique one. For all that she sees of the records and patterns of past lives of those who come before her, she is ever aware of the flaming presence of the Christ. This is a great gift. And because of this purity of heart and purity of vision, we are able to trust her with a worldwide endeavor of expanding the teachings in this hour when they are so needed.

Discrimination is a faculty that is such a fine line, such a razor's edge. For there are those dark ones and Luciferians whose wickedness and blackness is so great that if for a moment the Mother were to believe that that wickedness and blackness were real, the cause would be lost.

Take care, then, that you practice in developing this consciousness of knowing that only God-good has the power to perpetuate itself. All perpetuations of the energy veil occur by borrowing light from the one source. If you refuse to lend your light to the cause of the enemy, that cause will fail. It is as simple as that.

If you will close your eyes, that is, turn off the senses of physical seeing, and now meditate upon the inner seeing of light, I will come to you and expand your inner seeing. For I desire to give you a vision of heaven and a vision of the City Foursquare of pastel hue, of glorious floral arrays and gardens and birds singing and fountains playing and music gentle yet grandiose that comes from the fire-rings of the Great Central Sun. And every fire-ring has another form of music, another orchestration of millions of angels who release the soundless sound of the great Om and who release that sound as music.

Therefore, with the hearing ear of the soul, with the seeing eye of the soul, perceive this heaven. It is a dispensation which is given to you to have a glimpse of heaven and to retain the mem-

---

*The mantle of Mother of the Flame was transferred to the messenger Elizabeth Clare Prophet on April 9, 1966.

ory of heaven. For, you see, according to cosmic law, that which you are allowed to see of reality you must also be equipped to deal with in unreality. The greater the heights of reality which you behold, the greater the depths of darkness you will become aware of and for which you will be responsible to see not, to know not, but to transmute.

In the messenger's consciousness, then, there is now the awareness of the diametric opposite of the height which you are beholding. And in her mind's eye, she holds the balance so that you are not required to see the epitome of degradation which the astral hordes have chosen to make of the highest kingdom of God. Now you see, then, that to force the third eye is to come into an area of grave responsibility.

Gently, then, release your consciousness to your Christ Self, to your heart chakra, and be content to bask in the glow of love. For when you feel that glow of Helios and Vesta, of love-wisdom warmth upon the soul, you will know that the full-faceted mind of God and of Christ is also present, that God, who knows all things, is also in the basking of love, and that your consciousness, by being immersed in love, has also a contact at higher levels with all facets of that love, all ramifications of being and of the seven rays. But if it please the LORD, the Most High God, that you should only experience a portion of that total awareness within the heart, then I say, be content. Be discontent with human effluvia and invoke the flame to transmute it.

Be discontent with the actions and foibles of the ego and the pride and the will, but do not be discontent with the timetable of heaven's unfolding of the plan of your spiritual evolution. Have faith that you are in good hands—in the hands of angelic hosts and ascended masters, who dote upon you and who are concerned that you come up higher each hour, and in good trustworthy hands in the Keeper of the Flame² and in the Mother of the Flame.

Therefore, do not doubt your progress in this activity, for it is certain if you follow the teachings and practice them. Not to fret, not to worry, not to be concerned, but to know that if you do your part, heaven will multiply that part tenfold. This is the assurance of a Mother to her children, for the coming year will bring great progress to many of you. And yet many of you will not recognize footsteps of progress, for you will be so absorbed in the action of transmutation and you will not remember your former self and how far you have come from the point of origin.

Therefore this is an origin point of the release of cycles here in Mexico City, where there is an ancient focus of the heart chakra. And that focus was established by one soul who lived here who gave her life to the heart of God, who was a saint before it was known what a saint was or is or can be. By inner attunement, by intuition, but most of all by love for God, whom she personified in the light of the sun and the rays of the sun, this soul won her ascension by oneness with the heart of God, the heart of Christ and even the hearts of all mankind.

Thus [is] the record and the memory of one of those ancient priestesses who kept the flame in one of the twelve temples that surrounded the central temple of Mu. One life has left a record, and that one priestess did not fall with the others, did not forsake her duty and her calling to keep the flame. And she reembodied after that period of the temple experience and after the fall of Mu. And that final embodiment was the capstone whereby, you see, having been severed from the culture of Mu and from the precise memory of the rituals of the sacred fire, she nevertheless retained devotion, and devotion in itself, moving with harmony, became her victory and her crown.

Now you see why North Americans are often drawn to Mexico and Mexico City, because they desire also to find balance, which is the balance of heart. Yet you also have a focus of the heart chakra in St. Louis[3] and in Canada at the retreat of the Elohim

Heros and Amora. There at Lake Winnipeg, the release of love forms an arc to St. Louis, another arc to Mexico City and other arcs to South American cities, where some have kept the flame of devotion. And many have kept that flame, although not quite to that degree which was held by this soul.

Therefore I have brought with me this ascended lady master this day, whose name has not been revealed by the Brotherhood, whose name shall not be revealed this day. But in her devotion to my flame, to the Cosmic Virgin, many have called her Maria— Maria for Mary, for Mother ray. And that name will always be the impersonal-personal action of the feminine ray for all who espouse the raising of feminine life, feminine energies, for the exaltation of the masculine and of Spirit's release.

I am the guardian action of the immaculate conception, which is a filigree of lace pattern for each of the incoming avatars. Ten thousand and one mothers are being prepared, are receiving the veil of the Cosmic Christ, Maitreya. And that veil is a veil of innocence that is draped around each mother for the sealing of her consciousness from all evil, from all interference with the immaculate conception.

And the veil hangs to the ground, and thus the burden of having to look upon this world will be greatly relieved. For even though they do not know, these mothers will find that looking through the veil of the Cosmic Christ, the world and its density will seem a little far off, a little remote, a little removed. And those sordid aspects of human life will not register with as great intensity upon those who have the veil, for it is a veil of the secret-ray action of the going within.

Perhaps some among you are aware of having received that veil in this moment. Perhaps you did not know until this moment that you are a candidate to be the Divine Mother, the Mother of God, the mother of the incarnation of God. But now you know and understand that if you will do your part, heaven will bestow upon you every grace, every hope, every charity necessary to the keeping of the Word and of the inner vows.

And I would also say that when these avatars are born, they will also be born surrounded by an etheric veil—a special veil of white-fire substance that will seal them from the pounding and the beating of the rhythms and the harshness of the world. And this will enable you, as mothers of the Christ, to take that soul, through the early years of training to advanced years, to the place where divine manhood and divine womanhood will reveal to all mankind that God once again dwells with men.

I take into my arms the mothers-to-be. And Joseph, your beloved Saint Germain, stands over me with a consecration for those who bear the seed of Alpha. Holy, holy, holy art thou in manifestation, O man, O woman! For by God's grace you have been elevated to the place, the secret place of the Most High, where the Christ does appear as the thrust of lightning to the new year.

And those of you who are yet preparing, who have not received the calling for this cycle of lightbearers, remember, they are the first wave of beings. If their birth and incarnation are successful, then I am certain that the Lords of Karma will call forth other dispensations for other avatars to appear.

And so you see, the byword is to be prepared. For in the moment when you are prepared and when your consciousness is like crystal and the diamond of your being is centered in the Eye of God and you are in the center of that awareness, then, you see, you are a magnet. And from the farthest side of cosmos, a being of light will respond and will come to you and be born to you, as Jesus came to me and to Joseph.

So, we are here to proclaim that in the Aquarian age the Holy Family, the sacred Trinity, can be carved out as a destiny for all, as the salvation for all and as the greatest bulwark against the Luciferians, the fallen ones, the pride-bearers.

Remember that when marriage and holy union is a key to an

entire two-thousand-year cycle, that marriage and that union will come under the greatest attack of the dark ones that has ever been known before. And certain groups among mankind will revert to the tribe system and will affirm that it is not healthy for man and woman to commit their lives to one. And they will affirm that for the health and sanity of mind and body, it is necessary to go from one to one as animals—even lower than animals, for animals have a certain honor and a certain loyalty to one another.

So you see, precious hearts, the reason that I have released the rosary to you is because it is true, the family that prays together stays together. The reason that I have released the knowledge of the cosmic clock is because the Luciferians always, and remember that I said always, use the lunar energies and pit them against the holy union and the love of hearts united in service. You would be wise to follow the word of the Mother of the Flame to be diligent in calling for the transmutation, not only for yourselves but for all upon the planet, of the amplification of the electronic belt energies of the earth and of individuals.

As I pleaded to the children of Fátima to pray for the world, so I make my plea this day to you who already are praying for the world. But you see, it is always the case, those who are ready to assume responsibility are always called upon and given greater responsibility. But I tell you, as you increase your devotion and prayer, you will find that this body and the body of servers will reach the place where their awareness of light will create a critical mass that will burst forth and explode and be taken up and be multiplied, be absorbed and assimilated by millions among mankind.

And some of you ask, "Why are not greater numbers surrounding this focus and this flame?" You see, the numbers that are already here, though they be small, must reach a level of a certain requirement of holding energy and holding light and harmony.

You might say, then, that any failures on the part of Keepers of the Flame now associated with The Summit Lighthouse stands in the way of the total expansion and that any victory enhances the total victory.

You will see, then, that when this group of pilgrims has made the necessary sacrifices individually and collectively and passed the necessary initiations, then the Lords of Karma will say, "We will swell the ranks." For every one of you sitting here, five, ten, fifty, five thousand, could be drawn if I were but to raise my hand to Almighty God. But you see, I do not desire to see the weight of the multitudes and of their karma weigh you down and bow you down to the point where you can no longer function.

The Mother of the Flame is ready. She has been tested with the weight of many auras, many segments of the population, during certain periods. We know, then, that she can stand before the multitudes. But we are not certain that those who serve her, who are closest to her, who have the responsibilities of the care of the children, of the focuses, of the Church, of the administration, will also be able to withstand the great wave of the energies that come. For you see, every true teacher must hold the balance of light on behalf of every pupil until that pupil can carry his own weight and the weight of his karma and his electronic belt.

Everyone who is now tied to The Summit Lighthouse, then, has the grace and the action of the Mother flame holding the balance until he is able to transmute enough karma to hold the balance himself. Some of you have reached that balance and would stand fast no matter what. Others must yet learn how to handle vast quantities of energy that come suddenly as riptides, as tidal waves of darkness.

Many times just in the moment when you have concluded decrees and you are feeling a great bubbling joy and a childlike innocence, suddenly a wave of substance descends with a *whump!* and pounds upon your being. And some of you have handled that energy well, but others have put forth whirlpools and vortices of irritation that then, you see, can tip the balance of the inner core of devotees around the Mother.

Every messenger, prophet or avatar has that staff who have devoted themselves to upholding the flame so that when the avatar is holding the flame for millions, the inner circle can keep the flame for the preservation of the body temple [of that one] and for the details that surround life in this octave. To Jesus were assigned twelve disciples, Joseph and myself, the other seventy and many holy women who kept that flame while he labored in travail to carry the cross for humanity. And so you see, let not your minds enter the criticism of the Luciferians which is heaped upon you during this cycle of Capricorn. For the Luciferians whisper condemnation and they say, "If the messenger were pure, the activity would be worldwide and there would be millions here. If this were really the truth and really the Law, why isn't it every-where understood and proclaimed?"

I would remind you of the limited acceptance of Jesus the Christ and of his teaching, how many, many more turned away from the teaching than there were those who accepted it. And as the teaching became more intense, then many fell back and left the Lord, for they could not understand how they must eat the flesh and drink the blood of the Son of man. For their con-sciousness could not make the transition from outer symbol to inner reality, and yet the literal emphasis of that teaching was also true.

To activate the expansion on a world scale that we anticipate, it is our desire to prepare 144 sons and daughters of the domin-ion of the water element as the white-fire core surrounding the messenger. These devotees, when fully trained, fully harmonious, will comprise the locking of the light that will withstand all attempts of the dark ones to tear down the central flame and the focus where the Word of God passes from the plane of Spirit to the plane of Mater.

When you think of it, that this body temple through which I speak* is the only contact we consider sure and accurate that is also combined in the being of an initiate who has enough attainment to withstand the wiles of the devil, when you think how frail is the physical being and how it is the throat chakra that is the very nexus between heaven and earth, you will understand that heaven would much rather release the teaching into the hands of the few and preserve the life of the messenger than attempt to expand to the point where none could keep the balance of energy.

Now then, there are definitely certain numbers who could be counted this moment in the 144. I, then, will work with the messenger this year to see that 144 disciples and holy women are initiated into the Order of the Sons and Daughters of Dominion, that is, if those who are called and choose to accept the calling then will make themselves ready. And if you believe—by the love of my heart, by the sign of the fleur-de-lis and the forget-me-not—that you have already been called to be one of the 144, then make this known to the Mother of the Flame so that she may suggest and also deliver from my heart certain outlines for self-purification and for the strengthening of the fibers of the four lower bodies to be chalices for the living flame.

Then you must understand that in addition to this fiery core, the next ring of devotees must also surround the fiery core to protect the 144, and then another ring and then another ring. And each ring faces the center and determines to protect those in the next ring above. And by this hierarchy, this ladder of light as concentric forcefields, you will see the opportunity for all mankind to rise one day to the center.

I say, then, that some among mankind who would come to

---

*Refers to the messenger Elizabeth Clare Prophet. In 1973 the messenger Mark L. Prophet made his transition to higher octaves and is now the Ascended Master Lanello.

that center would find the white heat that is a coolness in the Mother, a concentration of such energy as to ravage their beings. To expose them mercilessly to this fire of God is not our wish. And therefore, you see, we are arranging that those of you who are graduates of the Ascended Master University should form the nucleus of activity, of service and of learning so that those who come directly from the mass consciousness may first feel the gentle fires and the release at a certain level of attainment which you have.

It is the responsibility of each one, when encountering a student, to at least bring that student to the level where you are. You can be expected to do no more, for you cannot impart what you are not, what you have not. And so, if you can bring a certain portion of mankind to your own level of devotion, then you can pass that student to those who are above you in training, advancement and levels of hierarchy. And this is how life is in your schools and universities. When a teacher has taught all he can teach to an artist, to a musician, he will then humbly recommend that his pupil be given higher training by a greater master.

We desire, then, that you should go forth two by two to give forth the teachings, to begin the leavening of mankind's consciousness, to prepare the way so that one day millions, having gone through the screen of your attainment and consciousness, can also sit at the feet of the masters so that they can take the extraordinary releases of fire which we will be giving in our dictations.

The century is wide with opportunity, yet the way is straight and narrow. Remember that you compromise not, that you do not allow students hungering after truth to cause a compromise of your energies, to lower your energies to their level. For your responsibility is to raise their energies to the level of their own Christ Self and your own Christ-attainment.

And so you see, it is no small matter. Hierarchy has a responsibility, the responsibility of keeping the flame and keeping open the door to octaves of light. We, then, await your response, and we shall see what you shall do in the first six months of 1974. And when the Lords of Karma meet once again, you will be apprised at the Freedom conference what additional dispensations for the expansion of the activity can be given.

In the meantime I say, go with God! Go with the Mother! Give gratitude for the presence of the light in your midst. And support the mission of releasing the teachings in print and on tape and on videotape for posterity and for people everywhere.

I am the guardian action of the Mother flame. And I take my leave of you now to go to minister to the people of Russia and the people of China, for their hearts are calling and they are tugging on my love. And my love responds and my angel bands come with me as we seek to give comfort to those souls who are waiting for this teaching. May you find a way to deliver it unto them quickly.

Until that hour, my love is the bulwark of their strength, their faith and their hanging on because of their great faith in the day of salvation and the day of the coming of Jesus Christ. Through tortures beyond your imagination, they have withstood. And they wait as true Christians, devotees of the flame, for the Second Coming of Christ.

I AM, then, the universal Mother but the very personal mother of each heart and soul upon Terra and upon other worlds, which I will tell you about at another time.

Adieu, precious hearts. I love you.

Mexico City, Mexico
January 1, 1974

11

The Flame within Your Heart

Keeping the flame through the midnight hour, as shepherds kept their flocks by night, so does the Keeper of the Flame, the Maha Chohan, keep the flame of life on behalf of mankind. In this service of light, you see how the spark ignited from one fire does bring forth rows and rows, tiers of the Christ consciousness. And yet all is the one flame.

And so, teach your children how God is one God, yet multiplied again and again. And so there is one Christ, one Lord, one begotten of the whole, and yet that infinite fire repeating itself over and over again—the old, old story of the incarnation of the Word. Look again and see how the sacred fire becomes the center of a galaxy, whirling fire sending forth other fires higher and higher.

And so you see, as you meditate upon the flame before you, the image of the face of God in the center of the flame. And so you see the Central Sun. So you see yourself. And so you know with absolute certainty that if you determine to be the Christ, to accept that torch from Father-Mother God on high, you can ignite a world, you can set afire the hearts of millions and billions of souls. And that energy is limitless. The fire is always there. The source of the energy is always there.

And so the threefold flame within your heart was lit at birth by the taper of the Maha Chohan, who came to you and to your mother's side, breathed the breath of life and, lo, the spark of immortality merged with the clay form, and the Word became flesh.

Some among mankind do not understand how Spirit could mesh with Mater. And I ask you, how can the fire, even the physical fire, mesh with any of the elements? It is not like any, yet the source of all, yet consuming all in the ritual of transmutation. And so, Spirit does indeed merge with flesh. Spirit is the fire in the core of the cell, the atom, the molecule, in the center of the heart and each flaming chakra.

So is the fire the gift of God to mankind in this season, when we, as the angelic hosts, celebrate the coming, not of one Son of God but of many, the coming of our Lord Sanat Kumara and the response of Prince Siddhartha of the clan of Gautama. So we celebrate the moment of the passing of the fire when the hand of God reaches out to the hand of man and there is that energy flow. And a god is born! And a universe is born! And solar fires echo the fire of creation.

So is life the passing of a torch. And so as you were given the kindling spark at birth to abide for a time, for a season, in this form, so you will know that as the cycles progress, as the cycles turn, there will come a time when the Presence of the I AM will take up that fire and take up that soul into higher octaves. And you will flow with that fire. You will go wherever it goes, for you have become one with the flame. And you will ascend on high, entering into etheric octaves and the planes of the Christ. And if you have prepared well and dipped into that flame with regularity and with system, you will find yourself wholly acceptable. And the flame that you are will merge with the flame that is, and the one flame out of which all came will be your identity— immortal, forever free.

I am your Cosmic Mother if you will have me as your Cosmic Mother. I am the Mother ray, and I flow wherever there is life aborning. I come and I place my cheek upon your own in the tender caress of a mother's love that you might know simply on this Christmas Day that he cares for you, that he cares for you, my children, that the Father is aware of your heart—your heart's longing to serve, to be free, to express individuality.

It is written that God is of too pure eyes to behold iniquity.[1] And yet, I say, the universal Christ is an aspect of the Trinity dwelling in the monad of God himself. And therefore, in the principle of the Logos and the very tender nearness of the Mother flame, God knows. For even the very hairs of your head are numbered.[2] So are the cycles of energy's release.

So mankind, so children of my heart, I come. I come to burn from you by a fire that is beyond the physical flame the scales of cynicism, the weight of the world, the burden of aloneness. I come to the aged, to the sick, to the dying. I come to those aborning unto those who are brave enough to take up the challenge of living for love. I come to one and all. And I come (as my angels come with me, Raphael and angels of the healing flame) carrying the taper of the sacred fire, and I touch it to your aura. And I come to burn away the dross, all impediments to your awareness of reality.

I come. And I am the Mother so close at hand, ready to step through the veil, ready to impart to you the knowledge of your mastery in time and space, the understanding of being an unascended master of cycles. And now I merge my aura with your own. Rest. Be at peace. For it will atone for every lack and every loss, filling to the brim your cup of life with sacred liquid fire flowing as water from the fount of everlasting essence.

So, then, in the name of the firstborn, I command the energies to flow into the matrix of the living Christ! So let the Word be made flesh! So let the fire press to the cause and core of all that would hinder the plan of life. So be immersed in the fire of the spirit of the Christ Mass, and know he cares for you. Know that he knows wherever you are, your thoughts, your feelings.

It is sometimes more than mankind can imagine that God— as a unity, as a oneness, as a whole—could be aware of a creation of duality, of manifold aspects. Yet, this is the nature of the Infinite One. And you can see were you to form a circle and to place all your candles in the center, there would be one fire, and that fire would be as God—God a magnificent flame, yet a oneness that is an infinity of aspects, of facets, of fires that can move and glow and focus individuality and then return and be the one flame.

This is what you are, my children. This is what he came to proclaim. This is Christmas. This is joy. This is the warmth of the eternal Father. He cares for you.

And so I say, knowing that you have the listening ear of the Almighty through angels upon angels upon angels, speak to God this night. Tell him of your desire to fulfill the plan divine, and ask for guidance. Tell him whatever is upon your heart. And pray for loved ones, for the sick and those who are sick because they have gone out of the way of cosmic law, those who are called sinners who have simply departed from the walk with life. Pray for them, for, you see, as mankind have invoked the Christmas angels, there are many emissaries of the Godhead ready with the energy of far-off worlds to answer your call and your prayers.

And mankind do not know that on Christmas Eve there is a very special flow, as Christmas Eve becomes the first faint rays of Christmas morn. It is a time for special intercession, for dispensations, for answers to prayer. For heaven, too, celebrates the birth of the Christ, and the gifts of God to mankind in this hour are gifts unto the Christ Self of each one to facilitate the Christ consciousness within the soul. And so, in celebration of the Word incarnate, there come the emissaries from on high to answer prayer.

So, then, I well remember that hour when the first Mother of the Flame kept the vigil for youth through the midnight. And I remember the hour of my coming unto her with the promise of the ascension, and I remember how the ascension was fulfilled. And standing with me this night is your own beloved Clara Louise, the lady Clara,[3] who assists in amplifying the power, the wisdom and the love of the resurrection. I recall these events for you, for I desire that you should understand the nonexistence of time and space and how a life of service passes so quickly, so quickly.

Behold, I come quickly! So comes the Spirit of the Lord. I say to you, the flame that is in your hand,[4] symbolizing the flame that is in your heart, is the promise of your own ascension. Far more than my promise could attest is this flame of life, which God the Father has placed within you, which God the Mother has nourished. Do you see, then? As tangible as the physical flame is the flame within your heart. And because that flame is real, you are real. You are real as sons and daughters of God. And reality burns through you now! For it is my will before the Almighty that reality should burn in you the awareness of your immortal destiny!

Some of you have thought, perhaps not too seriously, upon the hour of your ascension. Well, I say, think now upon it. For this cause came ye into the world. For this cause was he born, that you might be liberated from the rounds of rebirth and the rounds of density and the laws of mortality. And so, the birth of the Christ is the birth of the promise of the ascension as the liberation of *all* mankind.

I desire to impress upon this body and this consciousness and all of the body of God upon earth this night the reality of the ascension, the nowness of the ascension. For the goal *is* fulfilled now and the promise is now. For there is only the eternal Now, precious hearts.

And you will hear my words ringing in your ear ten, twenty, forty, fifty, eighty years hence when you make your ascension in the light. And you will have that flashback to this moment when I proclaimed, "The ascension is *now!*" And you will say, "Yes, my mother, it *is* now. It is now in this moment and there is no other moment in all eternity but the moment of my ascending consciousness."

And in that arc of light and in that flash to that distant point in time and space where you heard these words, you will suddenly realize that the arc that spans the centuries is the arc of transmutation whereby time and space are no more, infinity is one. And you will say, "There never really was any time, and I never really was ever locked in space but only a seeming, only the veils of maya. And so I AM alive forevermore! I AM alive forevermore. This is my natal day! This is my ascension into love."

So, then, if there is no time or space, I say, where is the cup? Where is the vessel that holds the clay, the sin, the error, the darkness, the rebellion and the pride? That cup, too, is but a point of reference that is no more the moment you contact infinity. Contact it now in my aura, in my presence. Know the Infinite! Know the Eternal! Know that there is no time or space or place within you that can hold the qualification of separation, of doubt or fear. For consciousness is one. Life is one. And only God can live in infinity! Only God is the eternal Now. I AM, you are that eternal Now and that vow I AM.

And so, precious hearts, if you would be free of sin, of darkness, of decay, be free of your consciousness of relativity. Go into the white-fire core of that flame within you and know the presence, the presence of reality. And keep that reference point. Keep it daily. Keep the flame. Keep the presence, keep the consciousness of infinity. And then, perform your works, your love and your loving in time and space, but always know that your reference point is infinity. And by your knowing this, you will not be caught up nor be caught in that relativity. It will not be altogether subjective, but it will be an objective awareness of a forcefield into which you project the flame and the fire.

And now you see the heat that can be generated by one flame. Now you see what many flames can do. Now you see the cross that is formed in these rooms by the configuration of your flames. It is the cross of life. It is the cross which you carry. Remember he said, "My burden is light."[5] For he knew the relativity of time and space, and to him that cross was a cross of fire. And that cross was the point of transmutation where all sense of time and space and the lodging of darkness in time and space was consumed at the point where Alpha meets Omega. Therefore, carry the cross of fire and win your crown by your awareness of the eternal Now.

Won't you think upon my words, meditate upon this experience and realize—in those moments that come now and then when you are caught up in the maya of moments moving into other moments, as crisis moves into crisis—won't you think of these words. Won't you think of this science of truth whereby you can be an inhabiter of infinity now and also a dweller of planes—planes known as time and space, planes where you project the infinity of your I AM Presence.

I came to give you a larger view. And do you know that this view of life is the view that Jesus held as he descended *consciously* into form? How few among mankind ever descend consciously.

Coming forth out of the I AM Presence, the star of his appearing, coming out of the fires of infinity, descending into that finite form, he proclaimed the eternal fiat and held within his heart throughout those thirty-three years[6] the memory of infinity. Be quickened by his memory. Be quickened, O my children, and you will nevermore be lost here below. But you shall always know I AM here! And I AM there! And, *lo*, I AM come to do thy will, O God!

So, the entire warp and woof of the creation is for the projection of light from your I AM Presence, for the exercise of light, and for your coming into the new dawn of the consciousness of the One.

I AM your Mother of fire. Fiery fire-star Mother, I AM within the flame.

Now I take my leave of you. And the angels who have come circle the earth with me as we continue our watch this Christmas Day. But we leave with you the token of our presence and the memory impressed upon your etheric body of your soul's habitation in the infinite light.

I love you, I love you, I love you forevermore.

Santa Barbara, California
December 25, 1974

12

Grids and Forcefields for the Hour of Victory

Children of my heart, come into the arms of the Divine Mother and find surcease from all of life's toil. Come into the heart of the Divine Mother and find there the chamber of light where the votive candle burns [in] a perpetual novena on behalf of the salvation of souls.

Angels of Raphael's band, angels of the Mother ray, come forth now! And let these children of the one light know the bliss and the love and the oneness of that love which is shared through the flame of the Mother.

I come to touch your hearts with the love of the Cosmic Virgin, that you might bear unto mankind that softness, that gentleness, that tenderness which melts even the hardest of hearts who have turned away from my Son. Yes, the soft answer turneth away wrath.[1] Won't you, then, be gentle toward one another, compassionate, forgiving, long-suffering, understanding that through love mankind might be drawn into the hallowed center of the law of life.

I come in the flame of love, and the flame of love has many facets. It is crystal clarity of a glass of the new wine that Jesus has partaken of in the Father's kingdom[2] with the saints and ascended beings who have returned to the lily fiery core of being in the ritual of the ascension.

And so that goblet now is suspended before you, not the goblet of the Last Supper but the goblet that is from ascended master octaves, which Jesus does share as that new wine of the

Spirit with all who have come to that level of Christ-awareness in the ascended state. This is the cup of the Christ consciousness, which he holds, receiving the essence of the Spirit of God.

You who would drink the wine with him in the kingdom, come into the heart of a mother. Come now and be purged of all desiring that is outside of God.

Do you not understand that you are bound by your desires? The desire to acquire, to be thought well of, to receive the adulations of the world, the desire for success, for things—all of these create a magnet of attraction, attracting to you the object of your desiring. And as these objects come into the center of being and the vortex that you have created, they displace the precious distillations of the new wine of the kingdom, of a mother's heart and the flow of a mother love.

Do you see also that that which is repellent to you, that which is anathema to you, is also a magnet, drawing to you, as Job said, the thing which you feared most?[3]

And so you see, the magnet of man's desiring has two sides, and he can never be free until he is free of all desire save God's desire for life everlasting. Desiring to be God, to be love, to be of service is not wrong desire. It is a whirling sun that replaces all carnal desire.

Do you not see, then, how the fallen ones hold up before the children of light the baubles and trinkets of this world, causing them, by a commitment of their funds and their energies, to become entangled in the commerce of the fallen ones who have the mark of the beast?[4] And so all of these things and all of these possessions reinforce the binding of the souls of mankind to the planes of unreality, to the planes which are a perversion of the body of the Mother.

Now, as you are in the aura of the angels of the All-Seeing Eye of Mary, All-Seeing Eye of Cyclopea, as you sit in the flame of living truth, which these spirits of fire have become, you see clearly, as though through crystal waters of a mother's love, all of the attachments, all of the burdens, all of the things of this world that have detoured you from the Path century by century. Yes, there is a way that seemeth right unto a man and the end thereof are the ways of death.[5]

Now then, let go. Let us suppose for a moment that there is nothing in this world that you desire or that can take you from the path of the fulfillment of God. Release, then, that desiring into the flame and feel yourself freeborn—a soul that is free to come and go from this house of clay, to leave the body at will and to return.

Your treasures are in heaven, for that is where your heart is.[6] And therefore you grace the earth with a presence and a flame, a ministering spirit, an arc of truth and a fiery lodestone, defending the children of God as a mother defends her flock.

Feel yourself, oh, so free from the things of the world, and see how God is to you all things, how he is love and compassion and mercy, your very self. And when you make that attunement with the Father and the Mother of life, you feel the flow of devotion that makes contact with the heart of a living presence. And you see how by your attention the flow is sustained, and you receive the gentle rain of love upon your face and you feel the caress of the wind of the Holy Spirit. And you move midst nature and the grasses and the trees and the flowers. And all of these are there to grace your path, and yet you are attached to nothing except the fiery flame.

And you see that the arc of your attention is the sacred flow. And through an unguarded moment or an absence of attention or a distraction, you lose the contact; and all of a sudden, you feel an absence and the loss of radiation. And you feel bereft and outside of the Presence of God, and so you renew your invocations and you place your attention upon the heavenly hosts and the Divine Mother. The contact is reestablished, the flow is restored, and you are whole again.

And so, having tasted of the new wine, of its flow into being, into consciousness, you realize that all of the desiring of your being and of your soul is to return to the center of being, where God is, to proclaim that being here and now, to be that fountain and that pool of living water that flows by the arc of your devotion. And so, you understand at last the meaning of his words "Pray without ceasing."[7] For the moment you cease to pray, you lose the contact.

What, then, is prayer? Prayer is the walk with God, the communion cup that is shared. Prayer is love for one another and doing the service of God in man. Prayer is a handiwork. Prayer is action. Prayer is the arrow shot from the heart, making its mark in world service. Prayer is the speaking of the Our Father and of the Hail Mary.

Prayer is loving life free. Prayer is seeing the good in all. Prayer is not taking offense nor being offended by any part of life, but loving and continuing to love and to love and to love. Prayer is the understanding that the flow of love is the balance which all life requires. Love is the union of Alpha and Omega, and prayer is the release of the energy of that union.

And as you release that energy through your heart to everyone, you soothe the frightened child, you soothe those who are possessed and obsessed by the fallen ones. You are the healing presence of life. And so you continue that long-suffering, that walk that goes on and on and on until you are called home to the throne of God.

Pray without ceasing.

There are some among mankind whose activities may be beneficial in the human sense, but they perform these activities for the benefit of the human and of the human consciousness. They do not make the contact with God. They do not desire to glorify his name and to invoke that flame. And therefore, with all of their living and all of their giving, they have not the flow of the arc of devotion. And therefore it cannot be said of them that they pray without ceasing.

Do you understand that perpetual prayer is the commitment of the heart as a living flame? It is the commitment to stand in life in defense of the Mother flame come what may. This is love and the overcoming victory of love.

So, then, as you set the cycles in motion within your being and consciousness, as you let the cycles roll for a twenty-four-hour perpetual novena of living prayer to my Son, to God the Father and God the Mother, understand that the momentum you carry in waking hours will cycle through and carry you through the hours of sleep. And you will find yourself beyond this plane, beyond this temple, your soul in the service of the light, continuing in that perpetual prayer.

Those who have not this momentum find that they are cast adrift in the astral sea in the hours when their souls are apart from the body form. Therefore, there is a discipline, there is a nurturing of a flame, there is a flow in the chakras that is necessary for you to be counted among those whose prayers rise as the incense of devotion, of distillation of the soul, of fragrance sweet unto the Maker and the Creator of all.

I am Mary, the Mother ray, and I come now with grids and forcefields for the hour of victory and of the victory of the Mother flame within you. Do you understand that a forcefield is a field of energy that is condensed, concentrated according to a particular pattern, a molecular pattern, as photons of light converge for a cosmic purpose?

A forcefield, then, is a grid of God's mind. It is like a strainer with a definite pattern and design. And as that strainer is placed upon the chakra of each one, the precious heart chakra, the energies of that chakra flow through the grid to release to all life everywhere a certain blueprint, an imprint of the mind of God. This is fohatic light! This is energy of the Great Central Sun! This is the dedication of life by the Lords of Flame from Venus!

And so, for the hour of victory, there is required a concentrated momentum of a release of certain types of energies across the planetary body. We come, then, bearing grids and forcefields designed by Omega for each one—a peculiar people with a peculiar pattern, so a specific invocation, so a divine calling. So let the action of the light, then, flow.

Now the angels of Mary and of Raphael come forth to those who make the call by free will silently now within. To you, then, come the angels, placing a grid that will be for the activation and the magnification of the blueprint of your heart chakra, which is destined to be the center of God's desiring, God's desiring to be.

The grids are placed upon you. And henceforth, the swirling of the threefold flame within your heart and its mighty outpouring and release will be according to a cosmic pattern that makes of you, one and all, a part of the *antahkarana* of the planetary body of world servers.

Needless to say, these grids of light are complementary. Each of them is unique, each of them interacting as the gears in the great wheel of life, interacting for a flow. This is the communion of the Holy Spirit.

As you are one in the flame of the heart, so all grids become one in the grand mandala of the Great Central Sun. As Sons and Daughters of Dominion and Keepers of the Flame are added into the consecration of these world servers, they who read or hear this dictation may make the invocation that that special grid and forcefield held in the heart of the I AM Presence be released and sealed in the heart chakra. And I will come with Raphael and it shall be done as the consecration of your life to service.

So, then, one by one we shall add to this matrix of light until 144,000 souls upon Terra are carrying that grid for the hour of victory, and that will be the fulfillment of a certain mandala. And from that point [and] beyond, there will be a multiplication of grids as more and more among mankind come into the forcefield of the spheres of the causal body of the Divine Mother.

So let the original 144,000 who receive the grid, who keep the momentum and who keep true to the law of life be counted as the fiery core of the causal body, as holding the torch of the virtues of the Cosmic Virgin in that fiery core. And let those who follow thereafter, then, be in the succeeding circles of the causal body until the entire planetary home, filled with light and with the light of Keepers of the Flame, is drawn into the sacred fires of the ascension and the hallowed circle of the Om.

As Above, so below, this is the hour of victory! So I come in grace, in beauty and in glory. So I come to seal all in the immaculate concept of your origin in purity. This is my love. This is my rosary, my offering this day.

I place about you now a garland of roses, a sacred garland of light. It is a gift of my heart gladly given, even as I gladly give my life that you might live.

And so let life be the eternal flow of Mother love as we commune each morning in the flame of the rosary for the victory of the souls of all mankind. So let it be, children of my heart.

Remember, at any hour when you seek the comfort and compassion of the Mother, call to me and I will take you in my arms and hold you close. And you will receive the comfort that you knew as a little child in your mother's arms. And then you will go forth again conquering and to conquer. This is victory. This is love. This is eternal life. I AM Mary.

Los Angeles, California
March 28, 1975

13

The Prayer of the Mother of the World

In the diamond heart of the World Mother is the light of hope, and hope is the fire of the resurrection unto the ascension of the Mother.

This is the year of the crown of the Mother's rejoicing. This is the year of the crown of resurrection's flame—a crown to be worn, a crown to be the focal point of light for the resurrection of sons and daughters of God upon earth.

I come with this crown of resurrection's fires. And I come to bestow upon your Mother of the Flame the crown of the Mother of the World for 1976, that the office in heaven and on earth might be sustained by our joint effort. I come with the Mother to be the Mother, to be the teacher, to be the bride of the Holy Spirit. I come with the Mother to be the beloved of the Buddha.

I will be in heaven and on earth her light and her flow, her crown and her Christ Child borning now in the womb of time and space. The Christ Child appearing is the one light in the hearts of all who would drink of the fount of the light of Alpha. And so you will see how the flame of the eternal Christos within her heart will magnetize the protection and the perfection of the coming avatars and for those who are already here living among you as the adorable ones.

I am Mary, the Mother of Jesus. That he might be born within you is my prayer. I am the Mother who knocks at the door of your heart. Are you ready to receive me that I might give birth to the Christ Child within?

I come to release the resurrection flame within your heart to resurrect the fiery destiny of your own work of art. I come to place the resurrection fires in the heart of America and in the heart of every nation where my name is pronounced as the Mother of God. I come to resurrect the purpose of light and to set the fiery matrix for rebirth, regeneration, clearing the way for the seventh root race.

This is the year of your opportunity to be the disciplined ones. This is the year of your opportunity to be freedom's sons and daughters. Such a year of joy, of newness of life, of miracles flowing from the hands of the Mother! Such a year of healing and of clearing the way by the waters of life!

I AM the Mother ray within you. And when you know me, you know the white goddess within you, whose energy will rise and take your soul to the place of the heart.

Let peace now be in the heart of the Mother. Let peace be in her soul. Let peace be in the hearts of her children, for all is well. And life is real and life is joyous, and life is the fulfillment of the wholeness of God.

I come to you in the midst of my novena in the Great Central Sun unto the Buddhic light and the light of ages. My novena is for peace on earth, goodwill, for enlightenment, for purity, especially for healing and for graces, and for souls to love one another, to minister unto one another. And my vigil with the Lord of the World is that freedom and God's will might dominate society in every land, from the least unto the greatest.

Each year at this time, I pass the novena, preparing for the new year. For I am seeking dispensations for the children of God. And I must give energy from my heart that the Almighty One might give to me those gifts and graces that are for the gentle caring, the understanding, the simple needs of little children and mothers and fathers—yes, the simple needs of the simple people of the world, many of whom have not any supply, not even enough to have shoes or proper clothing. And yet they come to the place consecrated in my name to pray with flowers they have picked, with their love, with their prayers, even their superstitions. These little ones are my own, and I am the only one who cares for them, not the state or the government or others who are too busy to notice these little lambs of God.

Precious ones, if you were I, looking into the eyes of the hopeful ones, who have no other hope but in the Mother ray, I tell you, you would respond as I respond. And God the Father, who hears my prayer, also responds. And I convey to them through my hands and my Sacred Heart the joy that makes them happy and for much of the time unaware of their poverty.

But, precious ones, if they are unaware of their poverty, the fallen ones are not. The rulers of this world who have within them that wickedness of the high places, they come to take advantage of my little children. In South America, in Central America, in this nation, in Africa, in the Middle East, in the streets of the great cities of the world, it is my little ones whom they seek. They seek to deprive them of their light, to take from them their energies, to keep them in a perpetual labor not of the love of God but in service to the state. They control them by keeping them in ignorance. And ultimately they plan to use them, to rally them, to stir them to support a one-world state under the direction of the fallen ones. They use my children because my children carry the true light of God.

I come to you who have a more than ordinary opportunity, who are educated, who have supply, who have understanding of advanced forms of government. I solicit your aid. My children need the arm of your protection, your love, your instruction. They need the ring-pass-not sealing them from being the victims of darkness. Take care of my children, Keepers of the Flame.

I come to you with my prayer. I kneel before the Christ Child born within you. I come to see the Bethlehem babe. And I know the light of that Child will enable you to raise up in purity the certain defenses against all of the sophistications and the weapons

and the fallen ones, who are moving in with their plots, so confi-
dent that they are able to overturn the plan of the Great White
Brotherhood.

They are duped by their overlords. They know not or they
believe not the prophecy of the coming of the Faithful and True,
my own beloved Son and the armies of heaven.[1] They have not
seen the hosts of the LORD camped round about on the hillsides
of the world.

And so, as the approaching armies of light and as the scurry-
ing of the fallen ones proceeds, I come. I come and I say, catch
them in your arms, my children—old and young, some tired and
ready for the next world, and some tired when they are born. Protect them from the Evil One. This is the prayer of my Son.

My Son did not declare that this world is evil. He asked that
the children of God might remain in the world to glorify God, to
enshrine a flame, to seal Mater for my coming in this age. His
prayer was and is today, as it is my own, the protection of these little ones.

Will you carry on with the service of Clara Louise, giving your
vigil for youth and the incoming children?[2] The need has never
been greater. Let them be protected from the chemicals, the harshness of the world, from those who have not the Mother flame or
the Mother light.

So many babies in cradles on Terra this night. I kiss them all
good night, each and every one. They wait my coming. They
breathe a little sigh in their sleep, and they know that I have been
there.

And sometimes, for many, this is the only real love of mother
which they feel in an entire day, so busy are the parents of this
world in other things. They do not understand the needs of little
children, how they wait—how they wait for the footstep of father
and mother, how they wait for the homecoming.

When you see your children, let your attention be undivided.

Let them know that they are the most important ones in your life. Let them feel your concern and your understanding of their dreams and their fairies and their dolls and their hopes for their future and their questions.

And when they say, "Mommy, I have to tell you something," it is not the something which they have to tell which is important. It is the telling in itself, for the telling is their communion with your heart. And sometimes when you say yes, they will forget what they had to tell you, they are so excited that you are listening.

You can be mother and father to millions of souls. You can come with me at night as your souls depart your body temples for etheric levels. You can assist these precious ones in form to feel the wholeness of God.

Many of you are here because I sealed you in my love from your very first breath, that you might be protected from circumstances of your own karma, which otherwise would have left scars too deep for you to appreciate the ascended masters. And so you see, the intercession of the Mother is all-including, all-encompassing, pervading the little aspects of life that make life worth living, the little needs, the gentleness, which bring the smile of joy and turn the rain into the sunshine.

There are many who have need of you this night, many who are calling out the name of Mother. They yearn for her coming. Be unto them Mother. Let your soul be infused with the Mother light of your own being and impart it, for this is the true and only healing. This is the true and only joy—the joy of giving and of watching the plants, the elementals, the sylphs and the undines, the children and people of all ages come to life because you have loved them. And this coming to life is the work of Mother in this age.

Join hands, then, in your souls and in your minds and in your hearts. Join hands for the victory of the Mother. And know that as you give The Mystery of Surrender[3] with me, you are allowing a very special order of angels to enter into the service of mankind, the order of the angels of light's surrender. And they come to minister to the children of God as they pass their initiations, and they intensify the mystery of surrender. [These angels] assist [the children of God] in weaning the consciousness from its attachments. They assist [them] in letting go, in becoming more of God, in recognizing all that must be given up in order to proceed on the Path.

I would like you to do for me another favor. I would like you to be concerned with the women's liberation movement in this nation and throughout the world. I would like you to take it upon yourself to instruct mankind in the true way of the liberation of the soul and of the feminine ray and of the true meaning of the impulses of the Aquarian age. I would like you to study the lectures of the Mother of the Flame and my dictation as a part of your mystery of surrender, my dictation which contains the special dispensation of the Lord Christ given in San Francisco.

And so, with this album of The Mystery of Surrender, you can go very far. You can enlighten souls that the women of America will not lose their light—the light which they ought to use in this year—in rebellion, in pride and ambition, in asserting the carnal mind as opposed to the light of the Christ. Do not ignore them and think them silly, but go to them and ask them if they have considered going within to find the Divine Woman, to find liberty, to find full creativity of expression.

Precious ones, there is such a work to be done by the women of America and the world once they make contact with the I AM THAT I AM. Let all, then, be diligent in listening to these lectures, in taking in the radiation and the dispensation of my dictation and in daily surrendering all of the aspects of the not-self as these are diagrammed in the Book of Revelation and as they form a part of the prayer "I Surrender."

No sweeter words were ever spoken, no greater love has ever flowed than that which comes from the soul who declares, "O God,

I surrender." And in the surrender is the relief from the burden of carrying your own burden. And your greatest burden, of course, is the carnal mind, the ego with all of its pains, all of its pleasures, all of its surfeiting in itself.

When you surrender, you take a deep breath and you know that at last God in you will work the work of the ages. Let it be so. Let this be the conclusion of our message, that God in you shall work the work of the ages because you have surrendered unto your Real Self.

I receive now a lei of lilies of the valley and white roses and camellias and gardenias, a beautiful lei which the angels of the light of surrender present to me. They place it upon me as the Mother of the World in Spirit, and I take it and I place it upon the Mother of the World in Mater. Together now, hand in hand, we will prove the science of the figure eight and the test of the eighth ray and the testing of the children in the eighth ray.

As Buddha prepares the way, giving his teaching in the Eight-fold Path, as Above, so below, within your heart, within my own, let light flow.

Anaheim, California
December 30, 1975

14

A Vigil at the Tomb of Matter

The Starry Mother keeps the vigil at the tomb of Matter. She awaits the coming of her Lord. She awaits the coming, the new birth of Father and Son and Holy Spirit in the threefold flame of the resurrection. The spirit of life encased in a form that does not pattern the law of the formless is thus crucified in Matter.

From the lowest to the highest forms of life, God the Father and the Son and the Spirit await the moment of the demonstration of the law of the rebirth. How long, O Lord? How long, O Lord, is the prayer of the saints? How long will God be crucified in Matter?

As the Mother waits for the birth of the newborn child from out the womb of time and space, so the Mother waits for the resurrection of the Manchild, for the freeing of the light of God. The currents of the resurrection are freedom, a flame. The currents of the resurrection are for the exoneration of every soul in the atonement. As long as there is separation and the sense of separation, Mother will wait with the Holy Spirit at the womb of time and space, at the tomb of Matter, waiting the birth of the eternal God.

I am Mary. Some have called me the Mother of God. Indeed, I mother the incarnation of God in all life, as you should also do.

Those who understand the true path of religion, whereby the soul is bound to God, must understand that every son and daughter and child of the flame must enter in to every aspect of relationship with God, must know God as father and as son, as daughter and as mother, as wife, as husband, as child, as the beloved one, as the guru, as the disciple. And so, to enter in to the relationship with God is to hallow life and all of the interchanges that occur between lifestreams. This is the purpose of incarnation and reincarnation and of karma and of the fulfillment of one's dharma.

The purpose is to know God, to discover the wholeness of God. And this can only be accomplished in time and space—on the line that is time, in the space that is God—there to experience portions of the whole until the individual soul thereby, through the interchange, contains the wholeness of God.

How can you become that which you have not experienced? Through your love of all life, you come to know God. In knowing God, you become God. In becoming God, you take him down from the cross. And he is free to be the expanded awareness of self, and that expansion of self-awareness is the purpose of creation. I have known him always, and he has chosen to let those among the evolutions of this cosmos know him as Mother, as I have carried the flame of Mother.

What, then, will mankind, through you, know God as? Will they know God as the artisan of the Spirit, as the Master Alchemist?

What will you be, precious children of the One? What will you be that mankind might find more of God appearing and that you might liberate that God appearing in the way of your own self-mastery?

How much of God do the children know by contact with your blessed self? Can they touch the hem of your garment, the very garment of your attainment, and thereby feel the quivering of the Spirit and the flow of our healing love?

On this day of the commemoration of the crucifixion of my Son, I would that that way might be carried in you—not through the death of the four lower bodies or even of the soul, but through the bringing forth in joy of an aspect of the Saviour on the cross of his attainment, of his courage and patience, his great love for his disciples and for the holy women. And even in the hour upon the cross, the fragrance of that love came to us as roses and lilies of the valley and the lilies and violets. And we were in the bower of God's heart, even as the lightning and the thunder and the rain came down as the sign of heaven that the Son of God was given that all mankind might live.

We had spoken of that hour in the chamber where the Passover was shared, where the bread and the wine were blessed and broken and passed to the disciples. We shared the knowledge of that supreme sacrifice made for the sake of science. We knew it from the Beginning. We knew it before our incarnation, even as your souls know the hour of your overcoming victory.

But somehow when the hour is come, the hour is clothed with the emotions, the thoughts and the feelings of the moment. And the weight of the powers of darkness and of Satan was very heavy as they had entered the heart of the betrayer and the mob, who were manipulated by the black magicians, by the Sanhedrin and those who had entered the synagogues.

As they used these precious lifestreams against the Christ, Jesus was also burdened that they were so easily manipulated, even as he knew that even they must play their role. And as he walked the stations of the cross—setting the pattern of your initiation for all time to come, overcoming the darkness on the lines of those stations by the flame of Alpha and Omega—his heart was troubled and burdened. And in his heart he wondered how mankind, who would follow after him, would gain that inner knowing to follow in his footsteps. And if they would gain the inner knowing, he thought, how will they then face the dreaded density of the dark ones, the virulence of the thrust of all of the legions and the powers of darkness and the fallen ones who came and Jesus declared that this was their hour and the power of darkness?[1]

And as he mused concerning the fate of the initiates on the Path and the members of the community of the Spirit and how they would overcome in succeeding embodiments, he met the daughters of Jerusalem weeping—weeping for his suffering, which was not so great a suffering for himself as it was the agony of concern lest those with lesser attainment and lesser understanding of God should come to this, the most magnificent of all initiations, and withdraw and walk the other way and leave the cross and use those powers which Jesus had of levitation, of dissolving the bodies, of removing himself. All of this he could have done at any moment, from the moment of the capture in the Garden of Gethsemane through the trial and through the stations of the cross.

We knew that we must meet, that our eyes must touch in the flow of the love of God. He knew that he would see me for the last time in this world, in that level of consciousness, and this was a part of the great drama of the initiation that must be portrayed. And the pull of our love was as the pull of the great starry bodies, who belong in the great fiery core of the One. Yet our understanding of the law that we were already one and would be one for eternity sustained us in that moment of the pain of parting, which is as a single tear from the Mother's eye.

The pain of separation and of the contemplation of death, although death is not real, lasts but for a moment, precious ones. And therefore you must see that sympathy for the *via dolorosa* only sustains that which is not real, either to Jesus or to myself or to any other sons and daughters of God who have passed through this passion of the supreme love of God in demonstration.

I AM the Mother, mothering life. I am the flame within you, encouraging you, urging you on to the next victory. I hold the promise of your immaculate conception. I have seen your end from your beginning and your beginning from your end. I have seen how God has fashioned your life to be a unique example of the initiation of the crucifixion, and each one of you will participate in that initiation in a very different way. For there are many who watch you on the path of life, many who must also overcome the cross of their karma, of all of their misuses of the sacred fire.

And they watch you to see whether you will be tempted, whether you will fall down before the prince of this world, who will come offering to you his power and his dominion over the cities and the nations of this world.

Many, many have gone the way of power. Power is as strong wine. It makes men and women drunk. It makes them cruel and tyrants, torturing one another, as though human life were as ants or cattle or less. And therefore, the power of God, the all-power of heaven and earth, which is given to the overcomer, is given after the resurrection, after the laying aside of all the things of this world. But those who have gained power (as Caesar, as Pilate, as the chief priests and elders of the people, as the doctors and the lawyers) and those who control the wealth of the kingdoms, they are the same as they always were. They are the same, and they shall remain until the harvest and the separation of the tares and the wheat.[2]

And therefore, you need not look far to find the instruments of the judgment of the Christ, the crucifixion of the Christ within you. The players will be there to play their parts. They will be there, precious ones. Of this thing you must be certain, that you are ready to play your part. Remember, millions of souls have walked the way of the Christ because my Son did not leave the stations of the cross.

Listen, then, to the teaching of the Mother on the stations of the cross and realize that you will walk these stations over and over again, transmuting, overcoming the planetary and personal cycles of karma, until you have anchored in your chakras the strength of Alpha, the strength of Omega, the fiery light momentum necessary for your fulfillment of this initiation. And God will not allow you to come before the tribunal of this world without the momentum of light that you require. God will not allow you to enter this initiation unless he is certain that you have all of the fire and the light and the increments of power and wisdom and love for the overcoming and for the victory.

And so you see, there is no need to turn back. There is no need to fear. There is no need to remain in wonder concerning the path of initiation. For the son and the daughter of God who are chosen to walk this path are carefully prepared, watched over as a newborn babe, as a lamb. So God sends his angels. God sends the holy angels to care for the ones who are experiencing the dark night of the soul, the overcoming of all the conditions.

Take care, then, that you do not tarry in that dark night by self-indulgence and self-pity or the boulders of self-condemnation or the blindness of pride and ambition. Take care that you remember to say with me, "I surrender." Take care that you understand that I said that he gave his life! He allowed the Christ to be crucified for the sake of science!

He was the great scientist of the age and of all ages. He proved—not by the power of the black magicians or of Satan but by the power of God alone—that this temple can be raised in three days.[3] In three cycles of the twelve, he proved the mastery of the threefold flame under the twelve hierarchies of the sun,[4] passing all of the initiations of the great solar hierarchies, who were in intimate contact with the Lord as he passed those hours in the tomb of Mater and as we stood without, holding the flame of the Mother as that counterpart of him who held the light of the Spirit of Alpha for all mankind.

Let those who would be worthy of the name *scientist* follow the admonishments of Leto[5] and all of the masters who are also scientists. For the proof of truth in the laboratory of the four lower bodies is your supreme calling.

They may question, they may argue, they may spread the lie that someone stole the body or that Christ never died upon the cross or that he was never resurrected. I tell you, the proof is in akasha, and the record of the Passion of my Son is recorded in the soul of every child of God evolving in this system of worlds. This is the great gift of the life of Jesus Christ—that God the Father has given to all of his children the record of the victory, the scientific proof! The account is there, right within the souls of you who will go and do likewise.

Who are they, then, who deny the Lord and his coming and his victory? They are the sons of Belial and of Satan and of Lucifer. They are the sons of darkness, who have not the soul and therefore have not the record of the victory. And therefore they testify of their father, the Devil, and he was a murderer from the beginning and abode not in the truth.

Therefore, look not to the prince of this world or to all of the fallen ones, who have the power of the prince of this world. They will not bear witness to the truth! They will tell you, you cannot know the truth that shall make you free. They will laugh and scorn you when you speak the word of truth because they say truth is relative.

Well, I tell you, precious ones, truth is not relative to any man or any level of human consciousness. Truth is the absolute manifestation of Almighty God within you! It is the witness of the flame of life! It is the perfectionment of the soul. It is the law of the path of initiation. And you have the promise that "Ye shall know the truth and the truth shall make you free!"[6] It is possible to know truth and to know absolute truth in time and space. And you must confirm and affirm your belief, your faith and your understanding in the science of truth of every word of Jesus Christ. You must understand it by the Holy Spirit, for the Holy Spirit will return to the Bible those passages and little phrases that have been carved out by the fallen ones to deceive and to confuse and to divide and conquer the children of the light.

Be wise, children of God. Be wise as serpents and harmless as doves.[7] Be wise and realize that for thousands of years the same fallen ones who tempted the Lord Christ have been after your souls, preventing you from the realization of God, tying into your own selfishness and sensuality, into your own darkness, and thereby tearing you from the credo, the teaching, the law, the flame, the love, the humility of Christ.

Therefore Jesus declared, "The prince of this world cometh and findeth nothing in me."[8] There was nothing in him—not a blemish nor a spot, not an anchoring point for the fallen ones.

You can be the same. You can be purged of those elements of your own creation that have enabled the fallen ones to trip you in the way of the cross. But you must be wise. You must study the teachings. You must know the Law. Even when Satan came to tempt Jesus in the wilderness, he quoted the law of the prophets. He quoted the scripture.

Jesus knew well the Law. Let the true Israelites, then, also know the Law, for the Law is the certain defense of the overcomer. Training in the Law will enable you to go before those who have the supreme development of the carnal mind as the identity of Antichrist and they will not be able to confound you with their lies. For the truth of the white magician is the rod that swallows up the serpents of the black magician.

See, then, that the Path is for you—the Path is for your over-coming. It can be won. It can be known. You can be free. But you must be alert. You must be wise. You must be diligent in your application.

Now I leave you to your own consciousness and to your own Christ Self and to your own flame of Mother. I give you that which God has already given to you—the supreme responsibility for your own victory. I shall be waiting in the wings of life to see your performance, for you are now the players in the great drama of the crucifixion of the Mother in the age of Aquarius.

Let us see, then, how quickly the drama of the sons and daughters of God will prove to the world once again that Christ lives, that Christ-mastery is the science of this age, and this science is equal to the *total* dominion of Mater!

288 Mary's Message of Divine Love

I am keeping my vigil at the tomb, waiting for your appearance on resurrection's morn. I am Mary, your Mother always.

Los Angeles, California
April 16, 1976

The Chart of Your Divine Self

The Chart of Your Divine Self is a portrait of you and of the God within you. It is a diagram of yourself and your potential to become who you really are. It is an outline of your spiritual anatomy.

The upper figure is your "I AM Presence," the Presence of God that is individualized in each one of us. It is your personalized "I AM THAT I AM." Your I AM Presence is surrounded by seven concentric spheres of spiritual energy that make up what is called your "causal body." The spheres of pulsating energy contain the record of the good works you have performed since your very first incarnation on earth. They are like your cosmic bank account.

The middle figure in the chart represents the "Holy Christ Self," who is also called the Higher Self. You can think of your Holy Christ Self as your chief guardian angel and dearest friend, your inner teacher and voice of conscience. Just as the I AM Presence is the Presence of God that is individualized for each of us, so the Holy Christ Self is the presence of the universal Christ that is individualized for each of us. "The Christ" is actually a title given to those who have attained oneness with their Higher Self, or Christ Self. That's why Jesus was called "Jesus, the Christ." *Christ* comes from the Greek word *christos*, meaning "anointed"—anointed with the light of God.

What the Chart shows is that each of us has a Higher Self, or "inner Christ," and that each of us is destined to become one with that Higher Self—whether we call it the Christ, the Buddha, the Tao or the Atman. This "inner Christ" is what the Christian mystics sometimes refer to as the "inner man of the heart," and what the Upanishads mysteriously describe as a being the "size of a thumb" who "dwells deep within the heart."

The Chart of Your Divine Self

We all have moments when we feel that connection with our Higher Self—when we are creative, loving, joyful. But there are other moments when we feel out of sync with our Higher Self— moments when we become angry, depressed, lost. What the spiritual path is all about is learning to sustain the connection to the higher part of ourselves so that we can make our greatest contribution to humanity.

The ribbon of white light descending from the I AM Presence through the Holy Christ Self to the lower figure in the Chart is the crystal cord (sometimes called the silver cord). It is the "umbilical cord," the lifeline, that ties you to Spirit.

Your crystal cord also nourishes that special, radiant flame of God that is ensconced in the secret chamber of your heart. It is called the threefold flame, or divine spark, because it is literally a spark of sacred fire that God has transmitted from his heart to yours. This flame is called "threefold" because it engenders the primary attributes of Spirit—power, wisdom and love.

The mystics of the world's religions have contacted the divine spark, describing it as the seed of divinity within. Buddhists, for instance, speak of the "germ of Buddhahood" that exists in every living being. In the Hindu tradition, the Katha Upanishad speaks of the "light of the Spirit" that is concealed in the "secret high place of the heart" of all beings.

Likewise, the fourteenth-century Christian theologian and mystic Meister Eckhart teaches of the divine spark when he says, "God's seed is within us." There is a part of us, says Eckhart, that "remains eternally in the Spirit and is divine....Here God glows and flames without ceasing."

When we decree, we meditate on the flame in the secret chamber of our heart. This secret chamber is your own private meditation room, your interior castle, as Teresa of Avila called it. In Hindu tradition, the devotee visualizes a jeweled island in his heart. There he sees himself before a beautiful altar, where he worships his teacher in deep meditation.

Jesus spoke of entering the secret chamber of the heart when he said: "When thou prayest, enter into thy closet, and when thou hast shut thy door, pray to thy Father which is in secret; and thy Father which seeth in secret shall reward thee openly."

The lower figure in the Chart of Your Divine Self represents you as a soul on the spiritual path, surrounded by the violet flame and the protective white light of God, the "tube of light." Your soul is the living potential of God—the part of you that is mortal but that can become immortal. The high-frequency energy of the violet flame can help you reach that goal more quickly.

The purpose of your soul's evolution on earth is to grow in self-mastery, balance your karma and fulfill your mission on earth so that you can return to the spiritual dimensions that are your real home. When your soul at last takes flight and ascends back to God and the heaven-world, you will become an "ascended" master, free from the rounds of karma and rebirth.

Notes

A Word from the Author

This excerpt is from Elizabeth Clare Prophet's "Service to Mother Mary," given July 3, 1984, at *The Flame of Freedom Speaks* conference, held in the Heart of the Inner Retreat, Park County, Montana.

1. For teachings on the cosmic clock, see Elizabeth Clare Prophet's *Predict Your Future: Understand the Cycles of the Cosmic Clock; The Great White Brotherhood in the Culture, History and Religion of America* (pp. 173-206); and *Seminar on the Cosmic Clock*, 2-audiotape album (Summit University Press).

2. The fourteen stations of the cross are fourteen scenes of the last hours of Jesus' life. They represent his mastery and sacrifice on behalf of mankind. First station: Jesus is condemned to death. Second station: Jesus is made to bear his cross. Third station: Jesus falls the first time. Fourth station: Jesus meets his afflicted mother. Fifth station: Simon the Cyrenian helps Jesus. Sixth station: Veronica wipes the face of Jesus. Seventh station: Jesus falls the second time. Eighth station: Jesus consoles the holy women. Ninth station: Jesus falls the third time. Tenth station: Jesus is stripped of his garments. Eleventh station: Jesus is nailed to the cross. Twelfth station: Jesus dies on the cross. Thirteenth station: Jesus is taken down from the cross. Fourteenth station: Jesus is laid in the sepulchre.

Foreword

1. Matt. 13:33.

2. Mother Mary, 1972 *Pearls of Wisdom*, vol. 15, no. 32 (published by The Summit Lighthouse).

3. Rom. 12:4; I Cor. 12:27; Eph. 4:12.

4. Rev. 12:10-11.

5. Acts 2:1.

6. Rev. 21:3.

7. Matt. 24:14.

8. Rev. 11:3, 10.

9. Rev. 12:5.

10. Rom. 8:7.

11. John 1:9.

Introduction
The Soul of Mary in Heaven

1. A root race is a group of souls who embody together and share a unique archetypal pattern, divine plan and mission to fulfill on earth. According to esoteric tradition, there are seven primary groups of souls—the first to the seventh root races.

2. Mother Mary, 1975 *Pearls of Wisdom*, vol. 18, no. 44, p. 230 (published by The Summit Lighthouse).

3. Ibid., pp. 231-32.

4. The Great White Brotherhood is a spiritual order of Western saints and Eastern adepts who have transcended the cycles of karma and rebirth and ascended into the heaven-world. They are known as ascended masters. The Brotherhood also includes the archangels and other advanced spiritual beings as well as some unascended beings. The "white" in the name denotes the aura of white light, the halo that surrounds these beings.

5. The Lords of Karma are the ascended beings who dispense justice to this system of worlds, adjudicating karma, mercy and judgment on behalf of every lifestream.

6. The God and Goddess Meru focus the feminine ray for the planet at their retreat, the Temple of Illumination, at Lake Titicaca in the Andes mountains, South America. The masculine ray for the planet is focused by Lord Himalaya at his Retreat of the Blue Lotus in the Himalayan range.

7. Rev. 1:6.

8. Rev. 21:9; 22:17.

9. See Elizabeth Clare Prophet, *The Lost Years of Jesus: Documentary Evidence of Jesus' 17-Year Journey to the East* (Corwin Springs, Mont.: Summit University Press, 1987).

10. Matt. 2:13.

11. Matt. 2:16.

12. Matt. 2:15.

13. Luke 2:46-47.

14. John 11:25.

15. See Mark L. Prophet and Elizabeth Clare Prophet, *The Lost Teachings of Jesus*, books 1-4 (Corwin Springs, Mont.: Summit University Press, 1993-1994).

16. John 19:26, 27.

17. For more on the seven aspects of the Christ consciousness, see *Lords of the Seven Rays: Mirror of Consciousness*, by Mark L. Prophet and Elizabeth Clare Prophet (Corwin Springs, Mont.: Summit University Press, 1986).

18. Acts 1:14.

19. See John of Damascus, "On the Assumption." (On the Web at www.balamand.edu.lb/theology/Jodorm2.htm)

20. John 1:14.

21. The twelve solar hierarchies act as step-down transformers for the energies of God and are referred to by the names of the signs of the zodiac. For more information, see "The Cosmic Clock," in *The Great White Brotherhood in the Culture, History and Religion of America*, by Elizabeth Clare Prophet (Corwin Springs, Mont.: Summit University Press).

22. Rev. 3:8.

23. Michael S. Durham, *Miracles of Mary: Apparitions, Legends, and Miraculous Works of the Blessed Virgin Mary* (HarperSanFrancisco, 1995), pp. 102-3.

24. Ethel Cook Eliot, "Our Lady of Guadalupe in Mexico," in *A Woman Clothed with the Sun: Eight Great Appearances of Our*

Lady in Modern Times, ed. John J. Delaney (Garden City, N.Y.: Image Books, Doubleday and Co., 1961), p. 54.

25. Frances Parkinson Keyes, "Bernadette and the Beautiful Lady," in *A Woman Clothed with the Sun*, p. 133.

26. Ibid., p. 137.

27. Rom. 3:9. Holy Amethyst, March 24, 1967.

28. *Fatima in Lucia's Own Words*, ed. Louis Kondor (Fátima, Portugal: Postulation Center, 1976), p. 62.

29. *Our Lady of Fátima's Peace Plan from Heaven* (Rockford, Ill.: Tan Book and Publishers, 1983), p. 1; and *Fátima in Lucia's Own Words*, p. 62.

30. William Thomas Walsh, *Our Lady of Fátima* (Garden City, N.Y.: Image Books, Doubleday and Co., 1954), p. 39.

31. *Our Lady of Fátima's Peace Plan*, p. 2.

32. Walsh, *Our Lady of Fátima*, p. 42.

33. Luke 22:42.

34. Heb. 12:1.

35. The ascended masters are enlightened spiritual beings who once lived on earth, fulfilled their reason for being and have ascended, or reunited with God. They are the true teachers of mankind. They direct the spiritual evolution of all devotees of God and guide them back to their source.

36. John 2:19.

37. I Cor. 6:19; II Cor. 5:1.

38. Acts 17:24.

39. Acts 17:28.

40. Ps. 110:4.

41. Walsh, *Our Lady of Fátima*, p. 50.

42. Ibid., p. 52.

43. Ibid.

44. William C. McGrath, "The Lady of the Rosary," in *A Woman Clothed with the Sun*, p. 194.

45. Walsh, *Our Lady of Fátima*, p. 120.

46. Durham, *Miracles of Mary*, p. 168.

47. Beloved Mother Mary, December 24, 1967. See pages 213-17, this volume, for the complete dictation.

48. See Thomas F. Brady, "Visions of Virgin Reported in Cairo," *New York Times*, 5 May 1968, p. 71; *Fatima Prophecy: Days of Darkness, Promise of Light* (Austin, Tex.: Association for the Understanding of Man, 1974), pp. 43-50; Jerome Palmer, "The Virgin Mary Appears in Egypt," *Fate*, August 1971, pp. 60-70.

49. Joseph A. Pelletier, *The Queen of Peace Visits Medugorje* (Worcester, Mass.: An Assumption Publication, 1985), p. 49.

50. Ibid., p. 139.

PART ONE

The Wisdom Aspect of the Holy Spirit
Fourteen Letters from a Mother to Her Children

Letter 1

1. John 15:12.

Letter 2

1. John 16:33.

2. The ascended masters have revealed in later years that Jesus did not ascend at the conclusion of his Palestinian ministry. After his crucifixion and resurrection he journeyed to Kashmir and at the age of eighty-one took his ascension from the etheric retreat of Shamballa. The messenger has explained that Jesus removed himself from Palestine in the ceremony on Bethany's hill. He left Palestine in secret so that "he would no longer be there, could no longer be sought after, looked to.... He had fulfilled his mission in Palestine." See Jesus Christ, June 27, 1993, "The Path of the Builders," 1993 *Pearls of Wisdom*, vol. 36, no. 36, pp. 522–23.

3. Phil. 3:14.

4. John 11:25.

5. Matt. 25:21.

6. Exod. 3:14.

Letter 3

1. Rev. 2:17; 19:12.

2. John 3:17.

3. John 10:10.

4. Gen. 22:16-18; Heb. 11:11-12.

Letter 4

1. Matt. 6:6; 14:23; Mark 6:45-46.

2. Heb. 13:16.

3. I Pet. 4:18.

4. Isa. 40:31.

5. Isa. 40:4; Luke 3:5.

6. Rev. 3:8.

Letter 5

1. Matt. 5:9.

2. Luke 10:27.

3. II Chron. 20:17; Exod. 14:13.

4. Matt. 6:21.

5. Luke 21:19.

Letter 6

1. John 14:6.

2. Luke 10:37.

3. Matt. 6:28.

4. Luke 22:42.

5. Matt. 25:40.

Letter 7

1. On Mother Mary's appearances at Zeitoun, a suburb of Cairo, Egypt, see pages 43-44.

2. Matt. 18:11-14; Luke 15: 3-7.

3. John 10:11-16.

4. Refers to "Understanding Yourself," a series of *Pearls of Wisdom* (*PoW*) by Kuthumi, Lanto and God Meru, printed as 1969 *PoW*, vol. 12, nos. 25-40, and available as *Understanding Yourself: A Spiritual Approach to Self-Discovery and Soul-Awareness* (rev. ed.), published by Summit University Press. Also available in *Pearls of Wisdom (1958-1998) on CD-ROM* (for information or to order, call 1-800-245-5445).

Letter 8
1. Luke 22:31.
2. Luke 2:49.
3. Matt. 7:20, 16.
4. II Cor. 6:14-15.
5. Matt. 5:8.
6. Matt. 7:15.
7. John 8:32.

Letter 9
1. James 1:27.
2. II Cor. 11:14.
3. Luke 22:31.
4. I Kings 3:16-28.

Letter 10
1. Hos. 8:7.
2. John 1:14.
3. I Cor. 3:19.
4. Exod. 16:3.
5. See Introduction, pp. 34-43.
6. Matt. 26:34; Mark 14:30; Luke 22:34; John 13:38.
7. William Ross Wallace, "The Hand That Rocks the Cradle Is the Hand That Rules the world," stanza 1.

Letter 11
1. Luke 23:28.
2. Matt. 8:29.

3. See *The Enemy Within,* by Mark L. Prophet and Elizabeth Clare Prophet (Corwin Springs, Mont.: The Summit Lighthouse Library, 2004).

4. Refers to the *Pearls of Wisdom,* weekly messages from the ascended masters to their students throughout the world. These letters are the intimate contact, heart to heart, between the ascended masters and their students. They are dictated to the messengers Mark L. Prophet and Elizabeth Clare Prophet and published by The Summit Lighthouse.

5. II Tim. 2:15.

6. Luke 2:49.

Letter 12

1. Matt. 5:6.

2. Refers to Saint Germain's August 29, 1965 *Pearl of Wisdom,* in which he said: "When the Master Presence of Life enabled mankind in this age to bring forth science and invention for the freeing of men from drudgery through streamlined methods, assembly-line production, increased speed and comfort in transportation and communication, it was a service intended to free men that they might give full attention to the culture of the soul. Contrariwise, these developments seem to have brought about a greater soul neglect and the spread of many types of infectious human nonsense....The nurturing of your own soul is serious business, but the world community also belongs to God. You live in a world of mechanical and cultural refinements while the true laws of life expounded are in the covered-wagon stages. If you are spiritual pioneers who adore the truth, *you will stand up now and be counted.* The battle for life is going on all around you. I commend you now to action!" (vol. 8, no. 35). Saint Germain's complete message is available on *Pearls of Wisdom (1958-1998) on CD-ROM.*

3. John 21:25.

4. John 14:12.

5. Matt. 27:51.

Letter 13
1. Isa. 55:7-9.
2. Matt. 24:22; Mark 13:20.
3. I John 3:2.

Letter 14
1. Matt. 24:40-42; Luke 17:34-36.
2. John 10:16.
3. Prov. 22:6.
4. John 1:1.
5. Acts 2:2.
6. John 4:14.

PART TWO

The Love Aspect of the Holy Spirit
**Five Mysteries of the Rosary by the
Mother for Her Children**

The Power of Spoken Prayer
1. John 16:24; Matt. 7:7.
2. Rom. 3:4.
3. Matt. 13:12.
4. Matt. 25:14-30.
5. Jer. 31:34.
6. Mother Mary, 1992 *Pearls of Wisdom*, vol. 35, no. 62 (published by The Summit Lighthouse), p. 708.
7. I John 3:2.

The Outline of the Rosary
1. Rev. 1:8.
2. See the Chart of Your Divine Self, pp. 289-92.
3. Exod. 3:13-15.
4. Mother Mary, April 20, 1973, "Communion Feast at the Temple of the Resurrection with Mary, Jesus and Lanello," published in 1973 *Pearls of Wisdom*, vol. 16, no. 30.

The Inspiration Mysteries

First Inspiration Mystery
Pss. 1:1-6; 19:1-2, 7-9, 11, 13-14.

Second Inspiration Mystery
Pss. 8:1-9; 9:1-2.

Third Inspiration Mystery
Ps. 23:1-6.

Fourth Inspiration Mystery
Ps. 91:1-16.

Fifth Inspiration Mystery
Prov. 3:5-6; Pss. 37:1-6; 100:1-5.

Sixth Inspiration Mystery
Ps. 121:1-8.

The Action Mysteries

First Action Mystery
1 Kings 17:1-14.

Second Action Mystery
1 Kings 17:15-24.

Third Action Mystery
1 Kings 18:21-24, 26, 29, 31-32, 36-39.

Fourth Action Mystery
2 Kings 2:1-2, 8-14.

Fifth Action Mystery
2 Kings 4:8, 11, 14-22, 32-35.

Sixth Action Mystery
2 Kings 5:1-3, 9-15.

The Revelation Mysteries

First Revelation Mystery
Rev. 14:1-10, 12-13.

Second Revelation Mystery
Rev. 19:1-10.

Third Revelation Mystery
Rev. 19:11-21.

Fourth Revelation Mystery
Rev. 20:1-15.

Fifth Revelation Mystery
Rev. 21:9-19, 21-27.

Sixth Revelation Mystery
Rev. 22:1-12.

The Declaration Mysteries

First Declaration Mystery
Matt. 24:1-13.

Second Declaration Mystery
Matt. 24:14-28.

Third Declaration Mystery
Matt. 24:29-42.

Fourth Declaration Mystery
Rev. 6:1-10.

Fifth Declaration Mystery
Rev. 6:11-17; 7:1-4.

Sixth Declaration Mystery
Rev. 7:9-17.

The Exhortation Mysteries

First Exhortation Mystery
Matt. 10:1, 5-20.

Second Exhortation Mystery
Luke 12:49-50; Matt. 10:32-42.

Third Exhortation Mystery
Matt. 12:33-42.

Fourth Exhortation Mystery
Luke 12:35-48.

Fifth Exhortation Mystery

Rev. 15:1-8; 16:1-3.

Sixth Exhortation Mystery

Rev. 16:4-12, 17-21.

PART THREE

The Power Aspect of the Holy Spirit
**Fourteen Messages of the Word of Life
to the Children of the Mother**

Message 1

1. I Sam. 3:1-10.
2. Matt. 8:20; Luke 9:58.
3. Matt. 25:21, 23.
4. John 14:2.
5. John 10:10.

Message 2

1. Luke 2:49.
2. Acts 5:1-10.
3. Heb. 10:9.

Message 3

1. Luke 1:52.
2. Luke 1:46-56.
3. Isa. 9:6.
4. Refers to the miracle of the sun. See pp. 42-43.
5. II Sam. 6:14.
6. II Cor. 12:2. According to Bible commentators, the first "heaven" of Scripture is that of the clouds or the atmosphere; the second, of stars; and the third, the abode of God.
7. Jer. 31:15; Matt. 2:18.
8. Ps. 16:10; Acts 2:27.
9. II Kings 2:11.
10. Damon and Pythias (or Phintias) were two youths of ancient Greece whose loyalty epitomized true friendship. According

to legend, Dionysius of Syracuse condemned Pythias to death but allowed him to leave the city and put his affairs in order when Damon pledged to take his friend's place if he did not return. Although Pythias was delayed in his journey, he returned just in time to save his friend from death. Dionysius was so impressed by the courage of the two friends, he pardoned them both and asked to join them in friendship.

Message 4

1. Matt. 5:25.
2. Beloved Jesus dictated through the messenger Mark L. Prophet on the following day, December 25, 1967.
3. Mark 15:39.
4. Refers to the parable of the talents, Matt. 25:14-30.
5. I Cor. 15:50.
6. The term *deist* refers to those who believe that the course of nature sufficiently demonstrates the existence of God and that God, having created the laws of the universe, no longer exerts any influence on natural phenomena.

Message 5

1. Luke 21:26.
2. Matt. 7:20.
3. Rev. 21:6; 22:17.

Message 6

1. Rom. 10:15.
2. Isa. 52:7.
3. According to legend, Leonardo da Vinci unknowingly used the same model for both Christ and Judas Iscariot in his painting of the *Last Supper*, in Milan, Italy. The legend says he first chose an individual to portray Christ. This young man was selected for the innocence and purity his face portrayed. Several years later, da Vinci searched for the model for Judas Iscariot. After weeks of looking among convicted criminals, he found his model in a prison in Rome—a man whose face would convey

the hardened image of one who would betray his best friend. When da Vinci completed the painting of Judas and the guards were about to take the prisoner away, this man revealed that he was the same model previously used to portray the face of Christ. This story is disputed by those who say there is no record that da Vinci used the same model for the two portraits or that his model for Judas had been a prisoner from Rome.

Message 8

1. Matt. 28.20.
2. Rev. 21:1-4; Isa. 65:17; 66:22; II Pet. 3:13.
3. Gen. 1:26-28.
4. John 10:10.
5. Mark 10:14; Luke 18:16; Matt. 19:14.
6. Pss. 48:1; 96:4;145:3: I Chron. 16:25.

Message 9

1. John 1:9.
2. Isa. 55:8.
3. Van Allen belt: a ring of charged particles surrounding the earth; one of two belts that surround the earth at very high altitudes, composed of charged particles trapped by the planet's magnetic field.
4. The spiritual retreat known as the Ascension Temple is located in the etheric octave, or heaven-world, at Luxor, Egypt. For further information on the ascension and the Ascension Temple, see Annice Booth, *The Path to Your Ascension: Rediscovering Life's Ultimate Purpose* (Corwin Springs, Mont.: Summit University Press, 1999).
5. Matt. 26:11; Mark 14:7; John 12:8.
6. Acts 10:42; II Tim. 4:1; I Pet. 4:5.
7. Mark 9:29; Matt. 17:21.
8. Decrees are a dynamic form of spoken prayer used by students of the ascended masters to direct God's light into individual and world conditions. For teachings and decrees, see Elizabeth Clare Prophet, *Violet Flame to Heal Body, Mind and Soul,*

pocket guide; *Spiritual Techniques to Heal Body, Mind and Soul,* audiocassette; and *Angels,* booklet of decrees, mantras, songs and devotions, with color-coded pages (published by Summit University Press).

9. Mal. 3:2, 3; Zech. 13:9; Isa. 48:10.

Message 10

1. On Mother Mary's appearance to Juan Diego, see pages 30-32.
2. The Keeper of the Flame is a title given to the Maha Chohan because of his pledge to all mankind: "I am keeping the flame for you until you are able."
3. Chamuel and Charity, archangels on the pink ray of love, maintain an etheric retreat over St. Louis, Missouri.

Message 11

1. Hab. 1:13.
2. Matt. 10:30; Luke 12:7.
3. Ascended Lady Master Clara Louise was embodied as Clara Louise Kieninger (1883-1970). In 1961 Saint Germain anointed her as the first Mother of the Flame of the Keepers of the Flame Fraternity. For years she had devotedly served in the field of nursing, taking as her motto *Ich Dien* ("I serve"). Later, as a dedicated student of the ascended masters, Clara Louise kept a daily prayer vigil for the youth of the world, the incoming children and their parents and teachers. She would begin every morning at five and decree for two to four hours, and sometimes till noon. She made her ascension at the age of 87 from Berkeley, California, on October 25, 1970.
4. Throughout Mother Mary's dictation, each one in the audience held a candle that was lit from the flame on the altar.
5. Matt. 11:30.
6. According to orthodox tradition, Jesus lived thirty-three years before his ascension.

Message 12

1. Prov. 15:1.

2. Matt. 26:29; Mark 14:25.
3. Job 3:25.
4. Rev. 13:16-18; 14:9-11; 15:2; 16:2; 19:19, 20; 20:4.
5. Prov. 14:12.
6. Matt. 6:19-21; Luke 12:33-34.
7. I Thess. 5:17.

Message 13
1. Rev. 19:11-21.
2. Clara Louise Kieninger (1883-1970) was anointed by Saint Germain in 1961 as the first Mother of the Flame of the Keepers of the Flame Fraternity. For years she had devotedly served in the field of nursing, taking as her motto Ich Dien ("I serve"). Later, as a dedicated student of the ascended masters, Clara Louise kept a daily prayer vigil for the youth of the world, the incoming children and their parents and teachers. She would begin every morning at five and decree for two to four hours, and sometimes till noon. She made her ascension at the age of 87 from Berkeley, California, on October 25, 1970, and she is now known as the Ascended Lady Master Clara Louise.
3. The Mystery of Surrender is the Fourteenth Rosary, which Mother Mary dictated to the messenger Elizabeth Clare Prophet as the culmination of the thirteen rosaries that she had dictated previously. See *The Fourteenth Rosary: The Mystery of Surrender* booklet and 2-audiocassette album, includes rosary, 2 lectures, and a dictation by Mother Mary, 3 hr., available through Summit University Press (www.tsl.org/bookstore).

Message 14
1. Luke 22:53.
2. Matt. 13:24-30, 36-43.
3. John 2:19-22.
4. In considering how "three cycles of twelve" can be equivalent to three days, it is helpful to understand the nature of solar hierarchies. Each of the twelve signs of the zodiac is ruled by a

solar hierarchy. And each solar hierarchy focuses the Great Tao, symbolized in the yang and yin of the T'ai Chi, which represents Alpha and Omega, our Father-Mother God. Therefore, through the yang and the yin, Alpha and Omega, the twelve becomes the twenty-four. Three times twenty-four is seventy-two—seventy-two hours, or three days.

5. On April 15, 1976, the day before this dictation, Ascended Lady Master Leto said: "You are co-creators with the great Alchemist of life, and therefore it is ordained by the flame within you that you should endow life with Spirit....As Spirit enters Matter, it gives Matter the impetus to rise back to Spirit." Leto suggested that we "meditate upon the crystal and its structure...as a means of contacting the plane of Spirit. For these emanations of the mind of God manifest in Matter are parallel to the energies manifest in Spirit. They are time-space coordinates of the coalescing of energy in infinity.... You will find that your visualizations will bring into manifestation elements of the Christ consciousness....You will see, then, that Matter is alive with the flame of the Spirit....It is energy ascending and descending from the very throne of God."

6. John 8:32.

7. Matt. 10:16.

8. John 14:30.

POCKET GUIDES TO PRACTICAL SPIRITUALITY:

Karma and Reincarnation

Your Seven Energy Centers *

Alchemy of the Heart *

Soul Mates and Twin Flames *

The Art of Practical Spirituality *

Creative Abundance *

How to Work with Angels

Access the Power of Your Higher Self

Violet Flame to Heal Body, Mind and Soul

The Creative Power of Sound

TITLES FROM

THE SUMMIT LIGHTHOUSE LIBRARY ®

The Opening of the Seventh Seal

The Enemy Within

Morya I

Community

Walking with the Master: Answering the Call of Jesus

Wanting to Be Born: The Cry of the Soul

Afra: Brother of Light

Saint Germain: Master Alchemist

Books from Summit University Press and The Summit
Lighthouse Library are available from fine bookstores
everywhere. For a free catalog or to place an order, call
1-800-245-5445 or 406-848-9500.
www.summituniversitypress.com

---

*also available as audiobooks

FOR MORE INFORMATION

Summit University Press books are available at fine bookstores worldwide and at your favorite on-line bookseller. Our books have been translated into more than 20 languages and are sold worldwide. If you would like a free catalog of our books and products, please contact:

Summit University Press
PO Box 5000, Corwin Springs, MT 59030-5000 USA
Tel: 1-800-245-5445 or 406-848-9500
Fax: 1-800-221-8307 or 406-848-9555
E-mail: info@tslinfo.org
www.summituniversitypress.com

Mark L. Prophet and Elizabeth Clare Prophet are pioneers of modern spirituality and internationally renowned authors. Among their best-selling titles are *The Lost Years of Jesus, The Lost Teachings of Jesus, The Human Aura, Saint Germain On Alchemy, Fallen Angels and the Origins of Evil* and the Pocket Guides to Practical Spirituality series, which includes *Karma and Reincarnation, Your Seven Energy Centers* and *Soul Mates and Twin Flames.* Their books are now translated into more than 20 languages.

LaVergne, TN USA
06 September 2010
196009LV00002B/5/A